Battle-Scarred: Justice Can Be Elusive

Memoirs of John F. Kippley

1963-2010

Battle-Scarred: Justice Can Be Elusive
Copyright © 2011 by John F. Kippley

All rights reserved. No part of this publication may be reproduced, stored in a retrieval system or transmitted in any way by any means, electronic, mechanical, photocopy, recording or otherwise without the prior permission of the author, except as provided by USA copyright law.

Other books by John F. Kippley:

    Birth Control and Christian Discipleship

    Marriage Is for Keeps

    Sex and the Marriage Covenant: A Basis for Morality

Co-authored with Sheila Kippley:

    The Art of Natural Family Planning (4th edition)

    Natural Family Planning: The Complete Approach

Author contact source: www.battle-scarred.info

ISBN: 978-1-4583-8791-2

Contents

	Introduction	v
1	Starting a Life Together	1
2	Our Canadian Experience	11
3	Great Unpleasantries: The Effort to Seek Justice	33
4	Salina, Kansas: 1969-1971	59
5	St. Odilia's Parish	65
6	The Years at Mount St. Joseph	73
7	Continued Dissent from *Humanae Vitae*	79
8	CCL: The Early Years	91
9	Crossing Paths in the NFP Movement	101
10	CCL: 1981-2001	121
11	Some of My Mistakes	131
12	The Whistleblower	137
13	More on Quality Issues	145
14	2002: Our Last Full Year with CCL	155
15	2003: Our Last Year on the Board	169
16	CCL Reneges on Its Agreements	191
17	Books, Health and Litigation	201
18	Two Settlements	219
19	The Extreme Makeover	225
20	NFP International	231
21	Matters of Justice	241
22	Learning from Mistakes	247

Introduction

Why does anyone write memoirs? If a person is famous, he might earn a lot of money. But if you're not famous, why bother? Who's interested? My own reasons are several.

1. Children. First, I am writing for my children and grandchildren. I deeply regret that I know so little about the lives of my own parents and grandparents. How did my grandparents meet? How and why did they come to Minnesota? Why did my dad, one of ten children, leave the farm? How did he become an officer in a construction company big enough to build at least part of the causeway connecting the Florida Keys? I don't know if my children and their children will ever read these memoirs, but at least when I am long gone, they will have some of the answers to some questions that might occur.

For them I hope to write something also about my earlier years. I start these memoirs with our marriage because that was the beginning of my life as a writer and very minor public figure.

2. Justice. Second, I hope these memoirs will have some small effect at bringing about an improved sense of justice and its practice both within the Church and the culture in which we live. Many Catholics are deeply involved in trying to rectify the greatest injustice of our day, the killing of unborn infants. Others are trying to rectify the injustice of erroneous sex education that leaves many young people with the impression that sexual sins aren't sins anymore. But there are other injustices as well, and sometimes these have to do with employment justice. Sometimes these deal with only one person or a very small group, so they are largely ignored even when they are publicized in the daily press.

In what follows, you may be puzzled at what appear to be some disconnects. Imagine a customer at a checkout counter who has just received too much change from the busy clerk. He recognizes that it would be unjust to take advantage of the mistake, so he immediately returns the excess to the grateful clerk. Then imagine that same person deciding to abrogate not only a previous agreement he had made but even a valid written contract which abrogation results in unemployment and/or other serious economic loss to the other party.

Why is there such a disconnect between the economic justice exhibited at the cash register and the economic injustice related to other persons? Of course, the ultimate reason for the mystery of disconnects and every sort of injustice is the mystery of Original Sin which Gilbert Keith Chesterton described as the mystery that helps to explain the mystery of our human condition.

Catholics and others need to realize that the whole purpose of Catholic social teaching is to bring about respect for the dignity and the rights of the individual person. It is to the unhappy reality of the more powerful taking unjust advantage of the weaker that much of the writing of the Old Testament prophets is addressed. It is to that still unhappy reality that the Catholic Church has addressed much of its social teaching including a whole series of encyclicals starting in 1891 and continuing to the present. It is still the case that many Catholics, including some in leadership positions, are quite unaware of Catholic social teaching or fail to see the connection between the encyclicals and day-to-day decisions. Most of us learn from examples, and sometimes specific examples can help sensitize the well disposed person to the demands of justice not just at the checkout counter but also with regard to contracts and employment issues.

3. *Humanae Vitae*. Third, perhaps these memoirs will shed some light on the teaching of *Humanae Vitae* and the dissent from it. I had the privilege of being an active participant in the debate prior to its issuance and a defender of its teaching in the ensuing years. I was obliged to read what the dissenters were writing, and their arguments did not then and still today do not make sense from the perspective of Christian discipleship. Ideas have consequences, and the dissenters, with one exception, almost never spelled out the theological and sociological consequences of their theories, logical consequences that were clearly foreseeable. I have been privileged to point out these consequences not only in the orthodox Catholic press but also in so-called "liberal" journals of theology and opinion.

4. Natural Family Planning. Fourth, since 1968, my wife and I have been active participants in what is called the Natural Family Planning movement. It's a disorganized "movement" that consists of various groups competing for a piece of the market that should be the entire adult population of the country and especially the adult Catholic population. The percentage of married Catholics who follow Catholic teaching regarding marital love and sexuality has dropped from approximately two-thirds a few years before *Humanae Vitae* to less than ten percent in 2010, if we are to believe the results of the latest government-sponsored survey. The time has come for the bishops of the Church to realize what they have to do—and then do it. If some bishops and priests have hoped that the "NFP movement" might do the job for them, it is now clear that such hopes were not well founded. Perhaps some ideas in these memoirs might be helpful to some of them.

5. For the record. In 1971 my wife and I formed an organization to provide practical help to live out the demands of married love as clarified by *Humanae Vitae*. Our association with that organization came to an abrupt end in 2003. Then we formed a new organization to carry on the work we started with the first. These memoirs will at least partially satisfy the curiosity of those who wonder what happened and why. George P. Schultz, President Ronald Reagan's Secretary of State from 1982 to 1989 has put it well:

> A living history requires tools of remembrance. So much of what we do today depends upon our understanding of the past. If we lose that past, we are also going to lose one of the important handles on the future.
> (*Wall Street Journal,* December 4-5, 2010, C2)

I certainly agree with Mr. Schultz about keeping records. I kept a diary during the conflict described in Chapters 2 and 3, and both Sheila and I kept good records during a second major conflict. Without these records, I could not have written this work as it stands. Perhaps this book can be part of the record.

6. Mistakes. Lastly, we have seen several situations in which certain mistakes cost people very dearly and left themselves quite unable to defend their rights. I have made more than my share of mistakes, some of which are reported in these memoirs. My hope is that inexperienced people can learn from my mistakes and from those of others and thus avoid some of these mistakes and leave themselves less vulnerable to injustice.

About the title: ***Battle-Scarred: Justice Can Be Elusive.*** The meaning of the title will be more apparent in some chapters than others, especially with regard to economic justice.

There is, however, another form of injustice. The 47 years from 1963 to 2010 have probably been the worst episode in the 20 centuries of Catholic Church history to promote its teaching on love, sex, marriage and birth control right within the Catholic Church. While the problem has been made much more difficult by the secular media, there's another important question. Has the Church in its dioceses, parishes and its local policies done what has been needed? Couples need and have a right to know the fullness of Catholic teaching on love, sex, marriage, and birth regulation. That includes the right to know about ecological breastfeeding and systematic natural family planning as practical helps for living that teaching. It seems to me that it's a form of injustice for those in leadership positions to do much less than they could do to promote acceptance of these teachings.

May this book help others to learn from my mistakes, prompt them to speak up for individual victims of injustice, and advance the cause of justice at least within the Church.

John F. Kippley
March 17, 2011

1. Starting a Life Together

Marriage always starts a totally new phase in life. For many of us, it's more like a totally new life. That's how it was for me.

I met Sheila via God's providence. I had moved to San Francisco in the summer of 1960 for health reasons. One night the previous summer in Omaha, my hayfever asthma was such that I didn't dare lie horizontally, and I wasn't ready to die. In a previous vacation to the Bay Area I had experienced perfectly clear lungs during the Midwest ragweed season, so I went west. By early 1962 I had not met the right one yet, and I had actually given up looking for a mate, so I had put the matter in the hands of the Lord and Our Lady. If I was called to the married state, they would have to provide. And they did!

One of the leaders of the Catholic Alumni Club (CAC) had asked me to head the Religious Discussion Committee, and I agreed to do the leg work if she would tell me what to do. One of her suggestions was to invite a priest to give us a talk about the migrant worker situation, and she even found a place to have it—Pat Chapla's apartment. Pat was a secretary in the medical-dental school of the University of California in San Francisco where Sheila was finishing her degree work. At Pat's invitation, Sheila was also at the meeting.

The melody of "Some Enchanted Evening" runs through my head as I write this. Some enchanted evening, you will see your true love across a crowded room…. The room wasn't crowded, but there was something about Sheila. She was pretty and she was willing to come to a meeting about migrant farm workers. She was also very shy at the time. Immediately after the formal meeting was over, she disappeared into the kitchen where I found her. If she had her druthers, she might have looked for a space behind the fridge. We talked, and, yes, she had played some tennis in high school. Later I would learn that she had been a ranked junior in Southern California. If I had known that and what it signified, I would have never suggested a tennis date. Ignorance was blissful, and she agreed to come with me to the CAC tennis outing on Sunday afternoon.

No one has ever mistaken me for a tennis player, but it was something to do occasionally for exercise. The best thing about that original tennis outing in Burlingame was the wind. It was that time of the year when the Sacramento valley heats up so much that it draws the cool Pacific air (and it can be quite cold by late afternoon and at night) through the Golden Gate and also over the coastal mountains. It provided somewhat of an excuse for my futile efforts to keep the ball in play. Fortunately, I provided a teaching challenge to Sheila rather than a tennis challenge. We kept up the tennis for years, and I shall never forget the time we played late in her ninth month of our first pregnancy. She was big as a house, and I figured she couldn't possibly move well enough, so I could finally beat her. Despite the fact that she had been trying to encourage me by saying that with practice I would eventually beat her simply because men are stronger players than women, she still had a competitive spirit. So whenever I was in danger of winning a set, she resorted to her surefire response—a high backhand she knew I couldn't return. And so it was that day as well.

Sheila and I had met close to the end of the school year in 1962. She returned to her home in the greater Los Angeles area for a short vacation, and then returned to work as a dental hygienist in San Francisco. I proposed on All Saints Day in a church after Mass. We married on April 27, 1963, lived in a third-floor walkup apartment very near the football stadium in Golden Gate Park, and in June we moved to start my career as a parish lay evangelist in Santa Clara.

Our first baby, Jennifer Ann, was born in mid-May 1964 at the Kaiser hospital in Redwood City, twenty miles up the Bayshore Freeway from Santa Clara. Sheila was well past the doctor's calculated "due date," and I thought they had missed it by a month, so I let the gas get low. That's a bad idea at any time during pregnancy, and it made for a nerve-wracking drive because we thought we didn't have time to stop for gas. As it turned out, we had plenty of time as her labor lasted 20 hours.

The Institute of Lay Theology

The position of lay evangelist was made possible by the insight of Father Eugene Zimmers, S.J. Father Z, as we all called him, started the Institute of Lay Theology (ILT) in 1959 to prepare men to exercise the Church's outreach to the uncommitted at the parish level. His vision was to have laymen conduct programs to attract uncommitted Catholics and non-Catholics alike to learn more about the Catholic faith. We would explain the Faith in a series of classes called an Inquiry Forum. We were called "lay theologians," but the reality was that we were lay evangelists, to use the contemporary term.

I entered the program in the fall of 1962 and graduated in June of 1963. It was a fascinating theology program. Our teachers were faculty members at Jesuit colleges, universities and seminaries. They would come to the ILT for short but intensive courses. We might have a course for three hours a day for three weeks straight. Our course on moral theology was taught by Fr. Gerald Kelly, S.J., one of the premier moral theologians of that time. An Old Testament course was taught by Fr. John Huesman, S.J. who was tan from a summer of archeological diggings in the Holy Land. The faculty loved teaching at the ILT because they could teach the heart of the matter and did not have to teach all the scholarly apparatus, the who-said-what-about-what sort of thing that is so much of academia. After reporting on our field work, we were awarded a Master of Applied Theology degree.

St Clare's Parish

St. Clare's parish was definitely not the sort of parish Father Z had in mind when designing the program. He had been thinking more of the growing suburban parishes of the late Fifties. St. Clare's was a very old parish, right across the street from the University of Santa Clara whose church is Mission Santa Clara. The parish had its share of new developments, but nothing like some of the other parishes of the area. The pastor who hired me was moved about the same time I arrived, but the new pastor, Fr. Raymond Prendeville, S.J., was also committed to the program.

The program got off to a good start, and we soon had a good number of enthusiastic volunteers. Sheila and I were welcomed by the parishioners, saw reasonably good numbers at the inquiry forums, and witnessed a considerable increase in the annual numbers of adult baptisms. It was very rewarding work, and it was a privilege to participate in this work of the Church.

Part of my work involved making door-to-door calls. This was quite different from visiting registered parishioners. These were cold calls seeking to find interest in the Catholic faith. I could take only about two hours of cold calling on a given day, and that was enough for the week. I would find so many people involved in invalid marriages that might possibly be validated that it was almost overwhelming. Sometimes I would get a rather rude reception. "I'm Catholic but I don't agree with everything the Church teaches." Translated: "I call myself Catholic but I use contraception."

I still remember a couple of encounters. One mother of seven children was in an invalid marriage. It was a simple matter. The couple had been married by a Justice of the Peace, but neither party had been married previously. I asked if I could help them get their marriage blessed by a priest, but she said no. "We're not sure yet if we want to be married." Well, at least she understood Catholic teaching. If they divorced from an invalid and therefore null-and-void marriage, it would not be difficult to get a declaration of nullity. But if they had a sacramental marriage, that would make them married for keeps.

An older man was also involved in an invalid marriage. If memory serves, he was previously married, then divorced and remarried to his current legal wife. When he told me that his first wife had died, I asked if I could help him get his current marriage blessed within the Church, but he declined. I assured him that under his circumstances, it would not be difficult. Nope, he said. "I will just have to take whatever punishment is coming to me.

Now that I'm so old that I can't sin, I'm not going to come crawling to God. I'll just take whatever I have coming." Despair. Refusal to ask forgiveness. Ready to go to hell rather than get on his knees, confess, ask for and receive forgiveness. I hope he changed before he died. Life is short, but eternity is forever.

The Inquiry Forum was the focus of our work. Mine consisted of 13 two-hour sessions, one night a week. This was not the easiest time to explain the faith. Vatican Council II had started when we were at the ILT and continued in session during the first two years of our service in Santa Clara. Change was in the air. People who were called theologians by the popular press were writing articles calling for the Church to change its teaching on birth control. Some would argue that the Church *could* change this teaching and therefore *should* change it to agree with popular sentiment and Protestantism. You could go into almost any parish and find a pamphlet in the vestibule trying to explain why the author thought the Church could contradict its former teaching and still say that it wasn't contradicting itself and could still teach infallibly. Of course, all such authors said they would accept the decision of the Church no matter what it was. That certainly wasn't the case; either they were deceiving themselves or they were trying to deceive others. Others didn't seem concerned about the Tradition; they just wanted the Church to accept unnatural forms of birth control. None of them pointed out that the acceptance of contraception would logically affect teaching about other sexual behaviors.

One session of the Inquiry Forum was devoted to explaining Catholic teaching on sexuality and birth control. It was challenging but productive. In my first year of teaching, I used the analogy of the vomitorium to explain the evil of contraception. I didn't have any particular problem with this argument, and I didn't experience any objections. Those who were arguing in published articles for contraception, however, were ridiculing it. So I looked for something else.

The Covenant Insight

For reasons I cannot explain, I started to explain the evil of contraception in terms of the marriage covenant. What makes marriage so special is that it is a covenant, not just a contract. This makes it partake of the most basic theme of the Bible, God's covenant with his people. It's unbreakable. It's for better and for worse. In God's plan, the sexual union is a covenant act. Sexual union is a privilege and a right only for a man and woman who have pledged a covenant of love with each other. In order to be validly married they have to covenant with each other for better and for worse. If they agreed to marry only for better but not for worse, there wouldn't be any marriage, just a situation of legalized fornication or prostitution.

So what about the marriage act? Should it reflect the marriage covenant? Should it reflect the faith and love and commitment they vowed on their wedding day? Should it reflect what really made them married—the commitment to love each other for better and for worse, no matter what? Well, yes, that's precisely what the marriage act ought to be—a renewal of the original marriage covenant. Contraceptive behavior within marriage, on the other hand, is a bodily statement that the spouses take each other for better but definitely and positively NOT for the imagined worse of possible pregnancy. That contradicts the marriage covenant. Contraceptive behavior is thus invalid as a renewal of the marriage covenant and is therefore dishonest and immoral. Body language is important. Our bodies are not just instruments of our minds. They are us. To engage in an act that is intrinsically dishonest means that I am acting dishonestly.

That's how I began to explain Catholic teaching against contraception, probably sometime in 1965. I first put this concept into writing in early 1966. One Saturday morning in what passed for winter in the Bay area, I attended a talk given by Michael Novak at a parish in Palo Alto. I forget the title and the general contents of his remarks, but during the question period it seemed clear to me that he was advocating a change in the received teaching on birth regulation. He wasn't at that time dissenting because this was still pre-*Humanae Vitae,* but he certainly wasn't supporting the teaching Tradition of almost 20 centuries, and he was encouraging couples to make their own decisions without discussing the matter with a priest.

I left the meeting feeling angry at this apparent effort to undermine the Tradition that had been reaffirmed so strongly by Pope Pius XI in his 1930 encyclical, *Casti Connubii.* Anger is a good emotion when it stirs you to get off your duff and do something to support the truth. As soon as I got home, I made a brief outline of five points that drew a similarity between the conditions required for the worthy reception of the Eucharist and the worthy marriage act. I typed the first draft in two days and titled it "Holy Communion: Eucharistic and Marital." The next summer I took a course from Fr. Barnabas Ahern, C.P., a well respected Scripture scholar, so I asked him to review it, and he graciously did so and made several helpful comments. *Ave Maria* magazine published it on February 25, 1967, exactly fifteen months before the publication of *Humanae Vitae.* It had mixed reviews. A monsignor called it blasphemous for daring to talk about Holy Communion and the marriage act in that way. A parish priest said it was very helpful in explaining the Church's teaching to his parishioners.

The USF MA Program

How was I able to have Father Barnabas Ahern review my paper? I had started to earn the academic Master of Arts in Theology at the University of San Francisco. Father Albert J. Zabala, S.J., directed a theology program that was noted for its international faculty and its very well attended summer sessions. The story was that there was wealth in the Zabala family and it was being generously bestowed on Father Zabala's efforts to build a significant theology library and program. In the summer of 1966 I had a course on the theology of St. Paul from Father Ahern and a course on the prophets taught by Fr. Bruce Vawter, C.M., author of a popular book, *The Conscience of Israel.*

One non-credit course was extremely well attended. The noted Scripture scholar Fr. Raymond Brown, SS, taught an evening course on scripture studies. I remember two things about it. First, it was at least two hours every night, and we would break at the halfway mark. Outside a cold wind and fog awaited us, definitely a waker-upper. Second, one night he was lecturing on contemporary speculation about the human knowledge of Jesus. He was very noncommittal, but it seemed to me that he was favoring the idea that Jesus did not have humanly usable knowledge of his own divinity until after the Resurrection. So I submitted a question in writing, as was the course policy, and he read it to the class after the break. "If Jesus did not have humanly expressible knowledge of his divinity until after the Resurrection, how do you explain his words of the institution of the Eucharist at the Last Supper?"

His reply was astonishing: "I have never thought about that." I admired him for his honesty but was amazed at such a clear and unfortunate break between his academic life and his priestly life. As a Sulpician priest, he was pronouncing the words of institution, "This is my Body…This is the chalice of my blood" every day. How could Jesus say those words if He did not know in every sense that He was divine? And how could He not have had that same knowledge when, the day after feeding the five thousand, he talked about his disciples eating his flesh and drinking his blood? And how could a priest who was interested in the self-consciousness of Jesus not realize this? Yet in his academic life, Father Brown was busy learning what every scholar and skeptic said about the consciousness of Jesus, and presumably he was teaching this sort of thing to the seminarians entrusted to his care.

That summer of 1966 I also had a course on moral theology taught by Fr. Josef Fuchs, S.J. I don't think any of us knew it, but he was, at the time, the principal author of the position paper of the majority of the papal birth control commission which argued in a very faulty way for the acceptance of contraception. I asked lots of questions in that course, and one day a priest thanked me, saying that I was asking good questions. The next year the same course taught by Fr. Fuchs was closed to the laity. There would be no more of those pesky questions that dared to question his personal views.

In October 1966, the commission presented its work to Pope Paul VI. I still wonder what the Pope's reactions were when he first reviewed it. I'm sure he was disappointed, but he might have felt relieved that the argument for contraception was so poor. In its objection to the majority position, the minority pointed out that the pro-contraception argument had no way to say NO to behaviors such as anal copulation and oral-genital copulation. The majority replied that they did not accept those behaviors, but they could not give any logical reason how they could accept some contraceptive behaviors and not accept heterosexual sodomy as a form of contraceptive behavior.

The reason that they didn't give any such reasons is that there aren't any. There is logic in human nature and there's logic in birth control, and they chose to follow the latter. For a more complete analysis of the majority report, see my *Sex and the Marriage Covenant*, (Ignatius, 2005, pages 304-309.) I think the Pope should have looked at that document for a week, taken another week to polish a reply, and then issued a statement saying that the debate is over, that the acceptance of contraception entails the logical acceptance of sodomy, and that there is no way that the teaching can be changed. He should have then promised an encyclical that would spell these things out in more detail and encouraged orthodox theological writers to point out the absurdity of the majority position.

More on Family

Early in our first pregnancy, I read an article that claimed that if a mother breastfed properly, her babies would be spaced about two years apart. The author said the properly breastfeeding mother might have ten children but wouldn't have twenty. I had no idea how we would support ten children, but it certainly sounded easier than twenty, so I asked Sheila a leading question, "You're going to breastfeed, aren't you?" Neither of us had come from breastfeeding families, and Sheila had never seen a baby nurse at the breast, but it sounded like a good idea to her. At her childbirth preparation classes, the instructor raved about breastfeeding and encouraged the women to attend the breastfeeding meetings of La Leche League (LLL). Sheila did so and learned once again about the baby-spacing effects of breastfeeding. She also discussed it with her doctor who pooh-poohed the idea and told her that no matter how she nursed, her periods would return within three months post-partum.

With our first baby, Sheila knew from her LLL meetings that she needed to nurse frequently day and night to maintain her milk supply, but we used baby-sitters just like everybody else used babysitters. We used pacifiers just like everyone else, and we thought we were on the inside track when we learned about a pacifier that was supposedly shaped like the human nipple when a baby was nursing. We also would not sleep with our baby so Sheila had to get up to nurse her during the night. In brief, we were thoroughly part of our culture, and Sheila did what is now called Western "cultural nursing." Sure enough, just like the doc had said, her periods returned by three months postpartum.

Our next pregnancy ended in a very early miscarriage, and that was followed by another early miscarriage. We then went to a Catholic fertility doctor who encouraged us to try again. Our next pregnancy resulted in a healthy baby who was born in 1966 on the day before the Feast of the Visitation of Mary to her cousin Elizabeth, then celebrated on July 2nd. That made name selection wonderfully easy. And to get way ahead of the story, our Mary Elizabeth named her daughter Elizabeth Marie.

With our second full-term pregnancy, Sheila had a different Ob-Gyn doctor who encouraged the use of the temperature method of natural family planning. He also knew that Sheila wanted to breastfeed so he encouraged her to breastfeed exclusively and frequently and to call him when she had her first period. When Sheila asked him about giving the baby water because of the hot summer, she was told not to give the baby anything but breastmilk, not even water. Sheila's pediatrician was also most cooperative and wished that other mothers in his practice would do exclusive breastfeeding. He also never told her to start solids. When she would ask, he said our baby was very healthy and doing fine. Mary had her first tooth at eight months, so Sheila took this as a sign to start solids.

Breastfeeding this time was a markedly different experience, and menstruation returned at 12 months. This difference led Sheila to research and then write her book on natural baby spacing, *Breastfeeding and Natural Child Spacing: The Ecology of Natural Mothering*.

Winding up in Santa Clara

I continued my evangelical efforts at St. Clare's. Then a parish up in East Palo Alto offered me a part-time position doing the same work, so I had two jobs. The second one gave me the privilege of working with Fr. John Sweeney who went on to become a legend of orthodoxy, holiness, and practicality in Santa Clara and the peninsula. (By practicality I refer to his founding Opportunities Industrialization Center West, a program that helped under-educated people get the skills needed for decent employment.) Then the University of Santa Clara had an unexpected opening and asked me to fill in for a basic theology course. So I was working three jobs and loving it. One night, however, I found out that my cardiovascular system wasn't in total agreement with my head and my heart. I was talking with an adult student after an evening class, probably about 9:30 or 10:00. All of a sudden, I had trouble breathing. I just couldn't get enough air to satisfy my need for oxygen. Something wasn't right. I asked my student to drive me to the ER room. As he did, I poked my head out the window to get more air. By the time Sheila got there, I was getting oxygen and had a few other tubes confusing the picture. She was brave, but she really bawled when she got home. She was really afraid I was a goner. Fortunately, it was just a warning. The doc told me I was working too hard, so I believed him. One of my associates was delighted to take the job in East Palo Alto.

I was happy to finish my MA work at USF in 1967. The commute had gotten tiring, and for a while I was a full-time student, staying in a dorm during the week and coming home Friday afternoon. By now we had two children, and they liked having daddy around. When I would get back on

Friday afternoon, one-year-old Mary would plunk herself in my lap and didn't want to move.

It was apparent to us as well as to Father Prendeville that maybe it was time to move on. He had generously allowed me to finish my academic work as things were winding down, and we told Father Zimmers at the ILT that we would like to work in a new parish. A parish in Saskatchewan had contacted the ILT, and the connections were made.

My adventure in California was complete. For me it was a great success. I had met and married the light of my life, and we had two living children plus two who had miscarried quite early. I had completed the ILT academic program and the USF graduate theology program, and I had experienced four years of parish evangelism with its joys and difficulties. It was a great seven years. On to Saskatchewan.

2. Our Canadian Experience

The interview with Father Emmet Mooney, pastor of Christ the King parish in Regina, Saskatchewan, and some of his parishioners took place in April 1967, and they were quite embarrassed by the weather. It was not only cold but an ice storm had covered everything with a reminder of winter. They feared that this guy from California would never move into that sort of frigid environment. I assured them that I was Minnesota tough and had delivered mail one Christmas season when the temp stayed at minus 35° Fahrenheit all day. However, what I couldn't get accustomed to during the April visit was the low temperature in the rectory where I was Fr. Mooney's guest, so I walked a mile or so to buy some thermal-knit long underwear.

One of the people I met was Marianne Schamber who lived with her husband Alex and their four children across the street from the rectory and church. Her next-door neighbor was moving and had a house to sell. This seemed providential, and I bought it before returning to Santa Clara. By the time we were ready to move, the Regina house was empty. Marianne had the key, so when we arrived our belongings were already in the house.

My 1958 Ford Convertible had accumulated over a hundred thousand miles, and the transmission was weakening. The problem was unnoticeable when the car was cool, but when the transmission was hot, it had almost no power in reverse. I told this to the prospective buyers, and we sold it to someone who didn't have a problem with the weak transmission and needed a car for one of his children. Aside from some rust around the headlights, it was still a beautiful automobile. We got a used Chevelle and set out on our trip, camping occasionally on the way.

We especially liked the campground in Bend, Oregon, and the only other campout that stays with me was Lake Louise in Banff National Park. We heard animals—probably bears—roaming around the tent at night giving credence to the ranger's warning to put all food in the trunk of the car. The temperature dropped well below 32° F., freezing our water and giving our sleeping bags a good test. We walked part way around Lake Louise to the point where glacial water flowed into the lake and gave it a distinctly gray color, a huge contrast with the deep blue at the center. I was carrying one-year-old Mary in a back carrier, and three-year-old Jenny did a great job on the first part of the walk. Coming home, she needed some help, so she became my second passenger, riding on my shoulders.

We quickly settled into our new home, and to our delight there were public tennis courts within easy bike-riding distance. That first summer we enjoyed the evening light and occasional tennis till close to ten o'clock. I began my new job on September 1, 1967.

Father Emmett Mooney

Father Emmett Mooney was in his early fifties and had become the founding pastor of Christ the King Parish in 1955. He would celebrate his Silver Jubilee of ordination to the priesthood in the first half of 1969. He was a complex personality, good in so many ways and yet totally lacking in his sense of justice, as will become clear later on, despite a doctorate in theology. He regularly made a personal visit to each parish home every two or three years if not every year. He directed the parking-lot traffic before the Sunday Masses as a way of making regular contact with parishioners, and he greeted people on the way out of church. He took pride in the parish lawn, fertilizing it himself each spring so it was one of the greenest and most weed-free, and mowing it each week as well. He was a great fan of the local professional football team, the Roughriders, and had regular social events such as monthly parish dances. He was the only pastor in all of Canada, to the best of my knowledge, to contact the Institute of Lay Theology and to employ one of its graduates. He was both frugal and generous, and I think he and the parish were largely responsible for the building of a new chancery office for the diocese, in my opinion a most worthwhile project.

On the other hand, he was known to be a loner. He listened to his handpicked group of advisors, but apparently he did not take easily to suggestions from others. For whatever reasons, parishioners who knew him well were betting among themselves that this new guy—lay theologian or evangelist—would not last a year. They had not yet met me so their betting against me was based solely on their knowledge of Fr. Mooney. Toward the end of that first year, I certainly wished that they had confided their reservations about the value of a three-year contract when I came up for the initial interview.

Friends and Neighbors

The front door of our house on Garnet Street faced the front door of Christ the King Church directly across the street. In the house to our left as we faced the church lived the Schambers who were great neighbors, teaching Sheila how to can various foods and sharing some of the moose meat that Alex brought home from his annual hunt. They are, unfortunately, the only Regina folks with whom we have kept in contact over the years with an exchange of Christmas cards. Ray Crozier helped me tremendously to transform our basement into a recreation room during the first winter. Wilf Oberthier and Harry Richardson laid their reputations on the line in trying to obtain justice when unhappy things happened in the spring of 1968 and continued happening all throughout the next 12 months. Dorothy and Ernie Lawby provided great support. In the weeks when Father Mooney was considering the employment of an ILT graduate, he frequently consulted with them, sometimes dropping by for coffee after the Sunday Masses. Dorothy would have a telling observation to make sometime after Pope Paul VI issued *Humanae Vitae*, the landmark encyclical that reaffirmed traditional Catholic teaching against unnatural forms of birth control. In short, apart from the conflict, my memories of our stay in Regina are happy ones.

In the house just south of us lived Stan Robertson, an older gentleman who had an interesting story to tell. He had come to this area maybe 60 years previously when the primeval sod was first being broken for cultivation. He worked a plow behind a team of beasts of burden (I forget whether they were horses, mules, or oxen). The mosquitoes were numbered in the billions or trillions, and they swarmed all around these intruders upon their ancestral breeding grounds. All the other men had to swath their heads and arms and hands in protective cheesecloth, but not Stan. They didn't bother him a bit. I told him that he should will his body to a medical school for scientific research to try to find out what made him so repellant to these pesky mosquitoes.

The Parish Job

A small room in the parish hall was converted to an office for me, and it was quite adequate. Soon I began our customary work of promoting and teaching the Inquiry Forum described in Chapter 1. There were no problems along that line except the customary one of attendance. It was difficult, as always, to get regular parishioners to bring non-practicing or uncommitted friends to a course on the Faith. At a meeting with Fr. Mooney and some of his advisors, I was criticized because the regular parishioners weren't coming to the courses on the Faith. Of course, exactly none of his advisors had showed up either. They were essentially asking how I was going to get people just like them to come when they themselves were not interested. Early in 1968 I conducted an afternoon class on the social teachings of the Church, and in one session I taught about participative management—the recognition of the dignity and intelligence of employees and seeking their input to the decision-making process. Some of the women thought I sounded Communistic, so they alerted their husbands who attended the next session. They were relieved to assure their wives that what I was talking about was considered enlightened management in the secular sphere, but they did not return for the rest of the course.

The Parish Council

The first out-of-the-ordinary task that Father Mooney gave me was to form a parish council. I dutifully asked him what sort of council he wanted—a "Yes, Father" council or one that would encourage initiative. I was not a big fan of parish councils since I considered them to be largely a waste of time, but this is what the pastor wanted. I told him that an initiative-taking council would involve inefficiency, debate and conflict. I didn't know how prophetic I was at the time. He told me to form an initiative-taking council, and I attempted to do so. It was a job-fatal mistake.

What follows now is a long quotation from a newsletter, *The Layman's Reporter*, written by the Committee for Justice and Truth, Co-Chairmen C.H. Richardson and Wilf Oberthier, editor C. Laughlan. This was published in the fall of 1968 for several weeks to inform parishioners about what led up to the pastor firing me in May 1968. Sorry to spill the beans so soon in the narrative, but as I reread, 41 years after the facts, the details written at the time, I thought this quotation was the most accurate and succinct way to describe what happened. It can be a bit confusing because I give the publication dates of the *Layman's Reporter* describing events that happened months earlier. I have retained the authors' headings and capitalization, but I have deleted the names of some individuals.

THE COUNCIL WITHOUT A CONSTITUTION

DISCUSSED AT FIRST COUNCIL MEETING
At the first meeting of the Parish Council on February 14, 1968, members discussed the purpose and objectives of the Council and the need for a Constitution. Mr. Kippley volunteered to send to each member of the Council a draft that had been worked up by the steering committee (Fr. Mooney, Dorothy Lawby, John Kippley and three others).

CONSTITUTION STUDY COMMITTEE
At the next meeting, members had the draft Constitution before them and decided to appoint a committee to recommend any changes. The committee consisted of Paul Mercier, Dorothy Lawby and John Kippley. They met for several hours and quickly agreed upon some alterations to the original draft.

THE BEGINNING OF THE END
If normal parliamentary procedure had been followed, the draft would have been reported in at the next meeting without further bother. It would have then been further scrutinized by individual members and subjected to debate that might have been very educational. However, Mr. Mercier went directly to President Benny Murphy and they worked out their own version. A copy was sent to Mrs. Lawby and Mr. Kippley who

were both disturbed by the drastic difference between the two concepts.

RULE BY FEW OR PARTICIPATION BY ALL

The Constitution Committee draft put the power in the Council as a whole. Each member, officer or working Guild Chairman, had an equal vote. The people who were in charge of getting the work done would participate fully in the decision making process and power.

The Mercier-Murphy draft put the power in a Management Committee which included the officers and as many others as the pastor wanted to appoint. The Parish Council as a whole, the people who did the work, was effectively cut out of real participation in the decision-making process.

PROBLEM SOLVING BY ELIMINATION

The Constitution Committee draft established seven Activity Guilds whose Chairmen formed a majority of the Council. The M & M draft gave the Management Committee the right to "disband existing guilds." "Management" unhappy with a Guild Chairman? Simple—just disband the Guild. By the way do you know what has happened to the Adult Education Committee?

NEVER SUBMITTED

The M & M draft was never submitted to all the members of the Council. Nor did Mr. Mercier ever report in the draft of the Constitution Committee. Instead, the Management group decided not to have a constitution.

Dated October 27, 1968

The Parish Council in More Detail

April 26, 1968. After those first meetings described above, the Executive Committee met in the evening of April 26 in Father Mooney's living room at 7:30. They decided that the Council would not have a constitution. A spokesman was appointed to tell me their decision, and at 9:00 they invited me to their meeting. The message was delivered: the executive committee had decided it was management and the rest of the Council members were workers. Management would make all the decisions. I said I was opposed to this decision. On November 3, the *Layman's Reporter* noted what followed.

Father Mooney explained that they had hoped for his cooperation but did not make it a condition of employment to go along with it. Instead he recognized the freedom of Mr. Kippley to oppose the decision of the executive.

Mr. Kippley still believes that he is bound by professional obligations to oppose the assumption of authority by a few. He feels he must support the teachings of the Church and oppose contrary views. He bases his opposition both on theology and on modern management practice. In theology assumption of authority by a few is contrary to the labor management teachings of the Church and to the entire spirit of democratization created by Vatican II. In modern management, it is axiomatic that good management in many areas shares the decision making process to the largest degree possible. Decision making develops people, and good management wants to develop its people so that their jobs become more meaningful. Unfortunately, the executive which decided that it was Management seems to have stayed with management theories popular in the 18th century and in the earlier part of this one.

The *Reporter* then added:

Fr. Mooney admitted to people before this conflict arose that he didn't really know how to get a parish council going. He assigned the task to Mr. Kippley with the explicit understanding that it was not to be a "Yes, Father" council.

However, the whole process of making the decision about the framework within which the Council would operate was done with the positive exclusion of Mr. Kippley.

Perhaps this is a good place to note the qualifications of the two co-chairmen of the Truth and Justice Committee and thus the authors of the text. C. H. Richardson represented the managements of a consortium of small businesses in their labor-management dealings. W. Oberthier was the human resources director at a large Catholic hospital. That is, they were both management people.

I should have taken this calmly, but I had become too involved with some of the parishioners. I didn't think of myself as taking sides with them in their relationship with our pastor, but that's what had happened. I had become too wrapped up in their excitement, and now I saw that he was crushing everything. So my adrenaline went to work in a way I had never experienced before, and it would probably kill me if it would happen again. I felt this big ball of energy coming up my throat. Fight or flight. If I recall correctly, I blew up; I was anything but meek and mild.

With the benefit of 20/20 hindsight vision, I can see that I should have played the role of the professional, the consultant, the teacher, but not that of an involved parishioner supportive of the other ordinary parishioners. I should have excused myself; I could have honestly said I wasn't feeling well; I would have done well to go on a very long walk. The effect was predictable. The pastor's decision simply deflated the legitimate hopes and excitement felt by these faithful parishioners. They recognized that he hadn't changed. They probably realized that my days were numbered.

That was April 26.

April 30. The next Council meeting was on April 30. *The Layman's Reporter* of November 17 described it this way.

> At the meeting of April 30, the executive garnered the votes of 3 of the 10 other Council members and managed to put through a vote which deprived the Council as a whole of having any effective decision-making power. The meeting was on an irregular date, four members were absent, and the majority of the Guild Chairmen voted against the motion.
>
> At the same meeting it was decided by a unanimous vote that there should be a coffee and donut get-together in the parish hall in May or June. At the meeting of May 7 it was decided unanimously to hold a parish picnic. It was also decided that the Adult Education Committee should publish a parish bulletin that would publicize the activities of the Council and other parish activities. There was also discussion about a parish library.

Things were tight. We alerted the ILT, and the parish did likewise. The ILT responded to the invitation from the parish and sent a new staffer, Brian Gagan, to calm the roiled waters. Brian, who had done the work of a parish lay evangelist since 1962, arrived the evening of May 2. No one notified me he was coming. Gagan explained that he had not personally notified me because he took it for granted that the pastor would do so.

May 5. Sheila insisted that Brian and I should get together with the pastor to try to work out a plan. We did so on May 5. We presented a typed statement of clarification for Father Mooney's review and assent or clear dissent. It included this statement:

> Therefore the pastor agrees in thought and in writing to allow the lay theologian to meet with other parishioners both individually and in groups, both in Council and outside of Council to discuss Church and parish matters even if it is known that the pastor and the lay theologian have different opinions on these affairs.

As reported in *The Layman's Reporter,* (November 17, 1968), Fr. Mooney gave his wholehearted assent to this. Both Mr. Kippley and Mr. Gagan felt that the spirit was such that it would have been excessively legalistic to ask Fr. Mooney to sign it. If you can't take a man's word of agreement to something that is in black and white, what's the Church coming to?

Exactly three weeks later, Fr. Mooney typed out the notice of dismissal to Mr. Kippley. No formal reason has yet been given...

At that May 5th meeting, Fr. Mooney also agreed that Council members should bring their proposals to Council for debate. He, the pastor, would have veto power. However, neither party explained this to the Council.

The ILT mission was not successful. As Brian wrote when I requested his recollection while writing this:

John, I knew forty years ago that I could accomplish very little, if anything, once I had conferred with Fr. Mooney. I came back and told Fr. Zimmers so, and hoped he would have more clout since he was the one who convinced Fr. Mooney to take an ILT grad. The fact I left ILT in the following year tells you how I saw our collective future.

May 21. Shortly before the meeting on May 21, the executive committee decided to cancel the after-Mass coffee party on May 26th for which they had all voted on April 30. At 9:00 p.m. they invited the gentleman who had already made all the arrangements. When I heard about it, I asked Mr. Kirsch why he didn't fight for his program. Mr. Kirsch replied that he didn't come to Church to fight and besides, who was he, one man against six?

At the May 21st Council meeting, Father Mooney was not present. The executive committee announced that they would be calling the chairman of each committee into executive session to discuss their programs with them. Bearing in mind the experience of Mr. Kirsch, I suggested that such program discussions be carried out in the open forum of the Council. The November 17th issue of *The Layman's Reporter* described what happened next.

Mr. Kippley used this meeting to explain that the conflict that was being experienced in the Parish Council was nothing unique but was simply a manifestation of the conflict in the Church as a whole. He explained that there are two schools of thought which are opposed. One wants an open Church, with discussions and differences out in the open. The other wants all the decision making carried on by a few in closed sessions, and not subject to review by others.

One member of the executive apparently couldn't stand the idea of openly expressed differences and walked out. The next morning, according to Fr. Mooney, three people told him to fire John Kippley. These people have never been identified.

At the May 21st meeting, I made the huge mistake of not telling the Council that the pastor had agreed in our meeting of May 5th that Council members should bring their proposals to the Council for debate instead of clearing them with him first. I should have told them that from the beginning our pastor had said he wanted an initiative-taking Council, not one that just said "Yes, Father." And I should have emphasized that the pastor would necessarily have the responsibility to veto Council decisions not in conformity with Catholic teaching and discipline and the right to veto decisions with which he simply disagreed as a matter of personal opinion. As it was, some of the Council members felt I was undermining the pastor and perhaps the Church. If memory serves, they waited at the parish meeting room until Fr. Mooney got back to the rectory, and it was then that they unloaded their displeasure with me.

Termination of Employment

May 27. On the morning of May 27, Father Mooney called me to his office at 9:00, a very unusual occurrence. With no explanation, he asked me to resign, and I told him I couldn't. He said that didn't surprise him since I never went along with his plans and then handed me a letter of termination that quoted the "grave cause" paragraph of the contract. I asked him what the grave cause was and he said that I had been creating discord and dissension in the parish. In what was to follow, he never provided any evidence for that charge. I was hired on his authority and I was fired on his authority. Giving any alleged evidence would have allowed me to respond and to explain. He carefully avoided that possibility. He said he regretted the timing since Sheila was due to give birth in a few weeks. He really expected us to put our house up for sale and move back home, wherever that might be.

Early that evening I asked a group of Cub Scout Leaders if they were aware of any discord or dissension that I was creating. None answered affirmatively. Someone asked why I was asking, and I replied that there were some rumors to that effect. I didn't tell them I had been fired because I didn't know these men and I thought the matter could be patched.

Since Fr. Mooney had not forbidden me to continue my courses, I taught class that evening. After class I asked the group if they thought I was creating any discord or dissension in the parish. Again, no one said anything. Finally somebody asked the reason for the question, and I told them I had been fired that morning and that "creating discord and dissension" was given as the reason. They were all surprised and shocked. Many wondered what they could do.

May 30. A few minutes before my 1:30 p.m. Thursday class started, Fr. Mooney came to my office and told me to clean it out and hand in my keys by 6:00 p.m. Friday. I said, "Are you sure you wouldn't like to sit down to discuss the matter?" and he just shook his head in the negative. He also gave me my paycheck for the month of May. At the Thursday evening class, many parishioners already knew the "news" via the grapevine. However, due to the presence of one lady who had identified herself as a fallen away Catholic, I didn't want to risk shaking her faith any more, so I was extremely cautious in telling them there wouldn't be any more classes. Several people stayed a long time after class and wondered what they could do. I told them nothing yet, that we hoped to have it settled by the weekend.

As indicated earlier, the Parish Council had voted unanimously to have coffee and donuts after Masses, to have a parish library, and to have a parish newsletter. The executive canceled the first, deferred the library action to seek funds from a diocesan office, but what happened to the newsletter? It was to be published by the Adult Education Committee. The first issue was soon ready to go, but the editor was waiting for the pastor's letter, a necessary component. It never came. That was his way of vetoing the idea.

After the termination, we held a meeting in our basement of people who were supportive, but it soon became clear that we could not expect any help by way of pressure on the pastor. First, there really wasn't any way anyone except the bishop could influence him. Second, they realized that it was just a matter of time before we moved somewhere while they would still be living in Regina. So I looked for a job, retained a labor lawyer, and tried to obtain either reconciliation or a settlement. This is how I summarized the first couple of months' efforts in my addendum to the last issue (Nov. 17) of the *Reporter.*

> I and others tried to get this whole business settled quietly. In the first week I asked Fr. Mooney both personally and through an attorney to sit down to discuss the matter. Refused. Then others went to see him individually without success; then a group of 50 parishioners elected 8 of their number to meet with the executive [committee] to discuss the issues. Refused. I and others asked the bishop to intervene; nothing came of it. Finally after seven weeks of having every effort at conciliation turned down, I did the only thing left: I obtained permission from the archbishop and filed suit.

I eventually found out that my three-year contract with the parish was unenforceable because I was not a signatory to it. The three-year contract had been negotiated between Fr. Zimmers of the ILT and Fr. Mooney. The latter had signed two copies and returned one to ILT which was given to me. Not having the employee as a signatory was a big mistake on the part of the

ILT and myself deriving from lack of experience in these matters. Eventually my lawyer excused himself from the case. The provincial government was one of the biggest clients of his large law firm, and there was no need to create unnecessary tension with such a valued customer. The inability to pursue my case for the enforcement of the contract through the law did not, however, preclude efforts to pursue justice in the public forum.

Another Blessing

As Father Mooney had indicated as he fired me, Sheila was due to give birth in a few weeks. Her pregnancy had been proceeding smoothly, and her doctor (a friend who had been a dinner guest at our home) had been going along with her desires to have a natural childbirth. Suddenly at the start of the ninth month, he announced that he was going to catheterize her after childbirth, something Sheila had not experienced with her first two babies. Her doctor was somewhat new to the practice of obstetrics, but he was adamant. To say that Sheila was upset is to put it mildly. It is not always easy to find a doctor who will accept a new patient in her ninth month, but fortunately we were able to find a good doctor who was willing to accept her. Everything went well, giving us a great blessing at a time of great turmoil. Margaret Geri was born in mid-June, about three weeks after the firing.

The Job Search

The summer of 1968 became known as the summer of discontent in the States—the uproar at the Democrat's national convention in Chicago, the racial riots in the Watts area of Los Angeles and elsewhere, and protests against *Humanae Vitae*. My immediate concern in June was that it could not have been a much worse time to search for a job. By this time of the year, contracts for the next academic year had been signed and the openings filled. About June 10th I received a call from George Hendrix, a lay theologian at St. Mary of the Lake parish in the western Minneapolis suburb of Plymouth. Hendrix had learned of my availability from Brian Gagan. I left on June 15th for two meetings. On the 17th I met with the Executive Board and passed with flying colors. On the 18th I met with the whole Board with the same result. (On one of these Boards was a former grade school classmate whom I knew as Joan Richter. We didn't have any time for conversation, so I didn't know where she was on the theological spectrum.) Hendrix told me that I appealed to the people at both ends of the spectrum because of my support both for the social teachings of the Church and for the sexual teachings of the Church. The motion to hire me was attached to a motion having to do with some financial matters so, strictly speaking, it wasn't a firm job offer yet. However, I was asked to attend a weekend meeting in early July to meet the other new staff members and get a better feel for the parish. I flew back to Minneapolis on July 4 for an unforgettable experience.

At our first "T-group" session, one of the young men began to tell a sad story about himself and he actually started crying. This was totally strange to me. I was thinking to myself, "C'mon, get a grip on yourself," and finally Hendrix put his arm around him to offer comfort and support. Then we had an evaluation of that performance, and the young man with the sad story criticized me very directly for not coming to his aid. This was touchy-feely at its max, my first experience with sensitivity training. I never knew whether the young man was genuine or was playing a part in a prearranged act. As part of our orientation to the parish, we were also given a huge printout of comments by parishioners. Some of them were very unhappy that the pastor, Fr. Tony Louis, had discontinued the practice of professing the Nicene Creed at Sunday Mass. At a meeting with some parishioners, one of them said that this parish was her last stop. She was on the far left of religious opinion, and if this parish was any less liberal, she would simply stop attending Mass. We were not given the opportunity to attend one of the regular parish Sunday morning Masses, so I thought we would be having Mass in the afternoon. Not at all. As the pastor was summarizing the weekend on Sunday afternoon, I asked him when we were going to have Mass. "Oh," he replied, "this whole weekend has been one big Eucharist." Apparently no one else found anything strange about this. As soon as I could, I started to phone a few parishes to find a late Sunday Mass, but after a few tries, I gave up. I still had to return the rented car and get to the airport.

When I got back home in Regina, I had some second thoughts about the job. Clearly, I did not fit in with the pastor or his associate, Fr. Tom Sweeney, whom I recognized from my seminary days; he had been a few years ahead of me. So on July 10th I started to type a letter reaffirming once again my orthodox Catholic faith. I was willing to work in that hotbed, but I wanted to make sure that I was free to work as a believing Catholic without being fired for that cause. As I was writing it, the phone rang. It was Hendrix. It seems that Fr. Tony and Fr. Tom Sweeney had decided that I wouldn't fit in, so the job offer was rescinded. Well, I thought, better now than after a month on the job, but how phony. Father Tony had gone on and on that Sunday afternoon about how everyone had been so open and how wonderful that was, but he couldn't be open enough to tell me and the group that he had some problems with my ordinary and orthodox Catholicism. Later, I found out that he was considered out in left field even by the liberal priests of the archdiocese.

A New Job

Back in Regina, I kept looking and a few weeks later I was employed as a Senior Management Analyst in the Research and Planning Branch of the Saskatchewan Department of Public Health. This was based on my previous experience selling IBM systems and hardware, and it was the cushiest job I ever had. It was an easy ten or fifteen minute walk from home; we had an hour and a half for lunch as was common in Regina at the time. I didn't have big responsibilities that I would carry home at least in my head if not my briefcase. It was a very short-lived experience.

I began working on August 20. On September 6, I had finished two and a half weeks of work, and my boss was away on a business trip. His next-in-command, a pleasant young man, called me into his office and gave me an early and informal job performance review. He told me that the young women I was helping with systems design had told him how helpful I was being to them. That was certainly welcome news. At 3:00 that afternoon, the deputy minister of health called my acting boss and said he wanted to see me. When my acting boss put down the phone he naturally asked me what this was all about. After all, new employees are not accustomed to being invited to talk with deputy ministers. I tried to make light of it, saying that maybe my salary had broken the budget, but both my stomach and my head knew otherwise.

Disemployed Again

The meeting with Deputy Minister Dr. S. L. Skoll, M.B., D.P.H., was very brief. "Hello, Mr. Kippley. I regret that in our first meeting I have to inform you that your job is not being filled." I replied, "Could you affirm that this decision was reached without any outside influence?" "No, I couldn't say anything about that, but you can see the minister of health if you would like to do so." "Yes, I would." End of meeting.

Back in the office, I reported what had happened, and a black pall covered the area. I had told some of them about what brought us to Canada, and what happened to my parish job. They knew this unhappy event had nothing to do with my job performance and everything to do with politics. At 4:00 that same afternoon, I met with the Minister of Health, Mr. Gordon Grant. He told me that at a Cabinet meeting that morning it was decided not to fill the position. According to my diary, I asked him, "Since the job was killed at the Cabinet level, I can't help feeling that it was political and that I am politically unacceptable to someone. Of course, in these cases one always wonders why." He did not make an ambiguous statement about finances or say that I shouldn't go away feeling that way. Instead, he merely said: "The Cabinet decided not to fill the position. We are sworn to secrecy. That's all I can say. I hope you can overcome the problem."

What was "the problem"?

An Unhappy Collusion of Pastor and State

My suspicion that this was the work of Father Mooney was quickly confirmed. On that very same day, September 6, on which I was disemployed by the Health Department, Fr. Mooney's attorney, Ed Bayda, wrote me a letter offering to 1) buy my house, 2) pay some moving expenses, and 3) pay some damages. The funds offered were insufficient, but even that small offer was contingent on this condition:

> Mr. Kippley must move himself and his family out of the Province not later than October 1st, 1968 and performance by the defendants and the Parish of Numbers 1, 2, and 3 above is entirely contingent upon Mr. Kippley moving out of the Province on or before October 1st, 1968 and remaining out of the Province.

By way of background, the employment of foreigners had to be approved by the Cabinet. This was normally just a rubber-stamp operation done after employment had already started. (I understand that after my case the procedure was tightened.) Canadian nationals were given preference for all government jobs, and that was the case for mine which had been advertised in the Regina paper, but apparently no Canadian had applied or my qualifications were better. I knew that my pastor was political, so after I started my new job I had remained very low key. I had told a couple of close friends that I was employed, but there was no jubilant gloating that I could now stick around and participate in the parish council.

The mere fact that I wasn't leaving town was a problem for my pastor, and somehow a parishioner who was a cabinet minister learned of Fr. Mooney's unhappiness. At the regular review of new employees, the parishioner blackballed me. Since approval had to be unanimous, one negative vote was sufficient to make me unemployed again. To put that in another way, through an unhappy collusion of church people and state people, I was being told in no uncertain ways to get out of town. The government was the biggest employer in Regina, and the church people didn't have jobs to fill. It was now early September. The cold weather ads were omnipresent on the radio. The utility bill would start going up, and I didn't have any income or any prospects of finding a job. Any business that was dependent upon government business would be taking a foolish risk to employ me. In the Province of Saskatchewan, politics was everything.

Disemployment

So what do you do when you've been fired without cause from your church job and had your state job dissolved? I started talking and looking. On September 9, Wilf Oberthier and I had a long conversation with another parishioner whose basic attitude was that if there's a problem involving an employee, the employee has to go, no matter what the problem or its causes. But he was shocked to learn the events of September 6. The next day he called Fr. Mooney who denied even knowing that I was working for the Province. The parishioner told him that he found that difficult to believe. For some time, Fr. Mooney continued to deny he had anything to do with it, but eventually he admitted to the priests that he had been involved, and still later his attorney would tell a lawyer helping me that a parishioner in the Provincial Cabinet had blackballed me.

On September 12, I interviewed for a job with Frank Proto at Saskatchewan Power. He found my qualifications okay for a job in systems analysis but said he would have to talk it over with the general manager. The next day I called him about 11:00, and he was interested in knowing who knew I had interviewed with him. He had already received a phone call from a minor Liberal politician suggesting that he have nothing to do with me. He was amazed at the speed of the effort. Months later, after I had finished taking some courses in secondary education, my advisor told me that he didn't think I would ever get a teaching job in the Province of Saskatchewan. I was politically a *persona non grata* simply because Fr. Mooney wanted me to leave town.

On Sunday evening, September 15, I participated in a panel on "Birth Control and Beyond." The organizers couldn't find any of the local priests to defend *Humanae Vitae,* so they invited me. A woman with a degree in theology was only too ready to criticize it. Her argument was amazing. She said she was *by nature* a loving person and therefore her acts were, by nature, loving. The encyclical condemned her acts of contraception as contrary to the demands of married love. Therefore, she concluded, the encyclical was wrong. I could hardly believe my ears. There are only three Persons in the universe who are *by nature* loving persons, and their names are Father, Son and Holy Spirit. God is love. The very nature of God is love. That cannot be said of his creatures. For a sinful woman to make the statement she made was simply preposterous. I thought it was so stupid that I thought it would be too embarrassing for her if I said so in the debate, so I remained silent on that key point. That was a huge mistake. The dissenters need to be confronted at every possible point with the amazing falsity and vacuity of their arguments. I was told later that Archbishop O'Neill said after the meeting that I was the only one to say anything worthwhile, but his subsequent handling of the dispute certainly showed no appreciation.

On September 18th, I talked with my former boss, Dr. Ramsay, who said he was advised as a good public servant not to write a letter of recommendation for me. He also told me that he had been told that I had been hired as a consultant, not as regular staff, and that was as much news to Dr. Ramsay as it was to me. Three weeks of efforts to find out why my job was dissolved brought only the repeated statement by the Minister of Health that it was a Cabinet decision and therefore secret.

Further, I couldn't even get a letter that would account for my employment history. The reply of the Minister of Health to such a request was almost humorous.

I am in receipt of your letter dated October 7, 1968.

I know that it has already been explained to you that since you are not a British subject, you could not, by reasons of The Public Service Act of this province, become employed as a member of the Public Service except by appointment by the Lieutenant Governor in Council. Since this appointment was never made, you were, from the Government's point of view, never an employee, and since you were not an employee the question as to the reason for the termination of employment cannot arise.

While you may find these circumstances unusual, I am confident that you understand the relationship between the Department and yourself to a sufficient extent to enable you to explain your activities during the period in question.

Yours sincerely, S. L. Skoll, M.B., D.P.H.

The night of September 18th, Fr. Godfrey Dieckman, OSB was in town for a lecture. In the social hour, I asked him about the possibility of having to sever communion with the local church in order to be loyal to the Roman Catholic Church. He answered that yes, that might be a possibility. There wasn't time to give him all the background behind the question, and who knows what he might have said if he had all the facts. I was beginning to feel excommunicated in a practical sense, and later I would use this feeling of practical excommunication and Fr. Dieckman's reply as an excuse for not worshipping with the church in the Diocese of Regina that I thought was flagrantly ignoring the Roman Catholic Church's teaching on social justice. That decision was truly stupid, and I regret it.

What Do You Do?

My situation was not enviable. By way of assets, I had three Master's degrees, some good experience in systems analysis and sales, good experience as a lay evangelist, a great wife and three small children, reasonable intelligence, lots of energy, and the Faith. Also, the Canadian federal government provided a monthly allowance for each child. I forget how much it was, but it was certainly enough to take care of their food and clothes. By way of liabilities, I was, for all practical purposes, unemployable in Saskatchewan in the areas of my knowledge and experience. Fortunately, our financial liabilities were limited. Our house payments were moderate, and we had no car payments. But still, the combination of house payments and general expenses would wear us down both financially and psychologically.

I worked up a plan.
1. I would seek public assistance if I was eligible.
2. I would keep looking for local short-term employment.

3. I would start looking for long-term employment back in the States.
4. Acknowledging the possibility that I might not find college employment in the States, I would prepare myself to teach in secondary education by taking local university courses.
5. I would write a book to defend *Humanae Vitae*.
6. I would do what I could to obtain a just settlement with the parish.

Lastly, I would have to do all of these things simultaneously. Since it might be confusing to read what I did in each area on a day-to-day basis, I have treated all of these subjects separately in what follows. There is some overlap including references to one or more of the subjects before they have been explained, so I ask the reader's forbearance.

1. Family Assistance

I have already described my initial efforts to seek employment. Within hours after I had interviewed for a job with Saskatchewan Power about a week after my disemployment by the Provincial Cabinet, a political operative had pressured Saskatchewan Power against me. The Province was not only the biggest employer but also, in many cases, the biggest customer, and certainly it was the most influential body in the Province of Saskatchewan. The chances of obtaining church-related employment were also nil. Under these circumstances, I felt justified in seeking public assistance commonly called welfare. If the state wouldn't let me work, I felt no compunctions about the state helping to feed Sheila and me; the federal government was already providing its standard child subsidies to help feed our children as it did for all families. I researched the regulations and soon fit into them. We could own a house but almost nothing beyond that of any value. On November 11, we sold our car to the Keiser family up the street who wanted a car for a college-age daughter, and every time I saw the car pull out of the driveway, a wound was reopened. I borrowed money from my younger sister so I could pay off the mortgage on our small house and not be burdened by mortgage payments.

On January 2, 1969 I formally applied for family assistance and for assistance with postgraduate education. The next day we were accepted for family assistance, but the education assistance was denied. We received our first check on February 4, but not many more. Political pressure was being brought upon the welfare office. On February 14, Jim McLaughlin at Welfare told me that he didn't think I would ever get a job teaching in Saskatchewan. On March 12, McLaughlin told me he could feel the pressure of the politics of my case in the office. Apparently there were some zealous Catholics in the office who were taking Fr. Mooney's side. Jim had heard that the parish was going to try to stop my picketing via a 19th century law prohibiting interference with a Church service on the grounds that the picketing was causing emotional disturbances to some people thus interfering with their worship. (This is covered in the next chapter.) On

April 16, my case worker asked me to come down to the welfare office. Someone had told them that I had received money in October and November. I explained that I had sold the car and that liquid assets had been converted to paying off the mortgage on the house. The interesting aspect of this is that it showed that the privacy of my bank records had been violated.

2. Local Short-term Employment

When spring arrived, it was common policy in Regina to discontinue welfare to all able-bodied men. Sometime in May my neighbor, Stan Robertson, hired me to paint his house, and I finished that in the first week in June. Then somehow I found a temporary job working at a Chrysler plant, riding my bike to work. The week of June 16th I worked the day shift, taking apart and putting up some new parts bins. The next week I worked the night shift from 6:30 p.m. to 3:00 a.m., except that on Friday we worked until 5:00 a.m. because of a mishap that caused 51 feet of shelving to collapse. I think I continued this job until just before we left Regina in mid-July.

I also picked up a few dollars by working as an itinerant photographer. My favorite photo of my dad was taken at his office, looking up from his deskwork. So I hoped others would like such a memory photo. In mid-April, I built a darkroom in our basement and bought a camera and darkroom equipment. On April 28, I paid my city business license tax and took my first pictures—Bill Cameron and Foster Barnsley. Bill was a friend, and Foster Barnsley is a non-remembered person in my diary; he may have been associated with the school where I did practice teaching. On May 1st, I made my first deliveries and began canvassing for business. When I finally concluded the business, I found it didn't make any profit after expenses for equipment and supplies, but it had provided a cash flow and the opportunity to do something constructive. Providentially, someone with whom I had invested some funds well before I met Sheila started to pay back the investment that spring, so once again we got by.

I also put in a couple of good days of volunteer work. The Wascana Creek flows in a northerly direction through Regina, and since the creek is usually blocked by ice farther north, it typically floods a bit. The flooding in the spring of 1969 was much worse than usual, so the call went out for volunteers to man the dikes. Free bus service was provided. After I finished some other work on April 14, I left about 3:00 p.m. I got a good workout and got home a little after 1:00 a.m. The first thing I heard on the morning radio was another appeal for volunteers on the dikes. I left home about 7:15 and put in a full day. When I got home about 5:00 that afternoon, I was so weary that I felt almost feverish.

3. The Search for Long-Term Employment

After the ill-fated search for parish employment in the summer of 1968, I realized that the best way, if not the only one, to use my theological education was to teach theology at the college level. I also realized that in the new era of post-*Humanae Vitae* dissent, there would be very limited interest in my services, especially after the publication of my future book defending *Humanae Vitae*.

December 26 in Canada is a holiday called Boxing Day. I spent the day typing envelopes to mail a résumé to all 230 Catholic colleges in the States. On the 27th I mimeographed the letters and my résumé, and I also typed a letter to 18 U.S. bishops about adult education programs. On Saturday the 28th I collated, stuffed and mailed the 230 letters. I noted in my diary: "Expect maximum of 8 letters expressing any interest." About the letters to the bishops, I noted "Expect at most one reply expressing interest."

My guess about the replies from colleges proved amazingly accurate. I received nine replies—seven by mail and two by phone. There were no replies to my letters to the bishops. On Friday, January 17, I had a call from Father Robert Levis at Gannon University in Erie, PA. He was interested in someone permanent and not just for a year or two. As I write these memoirs, I wonder what I might have said that gave the impression I was looking only for short-term employment, or why I had not corrected that impression on the phone. Was I thinking at that time of working for only a couple years and then going on for a doctorate in theology? I don't know. Working for him would have been great.

On Thursday, January 30 I started to make plans for the college interviews. By this time I was taking university courses and practice teaching, so I needed to get cleared for my absences. My professors and supervisor understood and obliged; fortunately, there would be no school on my absent days, so I didn't miss any practice teaching days. On Friday and Saturday I called seven colleges and made reservations.

On Wednesday, February 5, I caught a 9:35 a.m. flight to Boston for an interview at Stonehill College. The next day I flew to New York and rented a car to drive to Poughkeepsie to interview at Marist College. Leaving there, the front tire was low, so I stopped to have it changed. Back on the Thruway, the radiator boiled over because the radiator cap was off. Kept driving to Newark for a short flight to Philadelphia where I taxied out to St. Joseph's College for an evening interview. On Friday I caught an early morning flight to Baltimore for an interview at Loyola. That afternoon I flew to Scranton to interview at Marygrove. That same evening I caught an 8:30 flight to Pittsburgh, then Kansas City, two different airports in Chicago, and then to Salina, Kansas, arriving about mid-morning on Saturday for an interview at Marymount College. Next I left at 7:00 that evening for Denver, arriving about 1:00 a.m. Sunday, and interviewing with Loretto Heights. My final trip was back to Regina that Sunday, arriving home about 5:00 p.m. and attending 7:30 p.m. Mass at the Cathedral. As I read the account of this trip in my diary 40 years later, I was utterly amazed. At this point in my life, I think such a schedule would probably kill me.

At most of these colleges, it would be necessary to have an earned doctorate for advancement and continued employment. I noted in my diary, "At the end of the trip, the place that looks best from all angles is Marymount of Salina." On February 11, the Feast of Our Lady of Lourdes, Marymount phoned with an offer that I was happy to accept. I took four days to respond, and by the time I did, I had reason to think that my phone was being bugged, so I used my neighbor's phone to accept the offer. It was a matter of tremendous relief to know where we would be living and what I would be doing during the next academic year.

4. Postgraduate Education

Late in 1968 I didn't know if my efforts to find employment in college teaching would be successful, so I needed to be prepared for other options. At the end of the year, I started to cover my bets, and at the library I got the names of 3 schools with PhD programs in Industrial Relations – Cornell University, the University of Wisconsin, and the University of Minnesota where I had earned the MA in Industrial Relations in 1956. I wrote them in early January, and I recall that there was a bit of correspondence, but as soon as I had a contract with Marymount in mid-February, I lost interest in pursuing the doctorate.

The pursuit of an education degree was different. That could be done in Regina and at relatively low expense. On December 16, the day before I finished proofreading the handwritten manuscript of my book, I talked with a counselor at the University of Regina, a Mrs. Broome, about a degree in secondary education. That same day I also applied for a job with the Adult Education Department, but that went nowhere. The next day I talked with a Mr. Burgess about the university's elementary education program. Then I came home, picked up transcripts and walked to the main campus where Mr. Hersh Cramer gave his permission for late admission to the Bachelor of Education after-degree program.

On January 2, I registered for courses. On Monday, January 6, I arranged my practice teaching with Mr. Waddell who very considerately set it up at Lakewood School, just four blocks from home. Later that day and the next as well I did substitute teaching for Fr. Trainer at Campion. Friday, March 21, was my last day of practice teaching, and I noted in my diary that it was "a most enjoyable experience." My course work was finished by mid-April, and I delivered a term paper to Professor Deutscher's office early on Wednesday, April 16.

5. Covenant, Christ and Contraception, Alba House, 1970

On July 25, 1968, just 15 days after the end of my experience with the very liberal parish in the western suburbs of Minneapolis (reported previously), Pope Paul VI published his encyclical, *Humanae Vitae,* to respond to the birth control issue. It was a surprise to many who had been conditioned by eight years of pro-contraception propaganda by Catholic publications and speakers. Like everyone else, I quickly became aware of the rebellion stirred up by Father Charles Curran and his fellow dissenters. My reaction was different from that of many others. For some years I had been reading the arguments of Curran and company, and I realized that their arguments simply did not hold water in the light of Christian discipleship. After gallons of ink had been spilled, their arguments against the Church's teachings about love, marriage, and chaste sexuality were quite simple. They accused the Church of having teachings that are difficult to follow. What an astounding discovery by our dissenters! If the commandments of love were easy, why would the Lord Jesus *command* us to love each other as well as to love our enemies? The dissenters then concluded that today's Christians are free to abandon the difficult sexual teachings of the Church that require self-control and generosity. That is simply not an argument from a Christian perspective. It is nonsense, and very harmful nonsense at that.

The Lord Jesus made it crystal clear that if we want to be his disciples we must take up our cross daily and follow Him. I take it for granted that most of us, especially us men, have difficulties most days in saying no to various and sundry unwanted sexual images or temptations. So it's part of our daily cross to say no to these temptations. The fact that a teaching is difficult to put into practice is absolutely no reason for a Christian to reject it. It is rather an invitation to grow closer to the Lord Jesus.

I looked in various publications to see what big-name theologians were writing to defend *Humanae Vitae* and to point out how ridiculous were the arguments of the dissenters. I didn't find any such announcements in the Catholic papers. I was aware of an excellent 1964 book on the natural law and contraception by Prof. Germain Grisez written from the perspective of philosophy, but I was unaware of anyone writing on the encyclical from a theological perspective. So I decided to write a book in the evenings. I was no longer teaching the Inquiry Forum in the evening, and I still had a high level of energy. I would get started soon. Such was my thinking when I was working at the Health Department.

Suddenly, after the unhappy collusion of my pastor and a parishioner who was a Cabinet minister, a collusion that caused my disemployment, I had lots of time on my hands. I needed a quiet place, so on October 7, I started to write at the library of Campion College. Soon I continued my writing at the library of the Provincial Department of Health. My former acting boss came down one morning to inquire, and I assured him that I was writing a theological work that had nothing to do with my experience at the department. My routine was to write in the morning and then take care of other matters in the afternoon. I wrote in longhand, and it was quite easy to write. I had been following the controversy closely over the years and had developed a covenant theology to uphold the received teaching of the Church that was reaffirmed by *Humanae Vitae*.

On December 14, I finished the handwritten manuscript. Sheila then typed it, a fairly easy task for her since she was an excellent typist and had done part-time secretarial work as a Kelly girl during her college summers. A month later I finished proofing the typewritten copy, and on January 17, I mailed a review manuscript to Professor Hamilton Hess, a friend and professor of theology at the University of San Francisco, for his comments. In due time he responded with several helpful suggestions.

Finding a publisher wasn't too difficult. After several rejections, one of the rejecting editors suggested that Alba House might be interested, and they were. I sent them the manuscript in early 1969, and it was published in the spring of 1970 with the title *Covenant, Christ and Contraception*. Its key chapter argued that the marriage act ought to be a renewal of the marriage covenant, for better and for worse. It was a very simple and easy-to-understand "theology of the body" although we didn't use that term then.

Up to the time of its publication, I hadn't thought about teaching natural family planning. But as soon as the book was published in the spring of 1970, I had a feeling that a certain passage in the Gospels—Luke 11:46—applied directly to me and that I had to do something to provide practical help to live out the teaching of *Humanae Vitae*. It was as if God was pointing a finger right at me and saying, "Okay, you have done your best to affirm the teaching that so many think is a big burden. Now what are you going to do to lift the burden?" This was a prime motivation for Sheila and me to found an organization to teach natural family planning. More about that later.

The bottom line is that at least two good things came out of the very bad situation that we endured from the spring of 1968 through the spring of 1969—the 1970 publication of one of the very few books of that period that upheld the teaching of *Humanae Vitae* and the organization we founded in 1971 that would become the most complete and probably the largest NFP organization in North America. *Covenant, Christ and Contraception* quickly went out of print, but in 1976 it was republished by Liturgical Press as *Birth Control and the Marriage Covenant*. Somehow a Protestant couple at the Gordon-Conwell Theological Seminary obtained this very Catholic book, and in January 1980 they lent it to Kimberly Hahn who soon shared it with Scott. They credit this book with helping to persuade them to accept Catholic teaching on birth control while they were still Protestants, and they went on to become Catholics and do great work in the Church. They tell their story about *Birth Control and the Marriage Covenant* in *Rome Sweet Home*. For my book to have played a part in their journey made whatever pain was involved in its writing well worth it.

3. Great Unpleasantries: the Effort to Seek Justice

The previous five activities listed in Chapter 2 were largely dependent upon my own initiative but were also dependent on the cooperation of others. Except for my efforts at employment in Regina, nobody was actively trying to block my efforts in any of those five areas. The situation was entirely different with the effort to obtain a just settlement from the parish. The duration of the conflict calls for a separate chapter.

Father Emmet Mooney had not only signed a three-year employment contract, but he had also told me in the early months of our relationship that if and when our efforts at evangelization would be more productive in other parishes, he would be happy to finance such work for years. Thus when he decided that he didn't want me around the parish any longer, he could have made arrangements for me to finish out the three years in another parish. Or if he really wanted to see me leave town, he could have negotiated a mutually agreeable settlement that would see me leave town and might even be less than the compensation of the 27 months remaining on the contract. Both of those would have met the requirements of employment justice.

Instead, he thought he could simply run me out of town cheaply and quickly. He wanted me to "go home," but where would that be? Minneapolis where I grew up, or Los Angeles where Sheila had spent most of her life, or the San Francisco Bay area where we had previously lived? And where do you stay and what do you do when you simply "go home" without employment? And what if the prospect of professional employment then requires a second move? If we had been able to negotiate a just settlement, we could have moved back to Minneapolis and done my further job search from there. Not only Father Mooney but also his trusted lay advisors failed miserably to recognize both the demands of justice and the practicalities of living.

In what follows, the local church of the Archdiocese of Regina does not look very good. I am sure that upon realizing the treatment I received from the hands of the local church, some may wonder why I didn't simply leave the Church once and for all. The reason is a matter of faith. I believe that the Catholic Church was instituted by Christ for the salvation of all men. It alone has the seven sacraments and the fullness of the truth in its formal teaching. I am also aware that Jesus founded his Church on Peter whose weaknesses are well described in the gospels, and I am aware that Judas, one of the 12 Apostles, utterly betrayed him. I think it is completely unrealistic to think that 100% of the clergy in any age are going to be 100% faithful and holy. If 93% are faithful and loving, that's a better percentage than in the original Twelve. I think it is absurd to deprive yourself and your family of the sacraments and the fullness of teaching by leaving the Church because you have encountered one of the spiritual descendants of Judas. If you find the behavior of Father Mooney and his cronies deplorable, please join me in forgiving them.

Also in what follows, I don't look very good either. If you find it shocking that I would picket in front of my parish church, that's understandable and was certainly the reaction of many of the parishioners. I am not proud of some of the things I did, and I ask your forgiveness.

The Clergy and the Priests Senate

All during my employment at the parish I had been meeting regularly with a group of priests to discuss theology and related matters. They offered almost no support after I was fired at the parish. In fact, one of them told me that they were afraid that support for a parish employee's rights would mean that they couldn't fire a housekeeper or cook. Well, not arbitrarily, but certainly they could do so if the person simply would not or could not do the job.

It was simply amazing to see such ignorance of basic Catholic teaching on social justice, even on the part of the priests. To be sure, they may have known about the Church's social encyclicals supporting the dignity of the workingman and the work he does, but it is too easy to think that applies only to big corporations. They seemed entirely unaware that the real subject of the Church's teaching on social justice is the individual person. The whole body of Catholic social teaching, and it is considerable, exists to emphasize and support the dignity of the human person. This is how it differs so much from socialism and communism. Those isms have great plans for humanity in general, but they wreak havoc on the individual person. Catholic teaching focuses on the dignity of the individual human person.

After the priests realized what happened to me at the Health Department, they had more sympathy and indicated that they were working behind the scenes. It wasn't clear what they were trying to do, but they never accomplished anything. At first, they had a hard time believing Fr. Mooney was behind my loss of Provincial employment, but on September 26, Wilf Oberthier had two positive confirmations from priests that Fr. Mooney had admitted to his involvement.

I mentioned above that at least two good things came out of our experience in Regina—my book and the consequent organization to teach natural family planning. The third good thing that resulted from our experience in Regina was an improvement in conditions within the Archdiocese of Regina. Some years later I met a Regina priest at a conference, and I began to apologize for any difficulty I had caused him and his brother priests, but he cut me short. "You did some good," was his message. "Things are better in the archdiocese now." We didn't pursue it, but I like to think that the principles of justice were being more thoughtfully applied.

A fourth good thing was that these events were so extraordinary that I kept a diary. As I reviewed it for writing these memoirs, I was most grateful for it. I had been disemployed by the Province of Saskatchewan on September 6, and by the end of September the shock was wearing off, and we were devising a strategy to keep the matter alive until it would be resolved. Still, among all the bad stuff, there was still some time for some good things. For example, my diary noted: "Sat. 9/28 – Went duck hunting in a.m. 4:15. Got limit near Montmartre and home by noon."

We made no visible progress with the clergy in September, so Harry Richardson agreed to send a letter to all the priests and religious of the area. I drafted it for him, he signed it on October 1, and we mailed it shortly. As mentioned before, C. H. Richardson was a parishioner who professionally represented a consortium of businesses in labor relations. He helped me considerably because he had never seen such poor labor-management practices as he was now witnessing in our parish. My diary doesn't record any reaction to Richardson's letter during October.

On November 9th I called Fr. Gorski to find out whether there had been a Senate meeting. He said he was bound by secrecy but that he could say that the matter had been discussed, that a committee of three priests had been appointed to look into it, and that I would be contacted shortly. On December 5 or 6, I called Fr. Wadey, the pastor of Holy Rosary Cathedral and president of the Senate. By this time the committee of three had visited Fr. Mooney, but they were still waiting for a decision. The Priests Senate was still reluctant to set a deadline for a response, so we waited and waited and waited.

On December 7th Richardson and Oberthier met with Fr. Wadey late in the afternoon. Wilf came over after supper and told me that Fr. Wadey doesn't want me to bug him anymore. Somehow we heard that on December 10th Fr. Wadey got word that Fr. Mooney and his advisors still can't decide whether to accept mediation. On the 13th Richardson agreed to contact Fr. Wadey and to try to get him to accept the idea of putting an ultimatum to Fr. Mooney. Everything went dormant from late Advent to mid-January.

On Tuesday, January 14, 1969, the Senate discussed the matter again. On Thursday the 16th I called Fr. Emil Kutarna at Qu Appelle. He said the Senate was unanimously in favor of having the matter settled and that some representatives had been appointed to contact both me and Fr. Mooney. He was quite surprised to learn that I hadn't been contacted.

I told him that out of protocol the representatives had undoubtedly contacted Fr. Mooney first and had probably gotten either a flat refusal or the usual run-around about contacting his men and the lawyer. Running into that stone wall, the representatives probably thought it best not to contact me because it would give me more grist for my propaganda machine. I told him that the Senate would have to come to grips with the fact that Fr. Mooney would never agree to a settlement or arbitration or anything. The Senate would have to give him an ultimatum of losing his pastorate or agreeing to arbitration. He said he would check around.

Finally, on Sunday, January 19, Harry Richardson brought me a letter that was addressed to me but mailed to him notifying us that the Senate's efforts to settle the matter had failed. That same Sunday Fr. Mooney announced he was taking off on holidays, and the bulletin schedule for altar boys made it appear he would be gone for a month. It was a fine symbolic gesture saying that there's no problem.

The Great Stall

Father Mooney succeeded in getting me disemployed by the Province on September 6. His attorney wrote me on the very same day making a seriously inadequate settlement offer contingent upon my leaving the Province by October 1 and not returning. Fr. Mooney's fellow priests were aware of this by mid-September, but he managed to stall any action by the Priests Senate for more than four months. His strategy was simple. Do nothing and eventually this "trouble maker" would run out of money and have to leave town. "Trouble-maker" was his benign term for publication purposes, but his usual conversational term for me was "shit-disturber." His strategy worked with the Senate, and it almost worked with the archbishop, but more about that later. Suffice it say for now that it has never been clear to me how anyone who is broke can move a family and household goods, but logic was not supreme in this dispute.

Over the years, this episode would occasionally come to mind, and I would kick myself and wonder why I hadn't just gone back to see him to work out everything man to man. Reading my diary made it clear. He wouldn't agree to such a meeting. A college student who had served the parish admirably as an altar boy and in other ways and whose parents were among Fr. Mooney's most trusted consultants before the dispute tried to arrange a meeting between Fr. Mooney, himself and me. The young man pleaded for this as a special favor for all the good work he had done for years. The pastor told him that he simply could not grant that favor.

More than forty years later I have to wonder: If both of us could have foreseen how the dispute would develop, could we have found a way of reconciliation at the beginning instead of never?

A Means of Communication

The pastor enjoyed the advantages of money, time and the support of most of the parishioners. By and large they were nice people, but they were management-oriented folks who thought that if the boss did something it must be right. The boss had fired me. Bosses are always right. Therefore I must be at fault. They were ignorant of Catholic social teaching, and they were ignorant about what had happened.

Against the strategy of the Great Stall and the other advantages held by the pastor, we had to develop a strategy of education and, eventually, irritation. Accordingly, we published a news sheet to inform the parishioners. At first we hoped that they would influence the pastor to become reasonable, but repeated efforts by informed parishioners proved to be useless. We titled it *The Layman's Reporter*. It was usually just one or two pages, and we started distributing it on cars during Sunday Masses. We bought a hand-cranked mimeograph machine plus an adequate supply of stencils and ink, and that made it very inexpensive to publish. Wilf Oberthier and Harry Richardson were the publishers, and Colin Laughlan was the editor. I would write some of the copy, but it had to be approved by the others.

Fighting Back

At the end of September, we began to fight against the Great Stall and parish ignorance, and I think it is safe to say that everyone would agree that the next few months were not pleasant. In what follows now, I will occasionally quote from my diary, generally edited for punctuation and completeness, just to convey the flavor of what was happening. Sometimes I use no names or just initials instead of full names, especially where I think the actions reflect poorly on the person. Sometimes I use only a first or last name because that's all I recorded in my diary.

Sunday, 9/29/68. Colin, Harry, Sheila, and Neil Burns distributed the first issue of *The Layman's Reporter*. At the 9:30 Mass, two of Fr. Mooney's friends were in the parking lot to see who was doing it. At the 11 o'clock Mass we saw somebody sitting with a camera ready to take photos. At the wine and cheese party that night, parishioner Patrick Floyd told me that he heard that "they"—Fr. Mooney and his advisors—wanted to fight this in the courts because they knew that I didn't have sufficient resources to fight it for long.

Well, they were right on that one. But I still had good health, energy, and I needed to keep busy doing something in order to keep from going crazy. The strain of dealing with the parish stalling tactics left me not infrequently feeling like I was on the verge of a nervous breakdown. Activism resolved those feelings. The stage was set for something that neither the parish leadership nor I could have imagined a few months previously.

During that week, we composed the copy for the second issue, and we mailed the previously mentioned letter by Richardson to all the priests and religious of the area. I went duck hunting again on Wednesday, but my diary reported no results, so it must have been a fruitless day. On Friday evening Pat Flood came over to get more information first hand. Someone in the inner circle had told him that the parish had offered me $5,000 but that I refused it. I don't know where anyone got that idea; the reality was that they had refused my offer of a $5,000 settlement.

On Sunday, October 6, Fr. Mooney did not preach at any of the Masses and *The Layman's Reporter* was distributed without any problems. During the week I started to write a book to support the teaching of *Humanae Vitae*. It was during the week of October 13-19 that Colin asked for a joint meeting with Fr. Mooney and me but was refused.

The next issue (October 10th) reported Fr. Mooney's refusal to meet with Colin. It also told of the pastoral appointment of two of Fr. Mooney's friends to the Executive Committee. This report drew a violent reaction from one of them who phoned me after the 8:00 or 9:30 Mass and threatened to shut me up physically if his name appeared in another issue. He said he wouldn't kill me but wouldn't refrain from putting his fist in my mouth until I learned silence. I suggested that we talk later when he had calmed down.

This friend of Fr. Mooney was really a nice guy, just excitable. In our talk two days later, he expressed concern about people who were not only dropping out of active parish life but were in danger of dropping away from the Faith. The latter was a big concern of mine as well. We addressed this issue in the *Reporter* on October 27.

The controversy was getting to Colin. He was the editor of the *Reporter* and okayed everything in it. He was getting static from his fellow students at Campion College, and he was wondering if, based on the reactions of the students' parents, the *Reporter* wasn't doing me more harm than good. On All Souls Day, Oberthier, Richardson, Colin and I had a good meeting at which we agreed that the next issue would be the last with Colin as editor and would bring people up to date.

On November 3rd the Richardsons hosted the first of several home meetings to discuss the issues. Subsequent meetings were at different homes. The next day, a reporter with CBC News called me for an interview for radio and possibly for TV coverage. I said I'd let him know after talking with my attorney, Mr. D. K. MacPherson. I called Bill Cameron, and he planned to talk with Fr. Jake Kutarna to see if the additional publicity might be avoided by some common sense talking together. My attorney was out of town for the week, so I decided to postpone any further publicity until after the *MacLean's* article. There's more on that in the December narrative.

On November 8th Sheila celebrated her 29th birthday by being sick at night and all day with the flu. I stayed home too, dead tired from getting up twice with her and then two or three times with our second daughter. Sheila's mother called and we told her the bad news about our unemployment status. Two days later the Sebastians, a sympathetic couple, hosted the second home meeting. Harry Richardson called me at 10:00 in the evening to ask if I was suing for defamation of character, reinstatement, etc. No, I wasn't. I just wanted some simple justice and a way to leave town decently. This was also the week when I sold our car in order to qualify for family assistance.

The rest of November was relatively quiet. Parishioner Mrs. Shirley Haid received a reply from Gordon Grant, the Minister of Health in which he refused to discuss the question. The parish lawyer, Ed Bayda, obtained a delay in making his response, but he finally submitted his reply on the 26th, claiming he could not be ready for trial in January; but the next jury sitting would not occur until next June. The Big Stall had entered the legal part of the conflict. Late in the month I paid off the mortgage with funds borrowed from my sister Harriette.

November 28. Mom called this morning to tell me that dad died in his sleep this morning at my sister Joan's house in Connecticut where mom and dad had gone for Thanksgiving. The next day I borrowed $150 from Fr. Jake Kutarna for the round trip to Minneapolis. The same day I went to confession, Mass and received Holy Communion at Blessed Sacrament Church. I also had time to write an angry letter to my attorneys about being stalled by Ed Bayda.

On December 1st we were at the mortuary from 1:30 to 8:30. We buried dad the next day, and about 40 people came to the house for lunch. In late afternoon I made a hospital visit to my cousin Annamary who was dying of cancer.

I spent December 3 making all sorts of appointments and phone calls looking into educational possibilities. The next day I visited with Fr. Jack Gilbert who had been a seminary classmate and was now the assistant superintendent of Catholic schools, and then I saw Annamary for the last time. (She died on March 7, and mom took it hard, reliving the loss of dad.) I had lunch downtown with two high school friends, Peter Meyers and Peter Randall, and one of their good friends, John Olson.

Bishop James Patrick Shannon

At 4:15 the afternoon of December 4, I met with Bishop James P. Shannon who was an auxiliary bishop in the Archdiocese of St. Paul and Minneapolis. He had been ordained in 1946 and taught English and Greek at Nazareth Hall Preparatory Seminary where I had taken my first two years of college in 1948-1950. I had always liked him, and it would have been very difficult not to like him. He had the Irish gift of gab, generally had a big smile, and he had written a reference for me when I was applying at the Institute of Lay Theology. When Sheila and I made our first trip to

Minneapolis as new parents in 1964, I introduced Sheila and baby Jennifer to him. He had an earned doctorate in English from Yale, was then the president of St. Thomas College, and was just a few months shy of being ordained a bishop (in early 1965). I told him that December day in 1968 about our situation in Regina and asked him to write Archbishop O'Neill on my behalf. He said that other bishops didn't take him very seriously, but he would write anyway.

Then he asked me what I was doing. When I told him that I was writing a book to defend *Humanae Vitae,* a smile flitted across his face but then he regained his previous serious composure. With the benefit of hindsight, I should have asked him why he smiled. I would soon find out.

On November 23, just 11 days prior to our meeting, Bishop Shannon had written a letter of resignation to Archbishop Leo Binz of St. Paul, but it was not yet public. He wrote that he did not accept the teaching of *Humanae Vitae* and was thus resigning from his office as bishop. As soon as it became public, the liberals of the Twin Cities raised a huge cry of protest against the Church and *Humanae Vitae.* They took out a centerfold ad in the archdiocesan paper, *the Catholic Bulletin,* with a circled S O S in each of the four corners, SOS standing for Supporters of Shannon. They even had a demonstration down Summit Avenue, the broad boulevard that runs from the Cathedral in downtown St. Paul to the seminary on the Mississippi river. The former bishop soon pulled the rug out from under his supporters by announcing his intended marriage to a widow whom he had met out East in the mid-Sixties and who had been married twice before. I recall from the papers at the time that he said that her marital status was "divorced" but that she could easily be granted a decree of nullity. To the best of my knowledge, that never happened, and they lived together as man and wife but not married in the Church for many years. The former bishop died on August 28, 2003.

How could such a promising young bishop make such a tragic mistake? I think that one of his greatest assets proved to be one of his greatest liabilities. He was eminently likable and approachable. Shortly after he was ordained a bishop in 1965, he was made the pastor of a parish in South Minneapolis. This was a time when the Church's teaching on birth control was the subject of many attacks, and the most dangerous were the sophist arguments by our fellow Catholics. I suspect that Bishop Shannon absorbed these too well. It was also a time when those who believed the teaching that had been reaffirmed by Pope Pius XI in 1930 with his landmark encyclical, *Casti Connubii,* were silent. Pope Paul VI had said something in 1964 that was interpreted by many believing Catholics to mean that there should be a moratorium on public debate about birth control. That didn't slow down the future dissenters a bit, serving only to give them an almost unopposed monopoly of comment in the Catholic press. As mentioned in Chapter 1, in 1966, I couldn't take the nonsense and silence any longer, so I wrote an article that appeared in the February 25, 1967 issue of *Ave Maria* magazine.

I also suspect that because Bishop Shannon was so likeable and approachable, he heard a rather constant stream of complaints about the practical difficulties of living according to Catholic teaching. During these years, Dr. Konald A. Prem, a professor of obstetrics and gynecology at the University of Minnesota Medical School, made his one-night presentation on Natural Family Planning at parish after parish in the Twin Cities, but he would be the first to admit that more was needed. He also promoted the kind of frequent breastfeeding that normally postpones the return of fertility and provides a natural spacing of babies, but that part of the message was only rarely accepted. I think that a combination of factors led to many couples experiencing problems, and I suspect that many of them cried on the shoulders of a sympathetic Bishop Shannon. This is personal speculation, and there were certainly other factors such as his growing isolation from others in the hierarchy. Whatever the full truth, he was buried from the Church. May he rest in peace.

We were now into the month of December, so it's time for a further interruption of the narrative.

Maclean's Reports

A reporter named Linda Mitchell had picked up the conflict soon after it began in early September. She interviewed me and others, and filed a story with *Maclean's*, a national Canadian magazine, somewhat like *The Saturday Evening Post* in those days, at least in size. The magazine had a first page entry titled "*Maclean's* Reports." It was printed on buff-colored paper, just inside the front cover. Readers of the issue for December 1968 opened their magazines to a large print headline, "Why do they want to drive John Kippley out of Saskatchewan?" It was accompanied by a head and shoulders shot of me in front of the church. I found it interesting to reread, after 40 years, a reporter's view of the controversy so I am reprinting it here, even though I would have expressed some items differently.

> It sounds admirably progressive when church leaders talk encouragingly about "participatory democracy" at the parish level, as the Vatican II Encyclical did, for instance. Who, then, could have foreseen that a Roman Catholic lay worker who tried to put this concept into practice in Saskatchewan would not only lose one job with the parish and a second job with the government but would also become the target of an attempt to run him out of the province?
>
> In September 1967, John F. Kippley, now 37, moved his wife and three children from California to take a position in Regina as director of adult religious education at Christ the King parish. His qualifications included masters degrees in both theology and industrial relations and four years'

experience in adult education among Roman Catholic parishioners. Kippley says he and the parish priest, Father Emmet Mooney, had an understanding that the job would last at least three years. But eight months later, Kippley was fired, and the incident since then has split the parish into two bitterly opposed camps.

At first, Kippley seemed to everyone to be the perfect man to work in this prosperous, middle-class parish. An articulate, aggressive idealist, he had turned to theology after an unsatisfying stint in the business world. His job at Christ the King was defined by Father Mooney as "getting people off their keesters." That was certainly part of it, as Kippley saw it. Soon after he arrived he organized regular adult classes in lay theology, increased social activity among parishioners through a series of wine-and-cheese parties, and fielded a volunteer team of 100 men who canvassed the parish, requesting commitment and involvement from all members.

These moves gave the parish new vigor, but some of Kippley's ideas disturbed conservative parishioners—such as his insistence that with an annual income of $80,000 the parish should be able to set up a private welfare scheme for needy members.

His most important innovation, in Kippley's view, was the creation of a parish council of laymen. Through it, volunteers would carry some of the priest's administrative burden, and parishioners would have more say in routine church affairs.

By spring the parish council had passed several resolutions—in favor of coffee klatches after Mass, a parish picnic and a parish newsletter. But none of these projects became a reality. The newsletter was all but ready for publication in May; the editor needed only a column from Father Mooney and a copy of the parish mailing list. Father Mooney provided neither. At his urging the officers of the council abandoned the coffee idea, with Mooney explaining that "people are already too busy." (Later, after Kippley left, the picnic was also cancelled.)

Predictably Kippley was upset. "I believed that both Father Mooney and the archbishop should have a veto, but I also believed the people of the parish had a right to present their point of view."

While a vocal group of parishioners continued to support Kippley, his relations with Father Mooney cooled fast. One day near the end of May, Father Mooney summoned Kippley into his office and asked for his resignation.

"I said, 'No,' " Kippley recalls, "and he said, 'I thought you wouldn't' and handed me my dismissal.

"When I asked him the cause, he said, 'For causing discord and dissension.' "

Next, in a letter to some parishioners, Father Mooney wrote: "I would like to inform you that John Kippley is being recalled to San Francisco and will be leaving us on or before June 30."

"That was simply not true," Kippley says now. "I was not employed by the Institution of Lay Theology" (where he trained in San Francisco) "nor were they in the process of relocating me in any other parish."

Kippley appealed to Archbishop M. C. O'Neill for a hearing but was refused. He took his case to the senate of priests of the diocese, where it is still officially pending. Then he went to provincial Labor Minister Lionel Coderre, a Catholic himself, seeking mediation in the dispute. Coderre was willing, says Kippley, but Father Mooney declined.

By now, some parishioners were so incensed over Kippley's dismissal that they circulated a petition asking for a review of the case. Father Mooney refused, and to one parishioner he wrote: "We owe Kippley nothing. He has been paid in full, plus holidays, and we write 'finis' to an unhappy experience. There is no way that John Kippley can ever work in our parish again. There is no way he will ever work in any other parish of this archdiocese. . . Please God, the work will continue but never under John Kippley. For him, the game is over. He'd best pick up his marbles and go home as quickly and quietly as possible." This time he said the reason for Kippley's dismissal was "insolence."

After seven weeks of trying in vain for a public explanation, Kippley launched a suit against the parish, naming Father Mooney and Benny Murphy, a Regina lawyer, as president of the parish council executive.

Meanwhile, in August, Kippley went to work in a senior job with the provincial Department of Health. But as with most civil-service jobs, this one was technically temporary until the government ruled otherwise. Three weeks after Kippley began work, the health minister announced the cabinet would not confirm the appointment. His job, Kippley was told, "did not exist."

Perhaps it was only coincidence, but on the same day, the lawyer who acts for the parish wrote to John Kippley offering (a) to buy Kippley's house, and (b) to pay him $2,000 damages and costs "continent upon Mr. Kippley moving out of the province on or before October 1, 1968 and remaining out of the province."

Kippley went to the Regina *Leader-Post* with his story, but the paper refused to publicize it. He says he was told it was contrary to policy to print anything about a matter that was under litigation before it came to court.

Wilfred Oberthier, a parish member who has known Father Mooney for 20 years, says: "My field is industrial relations and I see the problem in these terms. It's not a matter of John Kippley right or wrong. It's simply that he was given no hearing before he was fired, nor any appeal after. Surely the church, of all institutions, should be bending over backwards in the interests of reconciliation."

But the church is not bending, and Father Mooney refuses to comment publicly on any aspect of the case. Meanwhile, John Kippley is out of work, and, at best, months away from any settlement of his lawsuit.

On top of that, a recent comment from his former boss in the government seems to carry the eerie suggestion that John Kippley has been relegated almost to the status of a non-person.

"I don't want him employed in the department," said Health Minister Gordon Grant. "As far as I'm concerned he was *never* employed here."

—Linda Mitchell

Increased Confrontation

I wish I could say that the publicity in a respected national magazine had caused the parish leadership to pursue a negotiated fair settlement, but that was not the case. The Great Stall continued.

When I arrived home from Minneapolis on December 5, I contacted my lawyer and was told that we did not have a legal case because of some technicalities, and we soon dropped it. I felt relieved for two reasons. First, they could not stall me in the courts any longer, and secondly, I preferred to carry on my campaign for justice in the court of public opinion. For the next two weeks my friends tried to advance the matter, all to no avail. By December 19, I was feeling frantic. The Great Stall was getting to me.

The best thing about the whole matter was that Sheila was a gracious queen throughout the ordeal. Not once did she nag me or accuse me of stupidity for having come here in the first place or for anything I had done or failed to do. She bore up under the stress extremely well. The next best aspect of the ordeal was the support of friends and neighbors. I don't know what we would have done without that support.

Let's summarize the situation. When I started to work at the parish in September 1967, Father Mooney told me to form a parish council. I told him that an initiative-taking parish council would involve friction, but he told me to go ahead with that sort of council. I was correct, so he fired me in late May 1968 for reasons never given beyond some non-specific, meaningless negative adjectives dealing with the predictable friction. He expected I would simply "go home," wherever that was. After I found employment as a systems analyst with the Health Department of the Province of Saskatchewan, he gave an earful to a parishioner who was a Cabinet member and who blackballed me, causing me to be disemployed. Efforts by others to arrange mediation or some sort of a decent settlement were repeatedly rebuffed. Efforts by the Priests Senate were going nowhere. Efforts to secure additional employment in Regina were met with political pressures to keep me unemployed. The parish leadership had decided on the strategy of the Big Stall, presuming that I would eventually run out of funds and be forced to leave town.

Patience had never been my great virtue, and it was now worn thin. This was the year of 1968 when public protest had become common. I thought I had done everything I could by way of low key efforts, to no avail. The thought of picketing a church would ordinarily be unthinkable. But since everything else had failed, it now appeared as something like that might possibly produce some results. I am not at all proud of what would now happen, and I still painfully regret that our publicizing the injustice being worked by my parish-employer may have led someone to leave the Church. That's always the risk of publicizing corruption. At the time I thought we were making it very clear that our objection was not to anything taught by the Church but simply to the fact that this parish, as an employer, was acting against the social justice teachings of the Church.

In addition to the conflict, I was writing a book to defend the teaching of the Church reaffirmed by *Humanae Vitae*. I was looking for a job locally, and I was preparing to look for a theology-teaching job in the States. I was still trying to get welfare assistance for my family, and I was enrolling in courses that would qualify me for secondary education. In all of this, it was not the work that was difficult; it was the seemingly endless waiting. It had left me feeling panicked and tremendously stressed. I needed something to give me an outlet, and it would be picketing. At least it gave me some additional human contact. I don't know what good the picketing accomplished, but I think it helped avert a nervous breakdown. Friends continued their efforts to negotiate with Fr. Mooney and parish leadership, and the Stall continued. I continued to look for a job.

On Sunday, December 22, I was prepared to picket, but there was no mention of it in my diary. I handed the *Reporter* to the walkers before Mass and put them on cars during Mass. Two women came to the house that afternoon to talk about the case. One was a visitor from Montreal and was shocked at the apathy in Regina.

Christmas Day of 1968 was very pleasant, and we had dinner with our next-door neighbors, the Schambers.

Picketing

Sunday, December 29, was my first day of picketing. The temperature was a chilly 34 degrees below zero at 10:30 a.m. Fortunately, we lived right across the street from the church, so the lack of a car posed no problem. I got a very emotional adverse reaction from T. S. who threatened to have me arrested if I put a *Reporter* on her car. I called her husband on Tuesday, informed him about his wife's threat, told him that I too would like to have the battle settled quietly, and he said he would talk it over with his wife.

Sheila helped with the picketing on Sunday, January 5. Father Mooney was in the parking lot asking people if they were "scabs" (for crossing the picket line). Some didn't know what he was talking about, but Joe M did, and Joe told him he didn't appreciate it one bit. Later in the afternoon Joe went to see our pastor to see if he could talk some sense into him. Joe told me that he had been contributing to the defense fund until we started to picket. Then he switched his money back to the church. Now he must have been in a dither. The picketing was not gaining me any friends—I heard one lady say "They should shoot him"—but that wasn't its purpose.

The next day I got a letter in the evening from Mr. Bayda, the parish attorney, telling me that if I didn't agree in writing to stop picketing and publishing news about the dispute by Wednesday, January 8th, they would start proceedings and seek an injunction. I began rounding up the media.

On Sunday, January 12, Fr. Mooney struck back. He called a parish meeting for 1:30. About 300 people attended—the parish hall was full. Al C. had the teens organized. Some confiscated Valerie Best's tape recorder. Others tried to get mine but did not succeed because I started to raise a fuss. Probably more to the point, Al recognized that my recorder required external electricity, and they had turned off the power to the wall plugs. One young man hovered over us like a personal Gestapo. He sat behind Sheila and edged up and began getting his hand in position to grab her clip board. I called him on it out loud and then moved Sheila's chair forward. Fr. Mooney talked for an hour, ripping me down.

The reaction of most was favorable to Fr. Mooney. They heard what they wanted to hear. I was the sinner who had abused him and the other saints. The people who had heard my side were generally sickened. Joe M. was neutralized.

More Publicity

Friends continued to try to work behind the scenes, and I continued to hold off on additional publicity at their request. When the Priests Senate admitted it had failed in its efforts at peacemaking with Fr. Mooney, we decided to try for more publicity. Linda Mitchell, the author of the

Maclean's article, taped a two-reel interview on January 20, and the next day Craig Oliver called about a short national TV shot. He was a fast worker and soon had me scheduled for videotaping while picketing at the 11:00 Mass the next Sunday, January 26. On Friday the 24th Beverly Monteith from CBC-TV in Toronto invited me for a TV interview the next day. They made the reservations, and I left for Toronto at 9:30 Saturday morning.

The television interview did not go well. The host seemed to want me to make some scathing comments against the Catholic Church, but they were not going to get that from me. I kept saying in one way or another that my protest was not against the Church or any of its teachings but against the fact that the local archdiocese and parish were failing miserably to put into practice the social justice teachings of the Church. It never aired.

On Sunday, January 26th, Craig Oliver came out with a TV crew. On a snowy, windy day he took shots of the picketing, of people coming to church, and of us mimeographing. I heard a nice old lady say "They should throw 'em in jail," and another gentleman asked me if I thought the church was a factory. On Monday the TV shots were shown, and on Tuesday Linda Mitchell's well edited radio interview aired. I received only one nasty phone call. On Wednesday we began distributing a petition for mediation or arbitration.

In the first week of February I interviewed for teaching jobs at seven colleges in the States. Upon my return I had reason to think our phone was being bugged. On Friday the 14th I couldn't get Terry Marner by dial so I had to have the operator make the call. Then during our conversation, an operator interrupted to say, "Ma'am, your phone is off the hook." Very strange. The next day when I called Marymount in Salina to accept their offer, I used my neighbor's phone.

The parish dance on Saturday the 15th was not well attended, and that may have had something to do with Fr. Mooney using the announcement time at Sunday Mass to decry what I was doing. The next day it was apparent that positions had hardened. Fr. Wadey wouldn't let me come down to see him. He would only give me the standard parish-as-righteous-victim line put forth by Fr. Mooney and his friends.

Sunday, February 23 saw an escalation. At the 9:30 and 11:00 Masses, supporters of Fr. Mooney removed copies of the *Reporter* from windshields and destroyed them. In the afternoon I received several phone calls. Most were critical but one person volunteered to help with the picketing.

A Turning Point?

Monday, February 24, may have been a turning point. I decided to talk once more with Archbishop O'Neill before I expanded my informational picketing. I literally had to drag myself to his office, and I broke down crying as I told him my future plans and how I didn't want to carry them out. When I said that I might be picketing the legislative building, the Cathedral, and some corporate offices that employed some of those who supported Fr; Mooney's actions, I think he listened in a new way. The upshot was that he asked for a couple days to think about it. When I saw him on Wednesday, he had talked with the parish people. He certainly didn't give me any assurances, but I think he said something to them that would change their absolute Great Stall to something a little more human. Still with no assurances, I needed to keep up the pressure, so on Thursday I made an appointment with the Saskatchewan Human Rights Association for the next Monday. That same Thursday, Wilf and Harry had a two-hour meeting with the archbishop that they hoped was productive because they thought they introduced some new thinking into his frame of reference.

On Friday morning, February 27th, the archbishop called Sheila while I was at school and told her that I was to attend an important meeting with some members of the parish executive committee that afternoon. Somehow Sheila reached me at school, and I asked Wilf to come with me. The exec would not allow Wilf to participate in the meeting when I was there so I met with three members of the exec at 4:00—to no avail. We were in two different worlds. I was seeking a settlement in terms of employment justice, and they were thinking only in terms of getting rid of a nuisance. Then Wilf and Harry met with them from 5:00 till 7:15 that evening. The executive committee upped their offer from $2000 to $4000, and they haggled about buying my house and moving expenses. Afterwards, Harry said he had never seen two parties in a labor dispute so far apart and with so many misunderstandings. The haggling continued on Monday and ended with the exec saying they would make me an offer.

Then, the executive committee got so ridiculous it became almost humorous. On Tuesday FW of the exec called Wilf to tell him that they didn't want to put anything in writing. During the rest of the week there was much back and forth about an offer that I insisted must be in writing and which they wanted to avoid putting in writing. I had a meeting with Rev. Hobson of the Saskatchewan Human Rights Association. I was to write a letter formally asking for support of the association. They would then write to the Archbishop and Fr. Mooney asking for their side of the story, and I could see their responses and offer a rebuttal.

On Monday, March 10 at 3:30 in the afternoon, more than nine months since my firing at the parish and more than six months since being disemployed by the Province, I went with attorney Ross Wimmer to Ed Bayda's law offices to view the agreement. Mr. Wimmer and I had to agree not to take the "agreement" out of the office and even not to take any written notes. No wonder they didn't want anyone to see it. The first nine paragraphs gave the parish version of the dispute and said that I was incompetent, etc. By signing the agreement, I would have been agreeing to that. Then it called for me to agree to remain entirely silent, to regard the matter as a closed issue, to do nothing whatsoever that could be construed as carrying on the dispute. Then it called for me to move out of the Province by May 1st and not to return for at least five years.

It then turned absurd. The parish would pay me $4,000 in relocation expenses to start 30 days after I left the Province, payable in eight monthly installments of $500 each. It added, however, that the parish was under only a moral obligation to pay these funds and that I had no legal recourse to recover them if the parish should cease payments short of the total. Further, if I ever broke my part of the agreement, I would have to pay back all monies received. No one in his right mind would sign such an "agreement," and they rightly feared that if we could have a copy, we would publicize it. Once public, the parish pastor and his executive committee would look absolutely ridiculous and unjust even to their defenders. Mr. Wimmer said very simply that if the pastor and exec were sincere about wanting to settle the matter for $4,000, they would have said so instead of creating such a document. I went to the library immediately and wrote down the salient features of the document as in this paragraph.

That same day I went to see Archbishop O'Neill for the last time. He told me that he was all through with the matter, that it was strictly a parish affair. I told him that if he had not given his permission to Fr. Mooney to fire me, we would not be in this position. (That had come out in some conversations with others.) He said that Fr. Mooney had done everything possible, and I replied that he hadn't done one thing. The archbishop quite obviously didn't want to do anything at all to settle the matter, so I left.

A Letter from Father Zimmers

By the time I got home, the mail had arrived, and I rejoiced to read the reply of Fr. Eugene Zimmers, S.J. to parishioner Benny Murphy. As the dispute had become irritating to the executive committee, on February 4th Benny had written on behalf of the parish to the Institute of Lay Theology complaining about my actions. If they expected a reply that would provide them with some propaganda, this surely wasn't it.

February 12, 1969

Dear Mr. Murphy:

In all my nine years of experience with about 125 parishes and pastors I have never seen anything approaching the way your pastor and parish council have mishandled this whole unfortunate affair with Mr. Kippley. There is no call for this kind of unchristian tearing at one another's vitals that you and John have been doing. He's only one poor guy against a whole group. You've backed him into a corner and have been closing in on him. So he fights back with every weapon at his disposal. It's just a matter of survival. Can't you understand that? If he had been more Christlike he would have let you people crucify him. But you shouldn't be surprised that a man with a family who has sunk his life's savings and his total future into taking a chance with the "open" Church should fight back when he sees that sacrifice and that future badly threatened.

And at the end of the two-page letter:

But you people ought to relax a bit also. It wouldn't have hurt you to have let the Priests' Senate mediate this disagreement. And even if they did conclude that you should make a just settlement with Kippley, it wouldn't be the end of the world. Surely the parish can stand it better than the poor guy at the end of his rope.

One can tell who the Christians are, Mr. Murphy, not by how much "reputation" they have or do not have, but by how they love one another and care for one another and bear one another's burdens.

I do not know how you and Kippley will resolve your dispute, but I do think you'd have more chance of arriving at an equitable solution if you would begin at least with the premise of "Love your enemies."

Sincerely in Christ,
Eugene R. Zimmers, S.J.

It was two days later that Jim McLaughlin at welfare told me the rumor that the parish was going to try to get an injunction against my picketing, as mentioned in the previous chapter.

The next day I began to share Father Zimmers' letter, and it received a fantastic reception. On Thursday, March 14, the Oberthiers, Sebastians, Glassers and Richardsons had a meeting to decide what they could do to bring the matter to an arbitrated decision. They decided to send copies of Fr. Zimmers' letter to various people, and by the next Sunday evening they had a crew mailing the letter, along with an explanatory cover letter, to the entire parish.

That Sunday, March 16, I distributed the *Reporter* at the door of the church. It told of the parish threat to take the offensive and described the offer they made.

On Monday, the group asked me to run off some more cover letters, and on Tuesday the group started to get phone calls, perhaps about 50 with 80% being favorable to their letter. On Thursday, Alice Sebastian and Carole Glasser persuaded me to refrain from picketing and publishing up through

April 5 to give them time to accomplish something behind the scenes, and I was only too happy to agree. On Friday the group worked out the wording of a petition for arbitration, and on Saturday they hustled and obtained close to a hundred signatures on a petition for arbitration.

The Counterattack

Passion Sunday, March 23, 1969. Fr. Mooney dropped a bombshell. At the sermon time in the last three Masses, he roundly defamed Fr. Zimmers, the members of the group seeking arbitration, and myself. Sheila went to the 9:30 Mass and left crying after about two or three minutes of his talk. Henri Soucier left a little bit later and then called me to tell me that he would help with anything. I called the Oberthiers and the word spread quickly. Carole and Wilf went to the 11:00 Mass and heard themselves slandered. Wilf tried to tape it, but the recording was poor and incomplete. I went to the 12:30 Mass and succeeded in getting a good recording.

Father Mooney started his talk without any ambiguity.

> During this past week many of you received a poison pen letter circulated at the instigation of John Kippley with the signature of Father Eugene Zimmers of San Francisco.

That's wrong on two counts. It wasn't a poison pen letter. It was simply a reply that found fault with both disputants but more fault with the parish. Secondly, it was most certainly not my idea to send it to the parish if for no other reason than that I couldn't imagine how to get those names and addresses. After reading Benny's letter to Fr. Zimmers, he elaborated some more on our sharing the letter with others.

> Kippley received or wrote to Father Zimmers requesting a copy and then, in his crude diabolical self, circulated it making it appear that it came from the four members of the parish.

Apparently it did not occur to Fr. Mooney that some of his parishioners might have acted independently, as they did, in meeting and deciding to take that course of action. About two-thirds of the way through his counterattack, he began attacking my supporters. Some might have had high motivations, he said, but then there are those others.

> There are others among them, however, who know their motives were not so noble. These people moved into the parish for the most part well after it was firmly established and all paid for. They didn't have to dig as many of you did to help put brick and mortar together to build this place. They didn't have to put on teas and bazaars in support of our school as many of you did to help pay for some of the bills... They didn't

slug it out organizing the parish dances and sportsmen's dinners or smorgasbords to help pay for this place and to provide a hall and sporting facilities for the kids as many of you did. When they came this place was organized and built and paid for, and some of these are the very people who have been fanning Kippley's flames over the past months and who wish in fact right now to destroy the parish that many of you have worked so hard to build and stabilized...

Well, I think that you people worked too hard here to build and pay for this plant to let Kippley or any radicals destroy it on you. . . Now I think it's high time that you do something about removing this stigma from your parish.

I put it to you this morning to decide who you want to run your parish—me and your elected parish council or Mr. Kippley and his few radicals...

I'll resign on Easter Sunday unless you people give me positive proof that you want me to stay on. This is not a threat. It's a promise. You make the decision.

It wasn't the sort of thing you expect to hear on Passion Sunday, but it certainly had passion and it had its effects.

The whole day was one of turmoil. At 1:20 p.m. I received a phone call telling me to "get out of town before it's too late," repeated twice. Ten minutes later I reported the threat to the Criminal Investigation Department (CID). I spent most of the day transcribing the tape.

The members of the group were flattened and greatly discouraged. They went that evening to see the archbishop, but he was his usual indifferent self, and they returned crestfallen and greatly discouraged. Meanwhile, a Save-Father-Mooney meeting in the parish hall was attended by over 300 people.

After class on Tuesday I cut a mimeograph stencil of the transcribed sermon. I had more talks with members of the group who remained demoralized for the most part. They were aware that a Save-Father-Mooney petition was going around and that it would get over a thousand signatures. They did not want to get involved in a numbers game, and they made that very clear to the archbishop. They had an unhappy first-hand experience with corruption within the Church, and some of them were crushed, but not all. Mr. Matt Gelowitz of the CID interviewed me, and I think he did the same with Fr. Mooney.

On Wednesday I mailed out copies of Fr. Mooney's sermon to all the priests of the city and of the Senate along with a letter of protest. On Thursday Carole and Alice released me from my promise of silence, and by the end of Friday I had seven others to help with the picketing on Sunday.

At the 11:00 Mass on Palm Sunday, March 30, eight of us picketed. Harry Richardson, Wilf Oberthier, Pat Davis, Terry Burns, Colin Scott,

Gordon Hunter, and Henri Soucier joined me in a slow moving line. At the 12:30 Mass I heard Fr. Mooney tell people to pray that the heretofore insoluble problem would be solved during Holy Week and for the hot tempered to hold their tongues, a reference to his visit from the CID. I left early and got a couple of picket signs reading "Let's Arbitrate" and "Why Fear Arbitration?" One of the first gentlemen out of church told me he would like to kick the stuffing out of me, but he declined to give me his name.

I painted some new signs for Good Friday and picketed for a half-hour before the 3:00 services. Louise Antonini chatted pleasantly with me, and afterwards she and her fiancé came over to chat. He thought my cause was futile; she said she couldn't picket yet but that she would have a talk with Fr. Mooney.

Wilf called and told me that his employer had put enough pressure on him that he told his boss he wouldn't picket anymore. He was the key Human Resources person at the large Grey Nuns hospital, and his boss, Mr. Stan Bourassa, had received several nasty calls about Wilf. Mr. B assured Wilf that his job was not in danger, but with the overall situation, Wilf decided he needed to keep his activities behind the scenes.

On Easter Sunday, I picketed at 9:00 by myself. At 9:30 and 11:.00 Sheila and the kids helped, and I did 12:30 by myself. Father Mooney made a triumphant speech in which he thanked people for their support and said he wasn't going to resign. This would be my last day of picketing but not because of what he had said.

On Easter Monday I was interviewed by Mike Shykula of the *Leader-Post* at 4:00. I wrote out my responses to his questions, and he thought they would be running a story later in the week if not the next day.

Morris Schumiatcher, Q. C.

I think it was through the Human Rights Association that I had learned about Morris Schumiatcher, Q.C. (Wikipedia says that **QC** refers to Queen's Counsel, a distinguished and experienced legal practitioner.) Counselor Schumiatcher had a good reputation not only as a lawyer but also as a person interested in human rights. At 2:30 on Tuesday, April 8, I had my first meeting with him, and it lasted two hours. He thought I might have a case for slander and conspiracy, asked me to be silent on any strategy, and to return on Thursday after he had reviewed all the material I had given him. On Thursday he decided that at present he would try for a negotiated settlement. In the meantime, he asked me to call off the public aspects of the dispute. The next day I called Mike Shykula at the *Leader-Post* to ask that he hold the story since Schumiatcher might misunderstand any publicity coming at this time. So on Sunday, April 13, there was no picketing.

On Monday I gave Fr. Zimmers' letter to Schumiatcher, and he liked it. This was the first day I went to help man the dikes on the flooding Wascana Creek and did the same all the next day.

Mr. Schumiatcher met with Ed Bayda on April 22. After some initial sparring about a suit for slander and conspiracy to injure vs. a parish countersuit for defamation of character, they got down to business. Bayda said that as he understood it, at the Cabinet meeting a friend of Fr. Mooney said that I was the guy causing all the trouble to Father Mooney out in Christ the King parish and that I would be a troublemaker for the government too. That was enough for him to veto my permanent employment. I wrote Schumiatcher explaining that my "causing trouble" for Fr. Mooney didn't start until after I was blackballed in the Cabinet and was thus disemployed.

At the end of April, I still had daydreams that the Archbishop would exercise his influence either to cause arbitration or a settlement, but almost three weeks later he had not replied, and I'm quite sure he never did.

Negotiations continued off and on between Schumiatcher and Bayda during the first three weeks of May. I was getting very antsy because time was running out. On the 20th I told Schumiatcher that my silence would end the next day. I planned to move ahead on five fronts: civil, criminal, ecclesiastical, publicity, and through the Human Rights Association. That's what I entered into my diary, but I don't know what I could have meant regarding civil and criminal. As one of the friendly lawyers in the parish had told me repeatedly by quoting from Dickens, "The law is an ass," so I don't know what I could have done along those lines. On May 21 Schumiatcher said we had a deal for $5,000 for traveling expenses. I expressed my unhappiness with the deal, and he said I would be very prudent and practical to accept the settlement, that it was the best we could do under the circumstances. He said he didn't fear the man trying to make money, even the usurer, much as he hated the latter, but he feared the man who sought power because that man will stop at nothing. I thought he was talking about my pastor.

After a few days and no check, I began wondering if the deal was being further stalled, but on the 28th Schumiatcher called to say he had the check and the releases in hand.

During the first week of June I was painting my neighbor's house and had too much time to think. I began having paranoid thoughts about Schumiatcher, but fortunately I recognized them for what they were. The next week my fears had calmed down, but in the third week I foolishly wrote the Archbishop, asking him to persuade the parish powers to change the terms of the agreement that amounted to a very practical excommunication from the Archdiocese of Regina. I then sent a copy of the letter to Mr. Schumiatcher who replied that I should desist from such letter writing.

The open dispute was ended, but we continued to get about one nuisance call each week, and the terms of the agreement remained a sore point. Dr. Schumiatcher had the funds, but he could not dispense them until he had a permanent address from me someplace in the States and proof of employment. With that combination, the executive committee could be quite sure I wouldn't be returning.

Dr. Schumiatcher was allowed, however, to advance $1,500 so we could buy a used car and a small two-wheel trailer to get us out of town. We were not successful in selling the house, nor did we have a place to send our household goods. We learned about a campground near Salina, so we had our camping equipment and some clothes in the trailer. We boxed up everything else and left them in our Garnet street living room.

We left Regina on July 20, 1969. The day is easy to remember because we stayed that night at a motel in Bismarck, North Dakota and watched Neil Armstrong make his first steps on the moon.

Reflection

A dispute of almost 14 months ended unceremoniously with damages to both sides. To be sure, we lost the battle for a just settlement and had to settle for nuisance damages. On the other hand, Fr. Mooney's victory was not without costs to himself. According to a 1985 parish publication, in the summer of 1971 he was transferred to St. Anne's parish, and I have been told that he publicly admitted that he had a problem with the bottle and that at one time he had hoped to be a bishop. I suspect that the dispute did him no good in either respect. The parish council that was quashed in the spring of 1968 came into being in 1972, but it wasn't until 1981-1982 that the first edition of "Parish News" was presented by the council.

What had we accomplished by not accepting the first official offer of the parish leadership to run us out of town? First, their $2,000 offer would have gotten us across the border with no specific place to go. The logical place to have gone would have been Minneapolis where I had grown up, but there we would have had a very hard time economically. With my dad failing, as my mom had been telling me for two or three years, we could not have moved in with them. Rents would be high for an unemployed head-of-family, and the anxiety level might have been even higher there than in Regina. So staying in Regina was probably not any worse financially than a move to the Twin Cities without employment.

The unanswered question is this: Why did Fr. Mooney want to drive me out of the province? That he wanted me out of Saskatchewan is evident both from his letter saying that the ILT was recalling me and I would be leaving by June 30 and by the letter that the parish attorney wrote me on the same day I was disemployed by the provincial government. Why could he not stand to have me around not as an employee but even as a resident employed by some other organization?

The Birth Control Issue?

Dorothy Lawby, as mentioned previously, was one of Fr. Mooney's most trusted consulters in the process that led to my hiring. The Lawbys, however, became very disappointed with his performance in the dispute, and Dorothy later volunteered her opinion that the big reason for my dismissal was birth control. As she explained it, Fr. Mooney had a doctorate in theology, he was close to the archbishop, and maybe he was hoping to be named a bishop some day, so he felt he couldn't directly undermine the Church's traditional teaching against contraception. Dorothy thought he was hoping that the lay theologian he was hiring would be like so many others who undermined the received teaching affirmed by *Casti Connubii*. In that way Fr. Mooney could stay silent on the issue but indirectly support the acceptance of contraception and remain popular with a certain part of the community.

If Mrs. Lawby's interpretation is correct, Fr. Mooney must have been sorely disappointed when he learned that I was doing a good job of upholding the teaching of the Church in my regular classes. When *Humanae Vitae* was issued just about two months after he fired me from my parish job and the Canadian priest, Fr. Gregory Baum, was gaining attention all throughout the English-speaking world for his dissent, Fr. Mooney may have felt all the more emboldened in his efforts to drive a pesky defender of *Humanae Vitae* out of the province. It may be significant that when the archdiocese got dragged into a debate on the encyclical in October, the organizers couldn't find a single priest to defend it publicly and had to turn to me.

Covenant Sexuality

The most positive aspect of this episode was the publication of *Covenant, Christ and Contraception* with its covenant theology of human sexuality. If we had moved, would I have found the time and the quiet to write it? During my three weeks in the provincial health department, it was my intention to write the manuscript, but I wrote not a single word until unemployment gave me months of unwanted free time. The hard-cover book was published less than a year after we left Regina, and it was highly instrumental in our founding of the Couple to Couple League for natural family planning in the fall of 1971. Msgr. William B. Smith, the great teacher of moral theology at St. Joseph's Seminary in the Archdiocese of New York, used it in the early Seventies and was instrumental in getting it republished by Liturgical Press in 1976. In 1980 it helped Kimberly and Scott Hahn accept Catholic teaching on birth control, and it is my personal opinion that their living the truth about chaste married love helped them to accept the rest of the teachings of the Church.

What is the covenant theology of sexuality? Its key statement is simplicity itself. "Sexual intercourse is intended by God to be at least implicitly a renewal of the marriage covenant." Over the years different people, generally graduate students in theology, have asked me where I got it. I would tell them that I didn't know, and I invariably added that if they ever discovered that I had lifted it from some other source to let me know so that I could give proper credit. Scott Hahn once told me that I was the first person to put into writing that simple concept—that the marriage act ought to be a renewal of the marriage covenant. Since Hahn is the best-read person I know, I will take his word for it. The concept has become so widely accepted that people no longer ask where it came from; there seems to be a general feeling it's been around forever, so to speak.

In short, I think that God gave me the covenant insight when I was teaching the Faith in Santa Clara. I think He gave me the time to author a book around that basic concept to support the teaching of *Humanae Vitae* at a time when the encyclical needed support, even from theological nobodies. I know that God was watching over us in a special way during our stay in Regina. With the benefit of years of hindsight, I now like to think that my unemployment was providential. While I certainly did not feel that way at the time, I have thanked the Lord for it many times in later years.

Years ago I wrote Father Mooney a letter of forgiveness, but he did not reply. Perhaps he had already gone to meet his Maker. May he rest in peace, and may we be good friends in heaven.

4. Salina, Kansas 1969-1971

The aftermath of a recent tornado was the first thing we noticed as we drove through Salina on our way to a campground just outside this city of about 40,000 at the time. It was not a regulated campground. It was just a place where anyone could camp without any sort of security or regulations. So it wasn't surprising that one night there was a noisy party going on in and around a nearby camper. We couldn't get to sleep, so I foolishly went over to the party boys and asked them if they could tone it down a bit. These men had apparently never heard a polite request before, and I was glad they treated it as a joke instead of beating me to a pulp.

A departing faculty member had accepted a position in Hawaii and was very anxious to sell his house at a reasonable price. We were delighted to find a house so quickly. In the mornings it was an easy bicycle ride to Marymount College, but the afternoon winds typically made it a low-gear effort all the way home.

The situation at the college was interesting. The president who hired me was no longer with the college. He had previously been associated with Notre Dame in South Bend, Indiana and came to Salina with the dream of making Marymount the Notre Dame of the plains. Accordingly, he refurbished his own office at a price of $25,000 and hired six new faculty members to handle the increased student population that he anticipated. The public rumor was that his wife was not happy in Salina and missed the overall Notre Dame atmosphere. At the end of his first year as president, he returned to South Bend.

When the new faculty members arrived, we found a new president, one of the sisters of the religious congregation that owned and operated the college. She was a most pleasant and competent woman, but she accepted the job only for one year, making it clear to all parties that this was a temporary position for her. She quickly organized a search committee, and in due time the college hired Dr. Emerald Dechant who arrived in the summer of 1970 for the next academic year. It quickly became clear to Dr. Dechant that he needed to balance the budget, and accordingly he laid off the six of us who had just completed our first year with the college. He was a realist, and he did us all a favor by giving us our pink slips in the early fall in order to give us the maximum time possible to look for our next jobs.

There was one thing, however, that differentiated my job loss from that of the others. After I left, my position was filled by the chaplain, and that was contrary to the contemporary rules of the American Academy of University Professors. According to the AAUP, colleges can disemploy a faculty member when financial reasons force the college to eliminate a position, but colleges are not permitted to fill that position with other, cheaper personnel. In my case, my classes were to be taught by the lower paid priest who was the college chaplain. We could have contested the termination, but by that time we had already decided that we didn't fit very well into Salina society. Besides, we loved Sister Magdalita, the academic dean. She literally shed tears when she discussed the termination with me, and we would not have wanted to cause her any additional grief.

The Kansas Abortion Law

During the academic year of 1969-1970, we experienced three things of special interest. First, in 1969 the State of Kansas passed legislation that allowed a mother to kill her unborn child for any reason whatsoever up to the time of delivery. Most people are surprised to learn that Kansas had such a liberal abortion law prior to the *Roe vs. Wade* decision of January 22, 1973. At the time, Kansas was strongly influenced by Methodist politicians, and the Methodist Body of Social Concern (I think that was the name of the organization) persuaded the Methodist church to accept abortion. Of interest to me was the fact that the Methodist church at this time had some reputable theologians, one of whom, Paul Ramsey, was totally opposed to abortion. I heard at the time that their recognized moral theologians were not consulted. This was to be strictly a matter of politics, not science and morality.

At the same time, longstanding Kansas legislation made it illegal to drink a glass of dinner wine at a public restaurant. This was brought home to us abruptly when my mother visited us. She liked to have a relaxing drink before dinner, so when the server asked what we would like to drink, she replied, "Scotch and soda." "Ma'am, you're in Kansas." I interjected we knew that much geography but wondered what that had to do with having a Scotch and soda. "Kansas is dry." I was soon informed, however, that if you joined a "private club" for a dollar or so, you could get drunk as a skunk. So in Kansas, a young woman could kill her unborn baby but an elderly woman couldn't have a Scotch before dinner. That's beyond Oz.

Not long after abortion was legalized, one of the hospitals in Salina offered to perform them. That called for a protest, and some of the religious sisters at Marymount agreed. They helped me paint a few picket signs, but they would not join me in picketing the hospital because they feared such a public confrontation would have adverse consequences for the college. So I went there by myself with a couple of signs and started to picket. Soon I was joined by a woman who identified herself as a Jehovah's Witness. I didn't keep a diary at the time, and I have forgotten how often we picketed, but I do remember that not one other person joined us.

Kansas Labor Law

In the spring of 1970, I got involved in a second event of special interest. I read in the paper that the president of the Salina firefighters union had been suspended by the city safety director who felt that the union president had used inappropriate language. Suspended? And most likely without pay? For using some emphatic and perhaps vulgar language that the safety director had himself probably used hundreds or thousands of times? I couldn't believe it, so I phoned the union president. Yes. The newspaper was correct. But there was nothing the firefighters could do because in 1969 the cities of Kansas did not have to recognize unions as official bargaining units with statutory and negotiated rights including appropriate grievance procedures. (When I was in Wichita in August 2010, I was told that's still the situation.)

This was an excellent demonstration of the need for good unions. As an informed Catholic, I was aware of Catholic social teaching regarding the rights of individual human persons, including their right to organize. I was aware of the prophetic writings of Sacred Scripture against taking advantage of the poor and weak. I had been educated on the great social encyclicals starting with *Rerum Novarum* by Pope Leo XIII in 1891 and followed forty years later by *Quadragesimo Anno* by Pope Pius XI in 1931, *Pacem in Terris* by Pope John XXIII in 1963, and most recently (at that time) by *Populorum Progressio* by Pope Paul VI in 1967. It was the latter that taught so clearly that there will be no peace without justice.

At the time I was teaching a course on Catholic social-justice doctrine, so one spring afternoon I went to the City Council meeting to give them a very short course on social justice. A photographer caught me in a classic prophetic pose with my forefinger making an emphatic point and my mouth wide open. One of my students, however, found it very helpful. He said that he had been having some faith-related problems, but seeing that short presentation of Catholic teaching made him extremely proud to be a Catholic and had really increased his faith.

The intended recipients of this lesson on social justice did not appreciate it. One of their officials quickly did a background check and soon was circulating a rumor that I had a "police record." Amazingly, this was picked up by some parishioners and used against me. (I had been asked to run for parish council.) Fortunately, a priest looked into this. He found that, yes, the police in Regina had a record on me; after all I had called them when I received threats "to get out of town before it's too late." He also found that there was not even an allegation of unlawful conduct. So he told those who were spreading the rumor that what they were doing constituted the sin of calumny and that they needed to stop it immediately, which they did. Fortunately, I was not elected to parish council.

I had touched a sore point, and the controversy lingered. I remember that a friend at the college told me repeatedly that I couldn't accomplish any good and that I was only hurting myself by continuing to support the firefighters. He was, of course, correct. In my first meeting with Marymount's new president, he told me that at his first meeting with some of the prominent city fathers whose cooperation he needed in fund raising, he was asked, "When are you going to get rid of the 'perfesser'?" Still, the president and I continued to talk for a while about a joint book-writing project he had suggested, but then it became clear to him that he was going to have to disemploy all six of us who had been hired just a year previously.

I don't think Dr. Dechant let the critics unduly influence his decision. He simply had a very difficult financial situation. Founded in 1922, Marymount was the oldest Catholic liberal arts college in the state. It had been strictly a women's college until shortly before we arrived in 1969. While becoming coed provided a temporary boost in enrollment, it was not sufficient for the long term, and the college closed in 1989.

Salina and *Humanae Vitae*

The third memorable event of our stay in Salina occurred in the spring of 1970. My book, *Covenant, Christ and Contraception* was published in the early spring. As indicated previously, once it was published, I felt that the passage of Luke 11:46 applied directly to me. Jesus had been criticizing the Pharisees, and then— "One of the lawyers answered him, 'Teacher, in saying this you reproach us also.' And he said, 'Woe to you also, scholars of the law! For you load men with burdens hard to bear, and you yourselves do not touch the burdens with one of your fingers.' "

I had done the best I could to defend and explain what so many were calling a great burden—the teaching against contraception reaffirmed by *Humanae Vitae* in the summer of 1968. The key insight in my book was the covenant statement: "Sexual intercourse is intended by God to be at least implicitly a renewal of the marriage covenant." Now I felt obliged to do what I could to help lift that "burden." By this time, Sheila had researched and written *Breastfeeding and Natural Child Spacing*. We were printing it on our mimeograph machine, and it was selling pretty well through her La Leche League contacts. We wanted to share these insights. About the time we arrived in Salina, we had learned about systematic natural family planning from an article by Dr. Konald A. Prem, and we wanted to share this too.

What should we do? We decided to have a meeting with other like-minded couples. Sheila knew some through her breastfeeding contacts, but we wanted a few more. We advertised in the parish bulletins of Salina and some surrounding towns, and two couples and three breastfeeding mothers showed up. We were excited to learn that some of them knew more about NFP and the budding NFP movement than we did. We said, "This is great. Can we work together to form an organized effort to spread the good word?" Utter silence. It turned out that our fellow NFP users were "closet NFPers." The social pressure was so strong against *Humanae Vitae* that they didn't want to be known as believers—even in their own parishes.

We were disappointed that we found no local support for forming an organized effort to teach NFP, but there were at least two good outcomes. We learned about two East Coast NFP organizations, and our follow-up convinced us we had to form a new organization. Neither of them had anything to say about breastfeeding as a form of natural family planning. In fact, it was treated as a problem to be overcome. That meant that at least implicitly they encouraged early weaning to get back to regular cycles as soon as possible. Furthermore, attending the NFP teacher-training weekend offered by one of the programs entailed travel expenses, a fee, book purchases, and babysitting expenses. Sheila was nursing a toddler at the time, and separation was not an option. Some later chapters will describe our future efforts with an NFP apostolate.

The second good outcome from this Sunday afternoon meeting was that we learned about *Sex, Fertility and the Catholic* authored by Don and Helen Kanabay. An associate pastor at St. Mary's asked us to instruct a married couple about NFP, and we used the Kanabay's book as the basis for our instruction.

Year Two in Salina

Our second year got off to an unsettling start when the president of the college gave pink slips to the half-dozen of us who had been hired the previous year. Once again, we sent letters and my résumé to Catholic colleges, but this time the return was less than previously. I remember interviewing at Benedictine College in the famous rail town of Atchison, Kansas. Father Dennis Meade, OSB, wanted to hire me but was frustrated by the then current procedures. Candidates were required to give a lecture to a committee made up mostly or entirely of students. My lecture was on the covenant theology of human sexuality and supported Catholic teaching on birth control. Father Meade liked it, but it wasn't what the students were looking for. Department heads at a few other colleges said they would keep my résumé on file, but the prospect of continued college teaching was not promising.

From some source, probably the Institute of Lay Theology, we heard of an opening for a director of religious education at a parish in the Twin Cities. I interviewed and was hired to teach adult education, to coordinate the CCD program for high school students, and to share CCD coordination responsibilities for junior high grades.

Because I was willing to move out of my chosen field, I was the first of our group of six to find employment. One of the others found a teaching position at the local Methodist-related college. The others were still without jobs when we left Salina. Moving was a pain. We rented the biggest U-Haul truck available, but since we couldn't get everything in, we had to do some last minute giveaways. Our pastor was pleased with the silver coffee service, the new house-owner was happy to have a good ladder, and my only real regret was that I couldn't find room for a hawk I had shot in high school. The taxidermist had done a great job with the wings outspread as if just taking off from the branch to which it was attached. The kid next door was delighted to have it.

Teaching college theology for two years was a great experience. Some of our other experiences in Salina were less than inspirational.

5. St. Odilia's Parish

The academic year at Marymount ended in late May or early June, so we were able to arrive at St. Odilia's parish in Shoreview, Minnesota, a pleasant and generally prosperous suburb north of St. Paul, sometime in June. The senior associate pastor, Father Clem, had arranged for us to stay in a nearby motel, and we soon found more permanent lodging at the Nob Hill apartments, perhaps a little more than a mile from the parish center. The distance was great, and I walked it regularly.

Konald A. Prem, M.D.
One of the first things we arranged was a meeting with Dr. Konald A. Prem with whom Sheila was scheduled to conduct a panel on breastfeeding and natural child spacing at the La Leche League's convention in Chicago that summer. Sheila and he needed to clarify who was going to talk about what. Dr. Prem was, at the time, a full professor of obstetrics and gynecology at the University of Minnesota Medical School, and he had researched breastfeeding infertility. (He never published his research, but it is now at www.nfpandmore.org.) He was a Catholic who accepted the teaching of *Humanae Vitae*, and he had years of experience with a temperature-based form of natural family planning (NFP). In 1968 he had published in *Child and Family* a detailed explanatory article on NFP, and it was one of our main sources of self-instruction on systematic natural family planning when we were in Canada.

After Dr. Prem and Sheila had completed their discussion about the breastfeeding panel, we asked him if he would be interested in helping us form an organization to teach NFP using trained user-couples as the teachers. He was aware of failed clinic and hospital programs, so he was immediately enthusiastic, saying that this concept was precisely what was needed for long-term teaching and support of user-couples. Both he and we were aware of the success of La Leche League and its use of volunteer breastfeeding mothers to spread the word and provide excellent support. What we proposed would follow the LLL model, and it proved to be an excellent working model.

La Leche League International held a huge conference in July 1971 at a hotel in downtown Chicago, and Sheila was privileged to be a panel presenter with Dr. Prem and Dr. Paul Busam of Cincinnati. As I write these pages, we are still in regular contact with Dr. Prem whom I last visited in the summer of 2009, and we have dinner with Dr. Busam once a month. Each year I try to phone Dr. Prem with birthday greetings—easy to remember since we share the same birthday, just ten years apart.

The conference was successful on all counts. The adults were pleased with the presentation by Princess Grace of Monaco and by actress Susan St. James who was giving a new and popular face to breastfeeding, and our kids were thrilled when white-suited Col. Sanders of Kentucky Fried Chicken stopped by our table to say "Hi" to them.

We started to teach natural family planning as part of the parish adult education program, and we can still remember the first class that fall. It was held in the parish library, and almost nobody was there at the appointed starting time. We decided to wait a bit, and within ten minutes there were about a dozen couples, more than enough so that we didn't feel we were just talking to ourselves. Our teaching notes consisted of a few pages of handwriting. Our audio-visuals were just ourselves, although we may have had a chalkboard.

The course was simple but complete, consisting of four two-hour classes. Sheila would teach the aspects dealing with ecological breastfeeding, and I would deal with matters of faith and morals. Dr. Prem had already had a hard day of work and suffered from narcolepsy, so he snoozed in the back of the room as we talked, but when it was his turn to teach the Sympto-Thermal Method, he was refreshed and as sharp as ever. He came to each class of the two courses we taught, and for some time he continued to come to the classes taught by our new teachers in the Twin Cities.

Dr. Prem always stayed after class to help couples with the interpretation of their charts, but he did not use standardized Phase 3 rules as we do today. With his wide experience, he would simply tell the couples if they were now in pre-ovulation infertility, or the fertile time, or when Phase 3, the time of post-ovulation infertility, had begun. He would also tell them with great confidence that if he was wrong about a Phase 3 interpretation, he would deliver the baby free of charge. He also told them that no one had ever taken him up on that offer. We looked over his shoulder and not infrequently would ask him how he arrived at his interpretations. By listening to his explanations, we gradually developed the several rules that we still use today. The occasion of one of his interpretations still stays with me. At the end of the meeting, a couple who had been unable to get to the class on time dashed into the room. They wanted an interpretation, and when Dr. Prem told them they were in Phase 3, the wife raised the chart and cried out for all to hear, "Fun city tonight!" while her husband's face turned beet-red.

Religious Education

Part of my job was to help parents prepare their own children for First Holy Communion. At St. Odilia's, there was no "First Communion Sunday," but almost every Sunday was a First Communion Sunday for one or more families. It was the parents' responsibility to prepare their own children whether they were in the parish school or in a public school. On Saturday mornings, we would help parents refresh their own knowledge about the Holy Eucharist. "We" refers to me and a religious Sister with whom I shared this responsibility. When parents thought that their child was well prepared, the pastor would have a little conversation with the child. The sticky part was the lack of faith on the part of some parents. One father asked me point blank, "How can I teach this when I don't believe it?" On the other hand, one of the advantages of this system was that the pastor would visit the family of each new First Communicant that same afternoon, and he did this with us when our oldest daughter, Jennifer, made her First Holy Communion.

Another part of my job was to find and train teachers for the grade school CCD program for public school students. For the most part, this was a pleasant task, but once again the problem of lack of faith reared its ugly head. I was talking with a young man who had volunteered to teach a course that would include some miracles, but then he said that he simply did not believe in miracles. I should have asked him to research the miracles at Lourdes, but I was probably too surprised at the time to come up with a positive suggestion. I looked further and found someone else to teach the course, but the episode illustrated something about the ongoing battle between faith and skepticism even among those willing to serve within the Church.

Adult education was part of my job, but parish adult education by now was, for the most part, dead. It was now a half dozen years since the end of Vatican II. The theological left wing had been doing most of the adult education that was supposed to play a big part in renewing and reinvigorating the Church. Their courses and lectures, however, essentially said in one way or another that Catholics really don't need to heed the actual teaching of the Church. Oh, it might be good material for discussion, but it was not something to which the believing Catholic was obliged to conform his or her conscience. The actual documents of Vatican II were consigned to the dustbin of history, while the so-called liberals promoted what they called the "spirit of Vatican II." I call them "so-called" liberals because the chief talking point of people who want to be known as liberals is the idea of letting all ideas be heard. What we soon found out was that the so-called liberals were more dogmatic than the dogmas of the Church in their heterodox refusal to let the actual teachings of the Church get a fair hearing.

The result was that those for whom Catholicism was fast becoming a folk religion couldn't see any reason to attend adult education courses on the faith—they had already imbibed the heterodox dogma not to take it seriously. On the other side, believing Catholics who had attended courses taught by the so-called liberals were tired of having their Catholic Faith ridiculed by those who were paid to help them, so they too could see no reason for attending courses to hear more of the same.

I think it was well before the Christmas season that I had decided that this was not the way I wanted to spend the rest of my working career. If I was going to be involved with education, I wanted to teach. My experience with college teaching was encouraging, but the job hunts had also convinced me that a PhD was necessary for such a career, so I started my search for an appropriate doctoral program.

The Graduate Theological Union in Berkeley had a program that interested me because of its flexibility. For example, instead of a standard doctoral thesis that almost nobody will or can read, a satisfactory book would fulfill the thesis requirement, and that sounded more feasible to me. I was well aware of the liberal bias at the GTU, but I was confident that I could absorb the good and discard the fluff and the heresy. When they offered me a tuition scholarship, I started to make mental preparations for the move. We didn't know about student loans, so we weren't sure how we were going to manage the rest of the finances. Our situation was also complicated somewhat by the fact that we were pregnant with our fourth child (actually the sixth counting two very early miscarriages), and Sheila was not about to leave the baby to support this endeavor.

That was our situation when Father Angelo della Picca called from the College of Mount St. Joseph in Cincinnati. Although his doctorate was in sacred music, he was the chairman of the theology department, and he had meant what he had written the year before about keeping my résumé on file. A faculty member had just resigned, and Father Angelo reached into his file drawer, called, and asked if I was still interested. Given the situation above, was I interested! It would probably mean the end of doctoral studies, but at that moment, a bird in the hand looked a lot better than two in the bush. I flew down for an interview, and we were committed to Cincinnati. Incidentally, the faculty member offered to withdraw his resignation the day after the phone call, but he was told that the job had already been offered to and accepted by someone else. When I took over his courses and saw some of the books he was using, it was easy to see why Father Angelo was happy to have his resignation.

Allow me to share one last memorable event at St. Odilia's grade school. One of the associate pastors accepted a position as chaplain on a university cruise ship for the second semester. He had been teaching religion to the seventh grade boys, and I volunteered to fill in for him. I don't know for whom I felt more sorry—the boys or myself. At any rate, the experience clearly demonstrated to me and probably everyone else that teaching religion to seventh grade boys was not my vocation.

Politics, Abortion and Birth Control

We had never been involved politically, but the abortionists were making unprecedented progress. All the action seemed to be in the Minnesota version of the Democrats—the Democratic Farmer Labor party, so somehow we got involved in their caucuses. The followers of George McGovern had put new rules in place, so it was open season. I remember talking with one old-line party member, a Catholic and a long-time trade unionist. He was the kind of guy on which the party had been built, and it was sad to see him being forced out by the New Left after years of service. A group of us who were believing Catholics attended a memorable caucus in the spring of 1972. Sheila and a friend were conversing with a university student who became really upset when she found out that Sheila was pregnant with our fourth. Very angrily she accused Sheila for being the reason why she, the student, would have to get herself sterilized before she got married. Sheila managed to calm her down a bit by explaining the baby-spacing effects of ecological breastfeeding, but the student illustrated all too well the effects of the anti-population propaganda machine.

We also got slightly involved with Minnesota Citizens Concerned for Life, one of the first and strongest anti-abortion organizations in the country. Dr. Jack Willke of Cincinnati had started to publish brochures with photos of the remains of unborn babies, and they were highly effective in mobilizing pro-lifers into action. In fact, when pro-life forces used them in a referendum in North Dakota in the fall of 1972, the voters strongly turned down a proposed easy-abortion law. That success may have been partly responsible for the horrible Supreme Court decision on January 22, 1973 that declared unconstitutional all state laws against abortion. It's quite possible that the Justices, especially Justice Blackmun who hailed from Minnesota, realized that if the voters had a real say in the matter, and if they were properly informed about the bloody reality of abortion, they would vote against abortion.

Our involvement with the anti-abortion movement also revealed how personal relationships can affect one's thinking about abortion and birth control devices that may act as abortifacients. One of the real activists that we dealt with was a woman married to a doctor. She constantly refused to acknowledge that the intra-uterine device (IUD) could act as an abortifacient despite whatever evidence we could show. Her reasoning was very simple: Her husband was anti-abortion. Her husband inserted IUDs for birth control, and he wouldn't do that if they could cause abortion. Therefore, the IUD was not an abortifacient.

It is that sort of reasoning that makes it important to differentiate between those who are pro-chastity, those who are pro-life, and those who are only anti-abortion. Pro-chastity people accept only natural ways of spacing babies within marriage and total abstinence outside of marriage. Pro-lifers who are not pro-chastity will not use any form of birth control that has the potential to cause an early abortion, thus ruling out every form of IUD and every form of hormonal birth control, but they may accept intellectually or use in practice other contraceptive behaviors. Some anti-abortion people who are totally opposed to surgical abortions will illogically accept birth control drugs and devices with abortifacient potential as well as other contraceptive behaviors.

Regrets

My biggest regret for the year is that we did not visit frequently enough with my mother who lived in a Western suburb of Minneapolis. Her apartment was not child-proofed, and there was nothing to do for our children ages three, five, and seven. Mom was 74 at the time, in overall good health, and quite independent. While she could no longer help physically at the St. Vincent de Paul shop, she still helped by doing the phone work to line up the other volunteers each week. She didn't need us for anything except to be family with her, and I regret that we didn't do more to create some good family-type memories.

My second regret is that I didn't make an effort to establish contacts with some of my former classmates who were now priests serving in the area. They had been ordained in 1956, and this class was hit hard by the crazy stuff that was being taught and practiced in the Church under the guise of "the spirit of Vatican II." One classmate told me point blank that everything we had been taught in the seminary was wrong. By this time I had accumulated two graduate degrees in theology, and I had yet to be taught anything that contradicted anything I had learned in the seminary. My friend was engaged in non-critical thinking, just non-thinking acceptance of the latest left-wing idea advanced by someone who was dissenting from one teaching or another. I met one of my former classmates at a religious educators meeting, and he seemed to be out in left field, but I was later to learn of others who were truly keeping and sharing the fullness of faith with others. I certainly wish I had done more to get in contact with them during my year back in the Archdiocese of St. Paul.

In 1996 I attended a celebration of their fortieth anniversary of ordination to the priesthood. It was alternatively encouraging and pathetic. At the closing dinner, the tables were arranged in a horseshoe so we could all see each other. After dinner we were each to say a few words about our respective lives and careers. When it was my turn I gave a very brief summary, but then one of my orthodox friends, Fr. Jim Reidy, asked me to say something more about my work in natural family planning. I started to say something, but I was quickly put down by one of the inactive priests. We had golfed together that morning, and perhaps he had heard enough and didn't want to give me a chance to say something good about *Humanae Vitae*. By prior agreement, if anyone thought that someone was talking too long, he could tinkle a spoon against a glass, and the speaker was to shut up, and that's how I was put down. Still, I said enough that a couple of interested priests asked me more questions when the formalities were completed. On the other hand, we had to listen at length to inactive priests who had apostasized from the Faith. One of them announced that he was opposed to all organized religion, and yet after the meeting he sounded excited about what I was doing. It was like listening to a horror radio show. You know the show is fictitious drivel, but you're too curious to find out how it ends. This was worse because it wasn't fiction. Dear reader, please pray for the conversion and salvation of all those priests who lost their way. And keep praying for those who are faithful. They need and deserve our support.

Ten years later I attended their fiftieth anniversary of ordination. The number was smaller, and this time there were no such recitals of infidelities. It was my understanding that almost all, if not all, of those who had left the active ministry and had married were now reconciled with the Church. This time there was more exchange of health-related information. As one of them said, any time a group of guys our age get together, it turns into an organ recital.

Summary

Our year in Shoreview was a good one. My predecessor had called himself an agent of change, and I think we managed to tighten up a few things, or at least we exposed one or two problems. The pastor and the associate priests were kind and friendly, and I would enjoy correspondence with Fr. Leo Kappahn for some years to come. The realization that I did not relish what I did at the parish clarified at least what I did not want to do for years to come. The call from Fr. della Picca seemed providential at the time, and I think it was. The prospect of teaching college theology again was attractive. We had started an organization to promote and teach natural family planning. We had successfully achieved pregnancy early in the year, and our youngest child, the one born in Regina, turned four about the time we were leaving.

Once again, we rented a truck—this time a bigger one—and started to load it. I didn't think we had accumulated anything during the year, but the truck seemed too small. I was just about ready to call a moving van company when my sister Harriette, who was visiting our mother and us at the time, intervened. Somehow with her cool head we managed to unload and then reload everything into the van and were ready to move. Unfortunately, pancreatic cancer took Harriette from us in July 2007.

6. The Mount St. Joseph Years

It took us the better part of three days to reach Cincinnati. I drove the truck, and Sheila, seven months pregnant, drove our Canadian Pontiac station wagon with our three girls. Father della Picca had made arrangements for us to unpack all our household goods into a room on campus, and the unloading went smoothly.

Doctor Paul Busam and his wife Rose welcomed us into their home for the two weeks it took us to find housing, and it was a most pleasant stay. For years thereafter, our girls called them Uncle Paul and Aunt Rose. We had met for the first time at the 1971 LLLI convention in Chicago where Paul and Sheila shared the panel of breastfeeding infertility with Dr. Prem. Sheila and Rose corresponded during the year. When we met in Cincinnati it was a case of being old friends who had met only once previously.

The Busams had been teaching natural family planning in Cincinnati for years. The archdiocese supported a clinic-type NFP service at Good Samaritan Hospital, and Rose and Paul took turns with others in teaching NFP classes. They were also very much involved in the effort to promote and teach ecological breastfeeding as a form of natural family planning. Rose was not only a La Leche League leader but also trained other leaders and gave talks at schools and other venues. Paul was a family-practice physician and a long-time member of the Medical Advisory Board of La Leche League International.

We were also welcomed by the academic dean, Jim Wasserman, Ph.D. and his wife Barbara. Jim and I were both interested in gardening, and they supported our efforts to uphold the moral teaching of the Church.

A New Birth Experience

We had made arrangements with the Wassermans to watch our children when birth was imminent, and early in the morning of September 14 we made the anxious phone call and Barbara soon appeared. At Good Samaritan Hospital, Sheila was attended by Dr. John Brunsman, probably the best doctor in the Greater Cincinnati area for natural childbirth. For the first time, I was present at the birth. He was well aware that delivery goes faster when the mother is in a somewhat upright position, so he had Sheila position herself on the delivery table accordingly, using the stirrups as handholds. Talk about fast, he was so surprised at the quickness of the delivery that he almost didn't catch our fourth girl, Karen Monique.

After we were done in the delivery room around seven that morning, I went home to shave and have some breakfast. After a bit, the phone rang, and it was Harold Grove, an editor at Harper & Row, a New York publishing house. We had sent copies of Sheila's *Breastfeeding and Natural Child Spacing* to several publishers and had told each of them that we were sending the manuscript to multiple publishers because we did not want the delay of going through one refusal after another until we found the right one. Mr. Grove said Sheila's book would fill a niche in their list, and he and I quickly agreed on the terms. It was a real pleasure to announce to Sheila when I returned to the hospital that she had a commercial publisher. Dr. Busam had also come by to check out the baby. We had previously made an agreement with Dr. Brunsman that if both the baby and Sheila were fine, she could leave the hospital as soon as she felt comfortable doing so. Thus, well before noon we were on our way home. The nurses seemed in shock. Apparently they had never witnessed a mother and baby going home so soon. The next day I was still very excited and had to tell my students all about it.

Teaching at Mount St. Joseph

The College of Mount St. Joseph is a liberal arts college founded in 1920 by the Sisters of Charity as Southwestern Ohio's first college for women. Expecting a significant increase in enrollment in the early Sixties, the college built an entirely new and beautiful campus that opened for the 1962 academic year. It had admitted a few men for some years but became officially coeducational in the spring of 1986. That's when they began actively recruiting male students for the Fall '86 semester. When I started in the fall of 1972, it was still predominantly a women's college of around a thousand students. In 2011 it was a thoroughly coed college of 2,100 students with athletic teams reaching their divisional playoffs in some sports.

The actual classroom teaching at the Mount went well as far as I was concerned, and I greatly enjoyed the interaction with the students and the informal interactions with faculty and staff. Particularly enjoyable were the regular lunchtime bridge games that I missed once I left. The formal faculty meetings were something else; I suppose they are necessary, but they were certainly wearying.

More Effects of Dissent

Early in the fall I found out what I was up against in teaching what the Church teaches. When we were reviewing Catholic teaching on birth control, a freshman told me after class that I was the first person she had ever heard say a good word about *Humanae Vitae*. She explained that at her Catholic high school the religion teacher brought in the little encyclical booklet but then contrasted it with a stack of books by dissenters. The teaching was obvious whether it was direct or implied: You don't have to accept the teaching of *Humanae Vitae;* you can believe the dissenters. I asked her the name of her high school, but she replied that she didn't want me making waves at her school. "And anyway, it wouldn't make any difference. I've talked about this with the girls in the dorm, and we all experienced the same thing." She also told me that all her friends who were getting married were going on the Pill, thinking it was morally okay to do so. We were now four years beyond the 1968 issuance of the encyclical, and it was systematically being denied and undermined in Catholic high schools, one of the places where it should have been defended and explained.

In section 17 of *Humanae Vitae,* Pope Paul VI had predicted that the acceptance of contraception would have dire effects including an overall decline in sexual morality. If you ask anyone who believes in God as the Creator of the universe, "Who put together in one act what we call making love and making babies?" he or she will answer, "God, of course." The next question follows logically, "What is contraception except the effort to take apart what God has put together in the marriage act?" That's exactly what it is. That question helps us to see the fundamental reason behind the predictions of the Pope. If a person or a culture thinks and acts as if it is morally permissible to take apart what God has put together in one area of sexual activity, it is very easy to take the next step to separate something else that God has put together. And then the next and the next. That is, if someone accepts the principle that modern man can take apart what God has put together in one important area of love and sexuality, there is no logical stopping point.

One of the immediate fallouts was a vast increase in the number of sexual partners who took apart what God has put together in the relationship of marriage and sexual union. Sacred Scripture condemns every form of sexual union except the non-contraceptive union of husband and wife. Therefore we can say in confidence that God Himself has put together marriage and the marriage act. The sin of fornication is the sin of two unmarried people taking apart what God has put together and acting sexually as if they were married. The sin of adultery is the sin where at least one of the sexual partners is married to someone else, thus adding the insult of injustice to the innocent spouse or spouses. These sins have been with us since the beginning of recorded history, but in the Judeo-Christian tradition, they were seen as sins, not as sport. Today, with fornication and adultery rampant, Western culture seems to have put aside any recollection that God Himself put together in an exclusive way marriage and the marriage act.

It didn't take long for college students to lose faith in the biblical teaching that the marriage act belongs exclusively to marriage—if they had ever heard it. Soon, colleges all over the country were dealing with the issue of fornication in the dormitories. It was frequently handled as a matter of visitation rights. First, college administrators disowned the venerable tradition that they were to act *in loco parentis*—in the place of the parents. They took refuge in clichés that the parents have had 17 or 18 years to educate their children about right and wrong, so they claimed it is the sole responsibility of the students, who are now adults, to decide whether to act as their parents would like them to act. Then they set dormitory policies that not only allowed fornication but almost encouraged it. That is, when the students argued that they only wanted to use their dorm rooms for socialization as they would use their living rooms when they were at home, the obvious answer is something like this: "Okay, but leave the doors open, and everybody out by 10:00 p.m. on weekdays and midnight on Friday and Saturday. After all, some of our students want to get some sleep, and there are adequate lounges on the first floor." Instead, administrations and faculties first conceded closed door visitation and then locked door visitation until the wee hours of the morning.

The question came up at the College of Mount St. Joseph during my first year there. One of the students had told me that lots of the girls were on the Pill. The inference from the student was clearly that this was for birth control. But even if the Pill was taken for acne or dysmenorrhea, it had the potential to give them a sense of sexual recklessness. It also gave the boys a new line—"and besides, you can't get pregnant." To which they could easily add, "So the only reason you are saying no is that you don't love me." The idea that it would be a mortal sin may not have been in the dialogue, and the breast-cancer risks of the Pill were not yet known.

Accordingly I registered my opposition to the proposed dorm visitation policy in a four-column letter in the student newspaper, *Mount News and Views*. Opposition against me was voiced in the next two issues by other faculty and students. The college chaplain preached against me at Mass, saying that I didn't know what I was talking about. He had been ordained for only three years, and I thought he was not only wrong in what he said but was abusing his role in the pulpit. It came as no surprise to learn that he left the active ministry in 1994. The only written support came from a parent in the form of a personal letter. The expanded visitation policy was implemented, and I have no way of knowing the actual results.

I have not tried to follow what happened at the Mount dorms, but the problem of dormitory life at many schools was made highly public by a group of Jewish students at Yale. In 1997 the "Yale 5" objected as loudly as they could and eventually sued Yale University that was forcing them to live in dormitories they described as Sodom and Gomorrah. They didn't appreciate what was going on as guys ran around in various degrees of dress or undress at all hours of the night and early morning. They didn't like the brochure that told them where to get condoms and 100 ways to "make love" without actually having sex. They wanted to live somewhere that respected their Jewish beliefs and cultures, not a brothel. They wanted to live off campus, not pay a dormitory fee of $6,850 to live in such obnoxious conditions. A judge ruled against them in 1998, not on a matter of facts but in favor of the right of the school to impose its policies on all students.

In brief, college dormitories for the most part have become like brothels, the difference being that in brothels the men pay for sex but in the dorms they get to try their powers of seduction and the girls give it for free. In early December 2009, the evening news reported that $219,000 of federal stimulus money had been granted to study the problem of coed hookups in college dormitories. A morning paper that week carried a different item on the same problem—a college was banning dormitory sex when a roommate was present.

To be sure, there are some exceptions. There are some colleges that try to put faith into action and recognize human weakness, so they have restrictive policies that seek to limit opportunities for severe temptation and consequent sex. However, the mere fact that a college advertises that it is "Catholic" or "in the Catholic tradition" or "founded on Catholic principles" is absolutely no assurance that it has a virtue-supporting dormitory policy. I suspect that the same is true of colleges that advertise themselves as "Christian" or "in the Christian tradition" or "founded on Christian principles." After all, even Yale could say the latter in the historical sense of "founded."

The bottom line is that parents who care about chastity need to ask very specific questions about dormitory life. If parents start hearing that the students are mature adults who make decisions based on what the parents have instilled in them, the translation is that your child will most likely be living in a brothel-like atmosphere. It provides a good reason for having your children attend a local college, if at all possible, and to continue living at home.

Leaving Academia

In academia, there's a saying, "Publish or perish," meaning that if you are hoping for tenure, you need to have a record of publications. In a relatively short time, I had accumulated a good publishing track record. My first article was published in a popular magazine in 1967. That was followed by my book, *Covenant, Christ and Contraception* in early 1970, "Continued Dissent" in *Theological Studies* in June 1971, a long letter in *America* in October 1973, and "Catholic Sexual Ethics…" in the *Linacre Quarterly* in February 1974.

As mentioned previously, Sheila and I had started an effort to provide the practical help of natural family planning instruction to live out the teaching of *Humanae Vitae*. We had started it as part of my parish work at St. Odilia's in Shoreview, and we continued to teach NFP courses and to develop the organization when we arrived in Cincinnati. By the beginning of my second year at Mount St. Joseph, it seemed as if I had two full-time jobs. When I was preparing classes, I was concerned about NFP matters; when I was attending to the latter, I was thinking about my classroom work. Considering the little feedback I had gotten from my academic publications,

I started to think I might make more of a difference in people's lives if I could work full-time in the NFP apostolate.

There was also another element. The theological atmosphere at the Mount seemed to be changing. Father della Picca sensed it, and shortly after I left he transferred to the music department, the field in which he held a doctorate. He was a priest, had an earned doctorate, and was still the department chairman, but he was so concerned that his orthodoxy in moral theology might mean the end of his employment at the Mount that he gave up the chairmanship and transferred to music. (If you have seen the initials ADP denoting authorship of the melody of the responsorial hymn at Mass, you have seen or heard his work.) I had begun to wonder if I would be able to earn tenure no matter how well I performed and how full my publication record. Those who publicly and academically supported *Humanae Vitae* were welcome only at a few colleges at the time (and not much has changed), and if there was widespread gratitude and support for my efforts while at the Mount, I did not sense it.

Thus early in 1974 we began negotiating with possible funding sources, and I was able to resign from my position at the Mount at the end of the spring semester. It had been a good two years.

7. Continued Dissent from *Humanae Vitae*

Perhaps emboldened by the publication of *Covenant, Christ and Contraception* in the spring of 1970, and realizing the need to reach a wider readership, I decided to enter the so-called debate about the teaching of *Humanae Vitae*. The dissenters had a near monopoly in the Catholic theological journals and religious magazines concerning *Humanae Vitae* and related issues, but an important change had occurred. Almost immediately after the encyclical was issued, the leading dissenters stopped arguing about the immorality of contraception and switched to an argument from authority—the authority of numbers—the majority on the birth control commission, their own numbers, and the numbers of Catholics who practiced unnatural forms of birth control. Little attention was being paid to the actual arguments of the dissenters and to the logical consequences of their arguments—and for good reason. The arguments for accepting marital contraception couldn't stand the light of examination, and the dissenters certainly didn't want to deal with the logical consequences of their dissent.

Michael F. Valente

One dissenter, however, made clear the logical consequences of dissenting from *Humanae Vitae*. In the spring of 1970 Bruce Publishing issued a truly astounding book, *Sex: The Radical View of a Catholic Theologian* by Michael F. Valente who was then the chairman of the Department of Theology at Seton Hall University. The back cover blurb noted that he was "probably the first, and perhaps the only, layman to hold such a position at any large Roman Catholic university in the United States…[and] is also President of the Institute for the Study of Ethical Issues" an organization not found by my Google search in late 2009. Valente identified himself as a revisionist. He was a proportionalist as were most of the other dissenters who argued against the universal condemnation of marital contraception. Proportionalism rejects moral absolutes, teaching that the morality of any act depends upon the situation, so it is ultimately just another name for situation ethics. The latter had a bad name and the term is easily understood, so the Latin-derived "proportionalism" sounds better, and its meaning was not immediately apparent. But Valente was different from the rest—he spelled out the logical consequences of rejecting *Humanae Vitae*.

> In the present situation, one has a choice. If one can abstract from the ideological fight in progress and escape embroilment in the theological controversy over orthodoxy and authority and institutionalism, then the choice is to heed the pope and the traditional interpretation of sexual ethics, or to opt for the revisionist tack on contraception and with it arrive at the destruction of the natural law doctrine and the recognition of the need to rethink the *whole* of sexual ethics (115, his italics).

He saw that taking apart what God has put together in the marriage act leads to taking apart the God-given connection between marriage and sexual union.

> A second conclusion is that if human sexuality can have a nonprocreative purpose to fulfill, then it is at least questionable that this purpose is fulfilled exclusively in marriage—which would utterly repudiate the tradition's insistence that sexual intercourse outside of marriage is strictly forbidden (121).

> If sexual activity can be guaranteed nonprocreative, it is no longer hemmed in by the rules and guidelines previously established out of reverence for the life of the potential child (121).

He then argued against those who would want to accept contraception but limit sexual intercourse to marriage and concluded:

> Thus if the use of sexuality outside the married state is to be forbidden, it must be forbidden on grounds apart from the natural law doctrine; for to accept the revisionist position on the liceity of contraceptive use in marriage is not merely to find an exception to the natural law doctrine , but to destroy it (126).

Next, after stating that there is no moral difference between using a condom and having anal copulation, he spelled out the further consequences more clearly than any other revisionist whom I have read:

> Likewise there is no difference between using the condom and *coitus interruptus* [withdrawal as in the sin of Onan] or any of the other so-called sins prohibited under the doctrine, such as masturbation, homosexuality, and bestiality (126).

I think it took some intellectual bravery to point out that a logical consequence of the revisionist acceptance of marital contraception was the intellectual, logical acceptance of bestiality—copulation with animals. To make his point, he explained it further:

> The case of bestiality provides an interesting example. The individual who finds sexual release in bestiality has carried the masturbatory model into the area of animal affection. Feeling the need for communication and affection, he apparently thinks that with an animal he can find the kind of relationship best suited to his needs. Such an individual may have such psychological fears about attempting to get close to another human person that he resorts to animals which he finds more docile and easier to communicate with. Denied such activity, he might never progress beyond wishing for it. Permitted it, he might indeed progress beyond it. But, in any case, where is the harm in it? (140).

I never saw Valente mentioned in the birth control literature thereafter. He had clearly stated what was involved in the intellectual acceptance of marital contraception. He had spilled the beans, and I suspect that he was not welcomed by the other dissenters. A Google search in late 2009 yielded some information. In 1975 he was still a Professor of Religious Studies at Seton Hall, and on January 1 of that year he wrote a short piece "On Homosexuality" for the *New York Times*. In August of that year he was scheduled to be a main speaker at the Second National Convention of Dignity, the organization that works to advance the interests of Catholics who identify themselves as gay, lesbian, bisexual or transgender. A blogger wrote that in the early Eighties Valente migrated to Santa Monica and was a co-founder of an organization whose stated purpose was to "provide participants with the opportunity to experience the truth about love, sexuality, and relationships so that frustration, effort, and scarcity in these areas are supplanted by mastery, spontaneity, and fulfillment." This organization held two-and-a-half-day workshops that took place over a weekend and were held in New York and Los Angeles. I don't want to imagine the content.

In the light of the Scandal that came to light in 2002, it is worth noting that Valente mentioned homosexual behavior as one of those activities that could be accepted according to the logic of accepting contraception. Little has been said about the very real scandal of allowing the revisionists to teach their doctrines in schools and universities that called themselves "Catholic," some of which were under the direct control of diocesan bishops. It didn't "just happen" that there was an unusual amount of sexual behavior between a few priests and young boys in the Sixties and Seventies. Men with same-sex inclinations were being admitted into seminaries, but worse yet, they were being fed the erroneous theories of the revisionists. Although they eventually got great attention, the actual number of priests committing sexual sins with young or adolescent boys was very small, but the harm both to the victims and to the Church was great. And most of the abuse did not deal with small children but with adolescents, a favored target of homosexuals.

"Continued Dissent: Is It Responsible Loyalty?"

When I decided to enter the ongoing post-*Humanae Vitae* debate, I was unaware of Valente's book, and perhaps that was providential. It was better to focus on the writings of the chief dissenter, Father Charles Curran who was teaching at Catholic University. I did so, and the result was "Continued Dissent: Is It Responsible Loyalty?" I analyzed Fr. Curran's decision-making principles and demonstrated that such principles were so open to almost anything imaginable that they could not say a firm "no" even to spouse swapping. In short, when the decision-making principles of the principal dissenter were applied to human sexuality, the norm became mutual acceptability.

The generally liberal theological journal, *Theological Studies,* published "Continued Dissent..." in March, 1971. I considered that as quite a compliment because TS would not have published a work of mere rant and rave. This journal is widely read by people who read and write theology, and I know that Fr. Curran read it because he made an offhand reference to it in our correspondence on another subject. No one objected to it. No one said I had created a straw man. No one replied to it in any way. It was completely ignored at the time of publication by way of any written response either in the journal or elsewhere or to me personally. Four years later, Fr. Thomas Dubay, S. M., wrote in the same journal about the alleged desire for a "debate" on the birth control issue and noted that no one had responded to my article.

So my article accomplished two things. First, it showed that the decision-making principles of the leading dissenter could be used to say "yes" to any sexual behavior that was mutually acceptable to consenting adults. Second, the lack of response showed that those who were calling for debate were hypocritical. If they wanted a debate, they would have responded to a devastating criticism of one of their prime leaders. In reality, the call for "debate" was then and remains simply a call for more venues in which the dissenters can put forth their sweet sounding but poisonous words without fear of articulate reply. ("Continued Dissent: Is It Responsible Loyalty?" is available at the NFPI website, www.NFPandmore.org,)

Human Sexuality: New Directions

The sexual logic of taking apart what God has put together in the marriage act continued to be acted out. Though it wasn't being publicized at the time, it was being applied by those with same-sex attraction and by those whose sexual attraction was especially directed toward adolescent boys or even pre-adolescents. Thus it was no surprise to some of us when, in 1977, Paulist Press published *Human Sexuality: New Directions in American*

Catholic Thought. It was subtitled, "A Study Commissioned by The Catholic Theological Society of America," and it was authored by Chairperson Anthony Kosnik and four others—William Carroll, Agnes Cunningham, Ronald Modras, and James Schulte. Nor was it any surprise to read their moral equation between sodomy and marital contraception.

> Homosexuality is not a problem to which a pastoral minister need only to propose and implement proper solutions. On the contrary, homosexuality is a question that moral theology has only recently come to appreciate in all its complexity, ambiguity, and uncertainties. Given the limits of our knowledge, counselors and confessors must keep in mind that they have no right to impose unproven views or questionable opinions on others, thereby interfering with their fundamental freedom of conscience. All else being equal, a homosexual engaging in homosexual acts in good conscience has the same rights of conscience and the same rights to the sacraments as a married couple practicing birth control in good conscience (216).

The overall context of the book is that the teaching of the Church on the subjects of contraception and homosexual sodomy is at best uncertain and more probably just plain wrong. The same would hold true for all other forms of sexual behavior between consenting persons. For some reason, thankfully, the authors have reservations about adultery, saying we need more evidence from the social sciences. "Thus, while remaining open to further evidence from the empirical sciences, we would urge the greatest caution in all such matters, lest they compromise the growth and integration so necessary in all human activity" (149). Far from the Commandment given by the authority of God, the authors look instead to the weak and tentative authority of the social sciences. Thus, "Thou shalt not commit adultery" becomes in their hands, "You need to realize there may be some not yet proven consequences, so be cautious."

If there still exist people who wonder how those priests who engaged in pedophilia (as it's called with preadolescents) and sodomy (as its called with adolescents and young and older men) could possibly bring themselves to do such actions, I submit they need to realize more fully what was going on in the Sixties and Seventies by way of so-called moral theology right in the seminaries. The book cover described the five co-authors as influential and powerful people in the Church. Father Kosnik was a professor of moral theology and dean at Saints Cyril and Methodius Seminary in Orchard Lake, Michigan and holder of other honors in the Church. Sister Agnes Cunningham was an associate professor of patrology and Church history at St. Mary of the Lake Seminary in Mundelein, Illinois, the seminary of the Archdiocese of Chicago. Father Ronald Modras was an associate professor of systematic theology at Saint John's Seminary in Plymouth, Michigan.

The quotation above is saying essentially that if a person has persuaded himself that sodomy or contraception is okay, then confessors and counselors shouldn't correct them, shouldn't affirm the teaching of the Church and shouldn't try to explain the reasons for that teaching. Certainly we see in this book's pastoral guidance no effort to tell such misguided persons that they are endangering their immortal souls by engaging in acts condemned by the Church as the grave matter of mortal sin.

Now, if a seminarian or priest who reads the dissenters' theological books and journals also has a same-sex or other deviant sexual orientation, what will he think? Will he think that he better find some way to get such thoughts out of his head because they are evil? Or will he think that maybe what he formerly thought was wrong really isn't wrong anymore, so he is free to follow his inclinations?

When it comes to sexual temptations, if the battle changes from resisting the temptation to an internal debate about the authority and truth of the Church's teaching, the battle is more than half lost. When a person debates whether a behavior clearly taught by the Church as the grave matter of mortal sin really is sinful, he has put himself (or herself) on a very slippery slope. Those who did their best to cast doubt on the chastity teachings of the Church have done no favor to themselves or to those they influenced, and the great Scandal of 2002 is largely the horrible result of their efforts.

The only good news associated with *Human Sexuality* is that it caused some of the hierarchy to speak out against it. Just after its publication I was meeting with then-Archbishop Joseph L. Bernardin of Cincinnati. He had been instrumental in funding our NFP organization for the first two years of its existence with full-time-employees, so I would make a report every six months. On one such occasion, the Archbishop had stayed up most of the previous night to read the just published *Human Sexuality*, and he was clearly distressed. He completely dismissed the statements of Paulist Press that they had published it just for academic discussion: "Sure, and that's why they hired a Madison Avenue firm to promote it?" I was surprised at his negative reaction because it seemed to me that the book was reflecting the sort of theological trash rumored to be taught at his own seminary. I felt like telling him, "I agree with your concerns, but it's my understanding that the errors you are complaining about are standard fare at your own seminary. You might want to do some house cleaning." But either cowardice or prudence prevailed, and I said nothing. To his credit, he led the charge and persuaded the bishops to condemn the book.

The dissenters had been claiming that their dissent was an exercise of responsible loyalty to the Church, criticizing a teaching they believed to be not infallible and in fact erroneous. My article in *Theological Studies* challenged that claim because it was clear in 1971 that dissent was not responsible loyalty. Without batting an eye at the demonstration that the principles of dissent could accept anything of mutual agreement between consenting adults, the dissenters continued their poisonous work.

The errors of the dissenters became even more clear under the massive spotlight of the Scandal brought to light in 2002. They became clearer yet in late 2008 when Mary Eberstadt published an article titled "The Vindication of *Humanae Vitae"* in *First Things.* Using the evidence unearthed by the social scientists, she demonstrated that Pope Paul VI was all too correct in his prophecy about the dire consequences that would be caused by the widespread acceptance of marital contraception. Yet, despite repeated affirmations of *Humanae Vitae* by Pope John Paul II for more than 25 years starting almost immediately after his election in 1978, despite the evidence of the moral disasters that have come from the dissent, despite the evidence of the social sciences, the dissent continues. Yes, the leadership has died or is getting old, but the second generation of dissenters controls much of Catholic education at every level. The unhealthy situation of the Church in the West didn't "just happen." It was caused by the refusal to believe the Church's teaching on love, marriage and sexuality and by the refusal to admit the evidence against the dissenters' blind faith in dissent.

In section 26 of *Humanae Vitae,* Pope Paul VI called it a "most opportune apostolate" for couples to teach natural family planning to other couples. Another chapter will describe some of the efforts to do that in organized ways. For the present I want to point out only this: Such efforts starting in the early 1970s were made in the midst of the massive dissent of priests, the massive acceptance of contraception by the Catholic laity, and the hands-off treatment by many bishops. The bad effects of poor seminary education continued throughout the first decade of the 21st century because many of the priests ordained in the Seventies and Eighties and even into the Nineties were now pastors and still thinking erroneously about the demands of marital love and sexuality.

Richard A. McCormick, S. J.

Father Richard A. McCormick, S.J., was a moral theologian who went from belief that the received teaching on birth control was unchangeable to being a dissenter from *Humanae Vitae.* It didn't happen overnight, but he made the change. Perhaps some day someone will chronicle his metamorphosis. My first brush with him occurred in 1973.

The Jesuit magazine, *America,* habitually carried periodic analyses of events and documents, so I was quite sure that it would be running a "five-years-later" article on *Humanae Vitae.* Accordingly on March 5, I wrote to the editor, Father Donald R. Campion, S.J., and asked to be considered as a candidate to write about the encyclical from the perspective of one who believed its teaching to be true. He replied that Fr. McCormick was doing the five-year review, but that I would be welcome to reply to his article.

Father McCormick's article, "The Silence Since *Humanae Vitae*," ran in the issue of July 21. It was a combination of the sad and the humorous. It was sad that he could accurately report about the various statements by national groups of bishops that while only one might be in direct contradiction to the encyclical, some of their support was "noticeably softer and less insistent than we have been accustomed to where major moral positions are being authoritatively elaborated and communicated." He also played the numbers game to great advantage, and he then concluded that "this dissent, to the extent that it is responsible, must be seen as a source of new evidence."

That was irresponsible because Fr. McCormick had to be aware that the basic core of dissent was morally disastrous. He most probably had read Valente's book arguing that dissent dissolved the whole natural law argument. He certainly read my "Continued Dissent..." since he was a principal writer for *Theological Studies*. Of course, he carefully avoided saying that the dissent was responsible, as a careful reading of the sentence quoted in the last paragraph made clear. The sentence is ambiguous, and it was that sort of careful ambiguity that aided the dissent movement so greatly.

The humorous part of his article started with his call for "a new communal reflection on the meaning of the reasons for the dissent the encyclical provoked." Such a reflection would have to start with Original Sin, but under certain conditions it might have proved fruitful. But would it really address the issue of hyper-fecundity caused by the almost complete desertion of the kind of breastfeeding that really does space babies? Would it address the issue of the Pope's two-year delay in responding to the reports of the papal birth control commission? Would it address realistically the pro-contraception propaganda effort within the Catholic media and the absence of any sustained effort to explain and defend the teaching of *Casti Connubii* before it was reaffirmed by *Humanae Vitae* which referred to its predecessor only in a footnote?

Father McCormick concluded as follows: "The best way to undertake this reflection is probably through a blue-ribbon committee to report back to the bishops." And his very last sentence was this: "My own reading of the experience and literature of the past five years suggests that now is the time to respond as a community to Pope Paul's gentle invitation to dialogue."

The most charitable interpretation of this is that he was simply deluded if he thought that such a blue-ribbon committee could come up with anything except a report divided along the lines of the reports of the papal birth control commission in 1966 unless all the members were selected exclusively from the ranks of dissenters or exclusively from known supporters of *Humanae Vitae*. The huge difference would be that that those who accepted the teaching of *Humanae Vitae* would now have Valente's book and articles such as my "Continued Dissent..." to shed light on the logical consequences of accepting marital contraception.

I responded with a single-spaced letter slightly more than six pages long. The October 20 issue of *America* published four replies to the McCormick article—two from priests and two others including mine. The first three replies took less than two columns; my reply was condensed to about three and one-third columns. Father McCormick replied to the first three in less than two columns; his reply to mine took four and one-half columns.

The first point I made was that the U. S. Bishops had broken the alleged "silence" in 1971 with their publication of *Ethical and Religious Directives for Catholic Hospitals,* and Fr. McCormick failed to mention this significant event. Nor did he mention that he was a consultant to a group that issued a statement of dissent from the *Directives.* Toward the end of his reply, he mentioned the dissent from the *Directives* only obliquely by citing other theologians who dissented from *Humanae Vitae* and in principle from the *Directives.*

His reply was essentially a non-response to the issues I raised. He spent almost 40 percent of his reply criticizing me for "politicizing theology" by using terms such as "the liberal establishment" and the "the theological left" as if these were not accurate descriptions of reality. He further criticized my linking the principles of dissent from *Humanae Vitae* with other aspects of the moral decline within the Catholic Church. Yes, I had, and I still think the association is undeniable. Not surprisingly, he ignored the principles of Fr. Curran and Michael Valente.

My final point was this: "A blue ribbon commission of *Humanae Vitae* acceptors to map out ways of promulgating knowledge about natural family planning and the traditional sexual doctrine of the Church might be an extremely worthwhile use of human energy today." He ignored it.

I asked the editor to print a rebuttal, but that was refused. The exchange proved only one thing. No "debate" about the merits of the teaching of *Humanae Vitae* was possible in *America* magazine.

My next brush with Father McCormick occurred in *The Linacre Quarterly* (February 1974, pp 8-25). As mentioned above, the U. S. Bishops issued *Ethical and Religious Directives for Catholic Hospitals* in 1971. It was an effort to keep Catholic hospitals Catholic, to direct them not to allow abortions and contraceptive procedures including sterilizations. The Catholic Theological Society of America (the same organization that would publish *Human Sexuality...*in 1977) promptly set up a commission to dissent from it, and their report was published in *The Linacre Quarterly,* November 1972, hereafter the "CTSA Report" or "Report."

Fortunately, the Report invited criticism by stating, "the obvious theoretical limit to legitimate dissent is the truth itself as expressed in the reasons for the dissent from a particular teaching." I introduced the substantive section of my reply this way: "In the first section of what follows I shall attempt to show that dissent from the *Directives* is not justified on the very grounds that are put forth by the dissenters in the CTSA Commission Report; in the second section I shall attempt to uphold a similar position with regard to the dissent from *Humanae Vitae.*"

That particular issue of the *Linacre Quarterly* had an interesting content. The editors gave first place to my 18-page article, "Catholic Sexual Ethics:

The Continuing Debate on Birth Control." Right after it was a complete reprint of Fr. McCormick's article in *America*, "The Silence Since *Humanae Vitae*," possibly because my article had referred to it. Then followed an article by a Catholic doctor, Vitale Paganelli, affirming *Humanae Vitae*, and then an article by Drs. John and Evelyn Billings on the "Ovulation Method" of natural family planning. After a progress report on the Human Life Foundation, there were articles on euthanasia by Fr. Peter Riga, on abortion by William E. May, and a book review of *Abortion and Social Justice*. In short, it was a substantive group of articles on some very serious subjects.

I don't regret writing that 18-page article, and I am indebted to the editors for not only publishing it but also for giving it the lead position, but I wonder if it did any good. If your purpose in writing is to make a difference and not just to strengthen your résumé, a lack of response can raise questions about the value of such efforts. In reality, if the article helped one doctor stay faithful to Catholic teaching in his medical practice, that made the effort worthwhile, but who knows except God and that possible doctor?

My last meeting with Fr. McCormick was sometime in the late Seventies or early Eighties. I was doing lots of traveling in those years, and by chance we met at O'Hare airport. Chicago had been shut down by a storm, and when it opened up, planes swarmed there from everywhere. So many were coming in that the gates were full, and my flight from Denver circled and circled. In the meantime, my connecting flight to Cincinnati departed, and Fr. McCormick had a similar experience. He was immediately ahead of me in a line for lodging, and I decided I might as well try to talk with this priest, whoever he was. So I asked where he was going and what he did, and when he said something about teaching ethics, I asked his name. I told him it was a familiar name and introduced myself. I don't recall if he remembered, but at any rate we had a drink that evening, and the conversation was pleasant. Father Richard A. McCormick, S.J. was born in 1922 and went to meet his Maker in February, 2002. I hope he made it to purgatory where, if my theory on purgatory is correct, he is still kicking himself as he is compelled to watch the continuing unhappy effects of dissent play out in the Church and in the secular culture as well.

Why the Dissent?

In his *America* response to his critics, "What Does the Silence Mean" (Oct. 20, 1973), Father McCormick listed the names of a number of dissenting theologians and clearly implied that they were good people just trying to do their job in theology. That is, they weren't trying to destroy or weaken the Church; they weren't deliberately trying to foster the sexual revolution in all its ramifications. Allegedly, they were simply wrestling with the problem of when does a physical evil—contraception—become a moral evil. They struggled to find ways to teach married couples how and when they could justify their use of contraception despite the clear teaching of the Church that such behavior constitutes the grave matter of mortal sin.

I have to wonder if dissenting theologians and priests haven't been wrestling with a different problem—the ancient but always present problem of suffering. They weren't spending their time and ink wrestling with the question of what constitutes a sufficiently serious reason for practicing periodic abstinence to avoid pregnancy. They had to be aware of systematic natural family planning, but they focused mostly on the difficulty of periodic abstinence. Since most of the dissenting theologians were priests, perhaps they had heard about these difficulties in the confessional or in personal counseling. Perhaps some of them had friends who suffered with same-sex attraction.

Nobody likes suffering, even though many will embrace it as part of Christian discipleship or even as necessary to achieve purely secular goals such as weight loss or athletic achievement. Only psychopaths really like to cause suffering, but others will knowingly cause it by their actions in the effort to relieve another type of suffering. Surgery comes to mind. I suspect that almost all priests enter the seminary and are ordained because they want to be helpful to others both spiritually and with the corporal works of mercy. They want to alleviate suffering in one form or another.

I suspect that many of the theologians who led the dissent movement thought they were doing a favor to married couples by letting them have contraceptive sex instead of experiencing the difficulty or suffering of periodic abstinence. I suspect that is also the motivation of the many parish priests who either dissent from *Humanae Vitae* or ignore it. They don't want their people to suffer unnecessarily.

That was certainly the motivation of the man who would become the first Pope and argued with Jesus about suffering. Immediately after Peter's confession of Jesus as the Christ, Jesus began to teach the apostles about his coming passion and death. "And Peter took him and began to rebuke him, saying, 'God forbid, Lord.! This shall never happen to you.' But he turned and said to Peter, 'Get behind me, Satan! You are a hindrance to me; for you are not on the side of God, but of men' " (Mt 16:22-23).

It seems to me that the dissenters and others who ignore the teaching of *Humanae Vitae* are like Peter in this episode, and the answer of Christ applies to them as well. One cross that has to be carried by every priest and every teacher of the Faith is the teaching of Jesus about the daily cross. When we water down the teaching of the Church, we are not being on the side of God, and considering all the problems of the sexual revolution, we are not being a true friend by leading anyone to accept contraceptive behaviors. I know through faith, experience, and the witness of others that the discipline required by the practice of chaste systematic NFP is good for me and for others. Yet I have never enjoyed teaching about the need to accept periodic abstinence, and I have insisted that NFP teachers should teach the rules that reduce abstinence to the minimum consistent with the evidence. It's just part of the job of everyone who seeks to transmit the content of the Faith that they need both to teach the doctrine of the daily cross and also to ease the "burden" of *Humanae Vitae* with good teaching about natural family planning.

8. CCL: The Early Years

While we were at St. Odilia's parish in Shoreview, Minnesota we started the Couple to Couple League (CCL) to provide the practical help of natural family planning (NFP) instruction. Our purpose was not to assist the depopulation of Planet Earth as the Zero Population Growth movement was noisily advocating. Our mission was very simple and it was a combination of three related purposes.

The Triple Strand

We wanted to teach couples how they could enjoy a natural spacing of babies through **ecological breastfeeding**. We had done the research and would publish it in early 1972. We knew that mothers who breastfed according to what we now call the Seven Standards of Ecological Breastfeeding would experience, on the average, 14 to 15 months of breastfeeding amenorrhea (the absence of menstruation due to breastfeeding). In 1971 this knowledge was even rarer than it is today. Every couple deserves to know this information about the way God has made woman.

We wanted to teach couples how to practice a form of systematic NFP—**the Sympto-Thermal Method**—as taught by Dr. Konald A. Prem and others. This was intended to help couples who truly had sufficiently serious reasons to postpone their next pregnancy or to limit the expansion of their families. Every couple deserves to know this information about how God has made woman with identifiable fertile and infertile times of her menstrual cycle.

We wanted to support the teaching of *Humanae Vitae*, and we wanted to do so in a way that is simple and easy to grasp. That's why we incorporated in the CCL course from the very beginning **the easy-to-understand covenant theology of sexuality.** As noted previously, its primary statement consists of 17 words: "Sexual intercourse is intended by God to be at least implicitly a renewal of the marriage covenant." I had first put forth the "renewal of the marriage covenant" concept in my 1967 article, "Holy Communion: Eucharistic and Marital," and we knew from experience that it helps people to understand why Pope Paul VI taught that marital contraception is "intrinsically evil or dishonorable" (HV 14). It was and remains today a basic and simple "theology of the body." Everybody deserves to know this basic information about God's plan for love, marriage, and sexuality.

These three subjects—ecological breastfeeding as a form of NFP, the Sympto-Thermal Method (STM) as the most complete form of systematic NFP, and the covenant theology to support *Humanae Vitae*—constituted the Triple Strand Approach to natural family planning. These are the principle charisms we brought to the founding of the League.

We struggled at first to come up with a name. At the time we thought that we would be teaching married couples, most of whom would already have children, and that turned out to be accurate for a number of years. We thought that if we had "natural family planning" in the name of the organization, some couples might find that embarrassing as they explained to their babysitters where they would be, so we wanted something ambiguous. We took our cue from section 26 of *Humanae Vitae* where the Pope wrote:

> Thus there comes to be included in the vast pattern of the vocation of the laity a new and most noteworthy form of the apostolate of like to like; it is married couples themselves who become apostles and guides to other married couples. This is assuredly, among so many forms of apostolate, one of those which seem most opportune today.

So we named our new organization "The Couple to Couple League" and within less than three years it was incorporated as "The Couple to Couple League International, Inc."

We modeled out teaching program on the program of La Leche League International. Sheila had been an active member since 1964 and had started the first chapter of LLLI in Saskatchewan. They had a series of four meetings, and so did we. They had a small central organization that supported its army of volunteers, and that was our goal also. It worked well for both organizations. We were not in competition with LLL; we routinely urged moms to attend the LLL classes, and they in turn frequently referred moms to us. LLL has carried Sheila's breastfeeding and natural child spacing books since the first commercially published edition in 1974.

The First Courses

We taught the first class in the library at St. Odilia's school. Years later I asked one of the attendees what that first class was like, and he joked, "An hour and 50 minutes of preaching and ten minutes of how-to-do-it." First things first. Still, he and his wife became our first teaching couple.

Sometime during the second series of classes we invited two couples to our apartment, told them that we would be leaving in June, and asked them to continue the teaching. They gulped, asked a few questions about materials and training, and accepted the invitation. Sheila had a special connection with both of the wives because of their common interest in ecological breastfeeding, and that helped tremendously. We provided some very brief teaching notes for them to teach the third series that started in May. Bill and Joan Cossette taught that series. Bill taught math at a public high school, so he had plenty of teaching experience, but this was something entirely new. From where we were at the back of the room we could see ample beads of sweat on his brow.

Quality Control

The Couple to Couple League "headquarters" moved with us to Cincinnati in the summer of 1972, and we continued to stay in close touch with our new teaching couples. Soon the St. Paul chapter trained a new teaching couple. When we learned that the new couple had taught the first class in something like 20 minutes, we knew that something was missing, so we enacted our first quality control procedure. The central office would do the training of new teachers, and we would provide teaching notes that all teachers would use.

A Full-time Organization

When it became apparent that I had two full-time jobs and would like to work full-time in the NFP apostolate, we appealed to the Archdiocese of Cincinnati and the Archdiocese of St. Paul-Minneapolis for support. Both Archbishop Joseph L. Bernardin and Archbishop Leo C. Byrne were open to the idea, and they appointed Fr. Leo Tibesar of St. Paul to negotiate on their behalf. I was requesting funding for five years, and they offered it for one year. I responded that one-year financing would be a waste of their money because there was no way we could be self-funding by the end of one year, so I would be spending my last six months looking for a new job. They came back with an offer of two years. I had hoped for more, but thought it was not impossible to be self-funded by that time. So the two archdioceses agreed in writing to fund CCL at the rate of a combined total of $25,000 per year for two years. The "in writing" proved to be important. Archbishop Byrne died on October 21, 1974 at the age of 66. As the administrators were examining things, they notified me that the Archdiocese of St. Paul would discontinue its support. Fortunately, when I showed them the agreement signed by Archbishop Byrne, they continued to honor it.

The funding continued from July 1, 1974 through June 30, 1976. Sometime later in 1976 or early 1977, I met with Archbishop Bernardin to make a periodic report. I suspect he thought I would be begging because when I told him that we were getting by financially, he was evidently surprised. He was a fully sophisticated person, but this was such a shock that his jaw visibly dropped.

Even before I was completely finished at Mount St. Joseph, I started to travel for CCL. On Monday, May 13, 1974, I taught the first meeting (of our four-meeting course) in Wichita. The next evening, I did the same in West

Point, Nebraska. Wednesday saw me teaching in Sioux Falls, and Thursday I taught in Strawberry Point, Iowa. I repeated this trip in June for the second meeting, and then went directly to Collegeville, Minnesota to attend Fr. Paul Marx's NFP Symposium held each year during the Seventies, generally on Father's Day weekend. I concluded the regular course in the four cities with similar trips in July and August. The result was that we recruited future teaching couples in Wichita, Sioux Falls, and Dubuque (from the Strawberry Point course), and the priest who brought me to West Point soon arranged for me to teach in Omaha where we soon recruited teaching couples.

Those trips were one of the highlights of my 32 years with CCL. It was exciting, and it was very gratifying to associate with the great clergy and laity who sponsored those courses.

Facilities

Our first "office" was the third floor of our house that was built in 1894. There were two non-air-conditioned rooms on the third floor. One had a floor vent for such heat as might rise that far; the other was warmed somewhat by a huge chimney in the center of the room. It probably worked fairly well when the furnace was fired by coal, but the gas-fired furnace was intermittent. The south-facing windows in one room were badly deteriorated by 80 years of sunshine, so they weren't impervious to drafts even with the storm windows I had installed. The basis for one of the standing jokes occurred in the summer of 1975. Sheila and I were teaching NFP in Florida, but I kept tabs on Ohio weather conditions. When I read that Cincinnati was suffering from a heat wave, I phoned our two part-time order processing staffers—Donna Kneip and Marguerite Gehrum—who worked on the third floor and asked them to take the thermometers down the basement lest they be destroyed by the heat, but I didn't tell them to take the week off. It was always good for a laugh. Donna and Marguerite forgave me, stayed with us for years, but never let me forget.

One of the first external signs of growth was the need for office space not in our house. In the summer of 1975, I asked a real estate agent to find us a location within two miles of our house so it would be within easy walking distance, and he succeeded. CCL bought an eight-room house in an area zoned for business just a block from St. Martin's Church which offered a noon Mass in those years. It was ready for occupancy without us having to make any renovations. It was 1.9 miles from home, and I'm sure that walking or biking that distance on most good weather days contributed to the good health I enjoyed. The only major renovation was the addition of air conditioning in 1976.

Four years later we needed more space and were able to rent the basement of a building across the street. That took considerable renovation by way of utilities and a few walls. It had no windows except for two small ones in the back doors, but it was adequate for our needs. We stayed in both places for some years before we consolidated completely into the basement office. A sharp increase in rent in 1994 sent us looking for another facility, and in the early part of 1995 the CCL office moved to a warehouse-office facility on Delhi Pike four miles from home. For some time I walked it. I would leave at 6:30, attend the 7:00 Mass at St. Teresa's Church that was at the halfway mark, and then continue. Coming home I would sometimes take a ride part way with one of the other employees. After a while, I would drive to St. Teresa's and walk both ways from there. Biking was somewhat of a challenge because of the hills, but it was also a frequent mode of travel. But gradually I drove most of the time.

The warehouse building needed considerable renovation. An engineering review showed that it lacked sufficient structural strength, so that was remedied. The second floor office area was mostly wide open, so we partitioned that. A fund drive enabled us to pay off the mortgage, and that was very helpful for our financial well-being.

Personnel

We were enjoying expansion in the ranks of our teaching couples during 1975, and I needed help with teacher training. Our friends in the Twin Cities recommended Jim Glover because he liked the details involved with chart interpretation. We welcomed Jim and Mary and their children to Cincinnati in early January 1976. Two years later Peter Walsh joined the staff as another associate director. He and his wife Kay and family came from Winona where Pete had been the Director of Catholic Charities. Pete would leave in the summer of 1980 to take a teaching position at a college in Winona, but in his short time with us at Central he was a life saver, taking care of the big project involving the renovation of the basement facility across the street. In the *CCL In-House Memo* for May 9, 1978, I described our respective responsibilities. JFK—Getting things started. Jim Glover—Teacher Training. Pete Walsh—Keeping things going.

A very important part of our early staff was our secretarial staff. Our first part-time secretary was Barbara Wasserman who endured well the cold and the heat of our third floor office. After a bit, she and her husband, Jim, moved to Hidden Valley, Indiana which was too far for her to commute. I can't recall the name of our next secretary, and she didn't stay very long. The employment of Betty Schwartz in March 1976 as a full-time secretary was a blessing, and in the summer of 1980 she was promoted to office manager. In 1978 we hired her long-time friend, Eileen Martin, another blessing who eventually became the mainstay of our order processing department. She started in her mid-forties and served for 29 years. Ginny Niehaus came with us on January 23, 1984, and just two months later we were fortunate to hire Ann Gundlach who had just graduated from the University of Cincinnati with a major in communications and a minor in journalism. She definitely added a professional touch to our newsletter and gradually brought it up to magazine status.

During the 2009 football season, the sport pundits would not infrequently comment about the ability of the Cincinnati Bengals to assemble a good football team with a number of second-chance players. Over the years, we assembled a similar crew. Our only employees who had been previously trained to do their jobs were the secretaries and communications specialist mentioned above; the rest of us—including me—learned on the job. I believed that a person who might not be a great success in one job could really shine in another position that made better use of his natural talents and desires. So I hired some people for our professional staff who didn't have outstanding résumés, and it worked. One gentleman had a problem with anger that I tolerated but would have gotten him fired elsewhere. Another person should have been a full-time writer and editor of a magazine where he could have used his literary talents to their full. He was sometimes a square peg trying to fit in a round hole with us, but for the most part he did fine work. A person we hired as a fund raiser proved quite inadequate for that task but his other talents made him invaluable.

An important part of the staff consisted of a small group called Field Representatives. This was a marketing effort that was successful in one respect but not successful enough in another way. We hired Bill Taylor in California to develop the program on the West Coast, and from his base in Sacramento he did this successfully from Alaska to Southern California. Yes, he arranged for me to teach a weekend seminar to recruit potential teachers in Fairbanks, and I learned that in that part of the world it is so cold in October that the snow is crunchy when you walk on it. I also learned that Juneau is so wet that just about everybody wears rubber boots most of the year. We hired Douglas Touchet in Lafayette, Louisiana, and he also was successful in building a great network of volunteer teaching couples in Louisiana and into parts of Mississippi and Texas. Unfortunately, despite the increase in the numbers of teachers, the numbers of couples taught overall dropped and we could no longer afford this outreach effort. Bill went back to school, did his doctoral dissertation on ecological breastfeeding, and went into college teaching. Doug went into parish work and gradually came back to being a full-time field representative.

Technology

At first we didn't have any visual aids except a chalkboard, so the St. Paul chapter developed the first teaching aid. It was a chart about 3 x 4 feet with an erasable heavy Plexiglas cover. I mean, it was heavy and bulky. There was no way that I could use it for teaching out of town. We wanted a uniform teaching program to be used by all our teachers, so we were forced to develop a slide presentation. Necessity is the mother of invention. We didn't know about commercially produced slides, and I don't know if we could have afforded them so we did our best. I printed the text of each slide with wide felt pens in several colors on sheets of white typewriter paper. The standard Kodak carousel held 140 slides, so that was our limit. I didn't want to use more than one carousel, especially when I was traveling. Once we had a set of masters, I set up a camera on a stand and shot a whole role of 36 frames for each slide text. When the slides were developed, we sorted those 140 boxes of slides into 36 sets of 140 slides each. Fortunately, we had some good part-time people who took care of these tedious jobs.

For good reasons, no one ever said my printing was artistic, and the Twin Cities chapter came to the rescue. One of their members, Les Heins, could print artistically so they soon furnished me with a new set of masters that we used for probably at least 10 years. Eventually we learned about commercial slide reproduction. They kept the masters on file; all we had to do was place an order and soon we had the finished slides, all numbered, collated and boxed. We were still using slides when our separation from CCL occurred in 2003.

It was about 1985 that CCL Central got its first small computer, a Kaypro portable unit in an aluminum case. If you touched that case after walking on a carpet, you got a spark of static electricity, and you lost whatever program was open on the screen—a nine-inch monochrome with green print against a black background. When doing a spell-check, you could see a little green dash going from letter to letter. Our next computer provided me with the opportunity to show the staff how to use it. After the initial demonstration, I was cleaning things up, but I went too far. When "Are You Sure?" appeared on the screen, I boldly clicked "Yes" and cleaned the whole disk. "Are you sure?" was good for a laugh for years.

Teachers and Students

The years 1971-1980 were exciting, and the numbers showed it. Sheila and I started as the first teaching couple (TC) in the fall of 1971 and taught about a dozen couples. Then things started to happen.

In 1972, four TCs taught 160 couples.

In 1973, six TCs in two states taught 591 couples.

In 1974, 13 TCs in six states taught 1053 couples.

In 1975, 26 TCs in 11 states taught 1802 couples.

In 1976, 76 TCs in 17 states taught 3005 couples.

In 1977, 137 TCs in 33 states taught 5092 couples.

In 1978, 191 TCs in 40 states were estimated to teach 7000 couples. The number was estimated because the 1978 annual report was released after the end of the fiscal year, but the numbers at that time were still accounted by the calendar year. The annual report also said that these TCs were active in 70 dioceses.

We thought this progression would continue, and we were hoping to teach 10,000 couples in 1980. The number for that year was actually 9,094 so we felt quite certain that the next year would see over 10,000 new couples taught, but we were wrong again. In fact, beginning in 1981 the numbers of new couples taught started a downward slope that averaged a 15% reduction each year until it finally bottomed out sometime in the mid- to late Nineties. By 2003 there were over 800 TCs, and that made it the largest NFP teaching organization in the country. The number of new couples taught, however, was still well below the number we taught in 1980.

Humanae Vitae plus 13

Why was this long-term decline happening? Were our teachers and our staff losing their enthusiasm or taking things for granted? By no means. We had more brochures. Our manual was improved and much more attractive than during the years of great expansion. Our teacher training was great, and our slide presentation was excellent. It had been working well for years. Our volunteers continued to promote and teach, but they were now suffering from low attendance and even no-show courses where not even one couple or person attended.

The reality was that 1981 was *Humanae Vitae* plus 13 years. As indicated previously, as early as 1969 freshmen in Catholic high schools were being taught to dissent without even knowing they were truly dissenting from the formal teaching of the Catholic Church. A student in fifth grade in the fall of 1968 could complete four more years of Catholic grade school, attend four years of Catholic high school and four years of college—Catholic or secular—and graduate in the spring of 1981 without ever having heard one word favorable to *Humanae Vitae*. It wouldn't have been so bad if the teaching of *Humanae Vitae* had simply been ignored, but what students were hearing in Catholic high schools and colleges was the doctrine of dissent.

When we started CCL in 1971 there was a large body of Catholic married couples who were looking for instruction in natural family planning. Some had very good-size families already. Some had been on the Pill for some years because Father So-and-So had told them it was okay to do so, but in their hearts they felt something was wrong, and they were greatly relieved to find out about effective NFP. But the market for NFP services changed tremendously during the Eighties, and those conditions continued all through the first decade of the 21st century. In the Seventies, it was not uncommon to have 25 or 30 couples in a course in Cincinnati; in the 21st century it is common to have only two or three couples. Where dioceses make a full NFP course a normal part of preparation for marriage, classes are full, but as of this writing, only six dioceses have that requirement.

Conferences and Conventions

Amidst the gloom of the conditions in the Church and the increasing difficulties we started to experience in the Eighties, there were still some memorable bright spots. I was privileged to participate in the first international conference of the International Federation of Family Life Promotion in Colombia in 1977, and that was educational, interesting, and fun. There's a bit more on this in the next chapter.

In 1978 I was privileged to participate in a conference sponsored by the Human Life Foundation in celebration of the tenth anniversary of *Humanae Vitae*. Held at the Roosevelt Hotel in New York, it left me with two enduring memories. In one session we were discussing various situations relevant to the practice of NFP, and I suggested that if we could get women to optimize their nutrition, that would help to reduce the problem of cycle irregularity. Doctor Tom Hilgers, who rarely agreed with me, then told the conference that he agreed.

Then, in the closing session, an experienced NFP teacher from another STM program engaged in some pretty serious criticism of me without mentioning me by name. He found erroneous this unnamed person's statement in his book on natural family planning that a married couple practicing abstinence during the fertile time could engage in non-genital activity that would be highly inappropriate for the unmarried. He continued in this vein until no one in the room had any doubts that he was talking about me. I was sitting in the back row, and Bishop Justin Driscoll of Fargo was standing right behind me. Larry Kane, the executive director of the Foundation, had organized the conference and had orchestrated it successfully to avoid open conflict, but now a challenge had been given. He knew he had to invite me to respond, and so he did. The tension was almost palpable as I walked to the front. I thanked my critic for his remarks. I said it was the first time I had ever been called a liberal, so I rather enjoyed it. On the matter of substance, I assured him that we had submitted the book for ecclesiastical review even though we did not print the *Imprimatur* and that my statements reflected the common opinion of orthodox moral theologians. That took about a minute, and I returned to my seat.

That same summer we had our first convention in Cincinnati. A sign made by Roger Carter said it all: "We are friends who have never met."

In 1979 we had a mini-convention in Columbus, Nebraska where my main memory is from the pizzeria where we had lunch. Someone at our table ordered a pizza with anchovies, but one bite ended her appetite for that fare. So we gave it to somebody else who said she loved anchovies. One more bite—and the same reaction. That same summer we taught a weekend course in Panama. A CCL member worked for the U. S. military in the Canal Zone and arranged for the chaplain to bring us down. Our four girls were old enough to have a live-in nanny for a few days (the youngest would be seven in the fall), and that experience helped them to develop a greater appreciation for their mother. Sheila was pregnant with Christopher, and again, it was a great experience for us.

Our third convention was at St. Thomas College in St. Paul, Minnesota from which my main memory is about a small child who was thought to be lost. What frantic searching we all did. If memory serves, the boy was finally found sleeping in the family van.

In 1981, we took our family on a three-week combination business and vacation trip. We visited CCL chapters from Cincinnati to Phoenix and then visited family in Los Angeles. Starting home, we spent a few days at Jackson Hole from which my best memory is the whitewater rafting on the Snake River. Then we had more chapter visits on the way home. Almost all of those visits consisted of great potluck suppers, and both the company and the food were fantastic.

Summary

The first ten years of my career in the promotion and teaching of natural family planning were marked by considerable success in terms of growth and also in terms of program development. By 1980 we had a standardized teacher-training program, a uniform system of teaching, and highly adequate materials. The rapid growth led us to think that soon we would be teaching enough couples in enough dioceses to start making a difference. The next twenty years proved the inaccuracy of such thinking.

9. Crossing Paths in the NFP Movement

The organization we founded was certainly not the only recently established NFP organization, and an interesting part of the Seventies was crossing paths with the other players in the fledgling movement. Sometimes we crossed swords as well as paths.

Early NFP Programs

The organized North American NFP movement actually began in France after World War II. An organization called Equipes Notre Dame (Teams of Our Lady) started the conversation between men and women about sexuality. According to Father Randall Blackall, former Family Life Director of the Diocese of Hartford, Connecticut, many WWII veterans welcomed a change from all the intense "guy talk" that they had lived with, and soon couples started to trust each other's experience with the fertility cycle. When some of the Equipes migrated to Quebec, they brought with them a temperature-based form of systematic NFP, and a number of French-speaking physicians rallied to help them.

In 1955 Gilles and Rita Breault founded **SERENA** (Service de Regulation de Naissance) in Quebec, teaching the Sympto-Thermal Method (STM) and pioneering the concept of ordinary couples teaching other couples. **Natural Family Planning of Connecticut** became the first American NFP organization in 1963, and in 1964 Dr. Claude Lanctot and his wife Anne brought the couple-to-couple mode of teaching from Canada to Connecticut. In 1965, the same year as the infamous *Griswold vs. Connecticut* decision, NFPA began publishing its newsletter, *Coverline*. In early 1966, Joe and Delores Smith, the Executive Chaircouple, were already writing in *Coverline* about the value of a federation of NFP organizations "which follow a broad program of couple to couple counseling." The federation was a good idea that still has not been realized. I was privileged to know John and Nancy Ball during the early to mid-Seventies. Sheila and I did not become part of NFPA when we started to teach NFP in 1971 because, among other reasons, of our interest in teaching ecological breastfeeding as a normal part of NFP. When we needed some charts for teacher training, the Balls graciously gave us a set they used in their own teacher training. The Diocese of Metuchen, New Jersey sponsored another early NFP program titled **Fertility Love Insight and Control** (FLIC).

In 1964 Archbishop Karl Alter of Cincinnati decided that married couples needed some real help with NFP, so he started a hospital-based clinic, and he personally attended each of the training sessions for the doctors and others who would staff it when it opened at **Good Samaritan Hospital** in 1965. Also in 1964 the First International Symposium on Rhythm was held in Washington, D.C. It was a joint effort by the Family Life Bureau of the national Catholic Welfare Conference and the National Federation of Catholic Physicians Guilds (NFCPG). Out of this came a Commission on Rhythm which by 1967 evolved into **National Commission on Human Life, Reproduction and Rhythm.** The NFCPG has since become the Catholic Medical Association.

Doctor Herbert Ratner (1907–1997) was heavily involved with the National Commission which took over the publishing of *Child & Family* under the editorship of Dr. Ratner. He was a key figure in pro-family and pro-life activities for at least 25 years. A frequent speaker at the CCL biannual conferences, his talk on generosity in having children inevitably helped at least a few attendees to give their children another sibling.

In addition, there were a number of Catholic doctors who taught NFP in their respective areas. Our mentor, Dr. Konald A. Prem, gave a one-night STM slide lecture at parish after parish in the Twin Cities. Dr. Edward F. Keefe taught the STM to his patients in Manhattan. He also developed the easy-to-read Ovulindex thermometer that more accurately measured a smaller range of temperatures—only from 96.0 to 100.0 degrees F.—and was the first to research and publish, in 1962, the physical changes in the cervix during the fertile time. Dr. John Cavanaugh had his own STM program in Kalamazoo, and there were others—Drs. John F. Hildebrand in Toledo and John Brennan in Milwaukee, to name two whom I knew personally.

Some doctors, unfortunately, also offered contraception in addition to NFP. In the late Seventies I was on a retreat with some folks from another NFP group including a doctor who was influential in the movement but who also prescribed the Pill. They knew this was a bone of contention, so his wife told my friends that if he didn't give the Pill, he would suffer a loss of income, and they had a son in medical school. This did not gain any sympathy from me. As I saw it, his income might drop to only three or four times as much as mine, and we were raising four children at the time.

As we proceeded through the Seventies, it was apparent to me that the NFP movement needed an organization that would represent all the different approaches and organizations that were competing with each other but which also had many common interests, just as a local association of competing car dealers represents their common interests to legislative and other bodies. In 1977, I talked with Father Paul Marx, OSB who was running the well attended NFP symposia at St. John's University in Collegeville each June. I thought he was the only figure in the NFP movement who would be acceptable to all the other players. When he was lecturing in Louisville, I drove down to persuade him of the need for a national federation and of its need for him to be its president. He was not persuaded, and there is still no such organization.

Lawrence J. Kane

Very soon after the promulgation of *Humanae Vitae* in the summer of 1968, the American bishops founded The Human Life Foundation to support the teaching of the encyclical by stimulating research, publications and the development of NFP services. I am not aware of any other national hierarchy that did this. The bishops gave it initial funding of $800,000, and it was money well invested. In reviewing my files, I was surprised to find considerable correspondence in 1972 with Larry Kane, the Foundation's executive director. Before my employment was solidified at the College of Mount St. Joseph, we were even discussing a possible position for me at the Foundation. In 1974, I had some differences with its chairman, Mr. Ed Hanify who was the chairman of AT&T. He was also the lawyer who got Ted Kennedy off the hook for his dereliction of duty at Chappaquiddick but then broke with Kennedy as a matter of principle when the latter opted for abortion. I have forgotten the subject of our disagreement, and Mr. Hanify had limited time so eventually he discontinued the correspondence. We were all scrapping for our existence, but I'm sure I could have and should have done things more diplomatically.

The event for which I most appreciate the Human Life Foundation was a comparative effectiveness study. First, Larry Kane persuaded the Ford Foundation, the Rockefeller Foundation and the World Health Organization to endorse the concept of a randomized prospective comparative study of the Ovulation Method (OM) and the Sympto-Thermal Method (STM). Then Dr. Philip Corfman of the National Institutes of Health funded it. Doctors John and Evelyn Billings had tremendous success in promoting their mucus-only Ovulation Method in the States, and in the developing NFP movement there were only a few of us who continued to stand up for a cross-checking system. The study was headed up by Dr. Maclyn Wade and was conducted at the Cedars of Lebanon Hospital in Los Angeles and ran from 1976 to 1978, and it was hoped it would settle an ongoing argument.

The results were interesting. The randomization assured that the number of couples in the study would be approximately the same. The study was designed only to compare total overall unintended pregnancy rates that include both perfect-use and imperfect-use pregnancies. The statistics were reported for couples when they were still in their training and for couples who had completed their training and were formally in the study. The Pearl rate refers to a formula that yields a number of pregnancies per 100-woman years. A Pearl rate of 2 would thus translate into an effectiveness rate of 98%. Because the results generated so much controversy by certain OM advocates I quote instead of summarize.

Measured from the beginning of training, the 12-month Pearl pregnancy rate for OM was 34.9 pregnancies per 100 woman-years and for STM 16.6 pregnancies per 100 woman-years.
Measured from the beginning of entry into the formal study phase, the Pearl pregnancy rates were 39.7 for OM and 13.7 for STM (p. 374).

In the next paragraph dealing with "Pregnancy review," some attention was given to "method" or perfect-use pregnancies.

During the study phase, 62 pregnancies occurred (42 OM and 20 STM). There were 36 user failures and six method failures in the OM group during the study phase. There were no method failures in the STM group.

To put that in terms of avoiding-pregnancy effectiveness rates, during the formal study, the total effectiveness rate was 60.3% in the OM group and 86.3% in the STM group. They did not publish a "method" or perfect-use rate, but "no failures in the STM group" easily translates into a 100% method or perfect-use rate. The six pregnancies in the OM group translate into a Pearl rate of 5.67 per 100 woman-years or a 94.3% perfect-use rate.

The researchers found statistically significant evidence in favor of the STM so the purpose of the study had been achieved. Dr. Gabriel Bialy monitored the study for the government and made the decision to end it sooner than had been planned; he considered it unethical to randomly assign additional couples into one system that he now knew was significantly less effective than the other.

The publication of the study in 1981 (*American Journal of Obstetrics and Gynecology* 141:368-376) was heavily criticized by advocates of the Ovulation Method. Certainly no study is perfect, but the critics seemed to forget that any fault applied to both sides of the study. Furthermore, documents in the NFP archives at Ave Maria University show that Monsignor Robert E. Deegan, who was the director of Health and Hospitals in the Archdiocese of Los Angeles and responsible for Catholic NFP services, selected the principal investigator and the hospital for the study. He also required that the archdiocese would be responsible for training the OM teachers and had the Doctors Billings come to California for meetings with the teachers.

As an example of how exposure to the truth sometimes really does help, consider this. Dr. Philip Corfman was a government representative at the 1964 meeting of the Catholic Physicians' Guilds, cosponsored by the Catholic Bishops, which was the first American international meeting on "rhythm." At this meeting he learned about the work of SERENA in Canada and a successful NFP study in the island nation of Mauritius off the east coast of Africa. Some 11 or 12 years later, he was providing funds for a still unmatched comparative study of two different systems of doing NFP.

The difficulty of running a comparative study is illustrated by the fact that the next such study was not published for another 30 years. In the latter case, NFP researcher Richard Fehring, a professor of nursing at Marquette University in Milwaukee, compared what he called the Cervical Mucus Monitoring (CVM) with an Electronic Hormonal Fertility Monitor (EHFM). The 12-month correct-use rates for unintended pregnancies were similar—2% for the EHFM and 3% for the CVM. The total unintended pregnancy rates were quite different—12% for the EHFM and 23% for the CVM. (See DDP *Current Medical Research*, Winter/Spring 2009, 20:1&2.)

One would think that after the Los Angeles study, diocesan family life directors and NFP directors would have mandated the teaching of the full STM in their diocesan programs, but such was not the case. One might think that the recently published findings of Professor Fehring might result in a diocesan demand for the teaching of a cross-check on the mucus system, but that is unlikely. The mucus-only advocates are well entrenched. Many couples do well with a mucus-only system, but the comparative studies support our conviction that couples deserve to be, and should be, instructed on all the signs so that they are intellectually free to make their own choices.

Two other accomplishments of Larry Kane and the Human Life Foundation stand out in my memory. In 1972 it held a conference of experts at the Airlie House in Warrenton, Virginia, and its proceedings were a prime reference during the Seventies. Kane also persuaded his Board of Directors to make a grant to Dr. Rudolph Vollman so he could finish his book, *The Menstrual Cycle*, which was then published in 1977 by Saunders, a medical publishing house. We found Dr. Vollman's work dealing with menopause very helpful.

For reasons that have never been clear, the bishops stopped their funding of the Foundation in 1983. It was said at the time that it had accomplished its goal of stimulating research and key publications, and that was certainly true even if incomplete. Kane immediately found other work, but fortunately he eventually came back to the NFP movement, this time as an archivist. As various members of the first wave of NFP leaders were moving out of the movement or retiring, they shipped their materials to Kane. Since he had remained above the fray regarding methodology, he was trusted and well liked by all the leaders in the movement who thus had no fears about sending him their materials. When Sheila and I visited him and his wife Isabelle in March 2007, we were amazed at his collection. In his basement he had an area at least the size of a single car garage filled with filing cabinets. He founded NFP Archives Inc, a non-profit organization to shepherd the care of these materials, and then negotiated for their transfer to Ave Maria University in Naples, Florida in 2009 where they are, as of this writing, being archived and will soon be available to researchers. There will almost certainly be several doctoral dissertations on the NFP movement, and authors will find these archives invaluable for their studies.

Our Mentor, Konald A. Prem, M.D.

Our first contact with Dr. Konald A. Prem was his 1968 article on NFP in *Child and Family,* a journal edited by Dr. Herbert Ratner. We read it in Canada, and it proved helpful when breastfeeding amenorrhea ended and fertility returned. When Sheila was invited to be with him and Dr. Paul Busam on the "Breastfeeding and Infertility" panel at the 1971 La Leche League (LLL) conference in Chicago, we were thrilled. As mentioned previously, when Sheila met with him at his office in Minneapolis to discuss who would cover what topics, we proposed the couple-to-couple idea of teaching NFP and he gave us his enthusiastic support. When we started teaching that fall, he came to each of our four meetings, and he continued to do that with our successors when we left for Cincinnati in the early summer of 1972.

Konald Prem was born in November 1920 and attended St. John's University in Collegeville where he and his classmate, Paul Marx, were football teammates. Entering college in 1938, he left to serve in the National Guard from 1941 to 1946, at which time he returned and finished his pre-med work at St. John's. He then entered medical school at the University of Minnesota, did his residency at Minneapolis General Hospital, and then completed his advanced education in obstetrics and gynecology at the University of Minnesota. After graduation, he stayed on as a staff member, rising to the rank of a full professor of obstetrics and gynecology and serving as Department Chairman from 1975 to 1984. I am not aware of any other advocate of NFP who has held such a high position in the field of medicine.

In medical school he received no training about birth control of any kind, natural or unnatural, but he did learn about the value of the temperature sign for diagnosing female infertility. In 1954 his reading of the medical literature and his own experience convinced him of the value of the natural methods of conception regulation, and he began to teach a temperature-based form of NFP. At first he taught individual patients, counseling seven or eight couples by phone in the evening after having put in a full day at the medical school. Then he started giving talks at one parish after another.

He was convinced that Carl G. Hartman's 1962 book, *Science and the Safe Period,* provided documented proof of the value of natural family planning, and in 1968 he published "Temperature Method in the Practice of Rhythm" in *Child and Family* (Fall 1968 7:311-327) detailing his own system. This is the article mentioned at the start of this section and one of the two sources from which we learned the STM form of NFP. Despite its title, this article taught both the temperature and the mucus signs. By the time he was advising us in 1971, he had also accepted the value of the cervix sign discovered by Dr. Edward F. Keefe. Thus in our first mimeographed edition of *The Art of Natural Family Planning* published in 1972, we were able to present the full sympto-thermal method of natural family planning based on changes in temperature, mucus, and cervix.

Breastfeeding as a form of natural family planning was another special interest of Dr. Prem. At the 1971 La Leche League conference mentioned above, he presented the results of a study he had conducted with LLL mothers. This paper was never formally published but is now available at the NFPI website, www.nfpandmore.org. One of his findings was that only 5% of the breastfeeding mothers in his study conceived before their first postpartum menstruation.

In 1974 Dr. Prem became the first Board-certified gynecologic oncologist in Minnesota, and he then went on to found a program in that specialty at the medical school. At the close of his career there, he regarded that as his greatest professional achievement.

Father Paul Marx, OSB (1920 – 2010)

I first met Father Paul Marx either in late 1971 or early 1972 when we were living in Shoreview MN. After I attended an evening lecture he gave, I was privileged to drive him someplace after the meeting. We had heard of him a year or two previously when Father Jan Mucharski visited us in Salina on his way to Fr. Marx's NFP symposium in Collegeville, and we were able to attend his 1972 conference the week of June 4 through 9.

Father Marx, born May 8, 1920, was a football teammate of our mentor, Dr. Konald Prem, at St. John's University in Collegeville during the late Thirties, was ordained a Benedictine priest in 1947, and then earned his doctorate in Family Sociology. In the Fifties and Sixties, as a professor at St. John's, he promoted natural family planning in his sociology courses. He liked to tell us newcomers to the pro-chastity movement that he used to be called Father Temperature. He clearly saw the connection between contraception and abortion, and he was both fearless and tireless in preaching and teaching the need to have good NFP teaching so as to stop contraception and then stop abortion. Of course, he was absolutely right but almost 40 years ahead of the times. He had a lonely life at St. John's in the post-*Humanae Vitae* years because dissent had taken its toll among his fellow monks and professors.

Father Marx founded the Human Life Center at St. John's in 1972, and his NFP conferences each June from 1972 through 1978 were the highlight of those years for many of us in the NFP movement. He brought in all the big names in the NFP movement. Australia, Canada, Austria, Switzerland, Latin America were all represented. Most of us were Catholics, but if a Protestant or secular person wrote a book in favor of NFP, Father Marx let us hear them speak. The attendees constituted the leadership of the NFP movement which was more of a ghetto of orthodoxy than a real movement at the time.

Unfortunately, in his enthusiasm to promote NFP and to welcome non-Catholics, Fr. Marx at least once engaged in some wishful thinking. An author of an "NFP" book suggested oral-genital copulation as a way to avoid abstinence during the fertile time. I told Fr. Marx that I didn't think he should be selling that book. In due time the author changed the book, and Fr. Marx said the author had come to agree with Catholic teaching on marital chastity, but I was still skeptical. The author spoke at Fr. Marx's 1978 conference and described the relief work her group had done after the 1976 earthquake in Guatemala. As was customary, there was a microphone in an aisle for after-lecture questions, so I got in line. The lady just ahead of me used her mike time to lavish praise on the speaker for her relief work, emotionally calling her "America's Mother Teresa." I asked the author if the change in her text represented a change in her convictions. She replied that it did not but that she had changed it to make it more acceptable to Catholics. She added that she still couldn't figure out why Catholics were hung up on completed oral sex. My skepticism had proved right so I left the auditorium, very disappointed that Father Marx had not simply asked the author about her convictions instead of making assumptions and having her as a main speaker at his conference.

There may have been a conference in 1979, but by 1980 things were not going well for Father Paul. As he describes events in his 1997 autobiography, *Faithful for Life* (HLI), he was invited to attend the International Synod on the Family in Rome that year, but while he was in Rome "a decision was made by abbey/university authorities to force me to take a year's sabbatical, ostensibly to rest" (112). I had read a news story about him driving off the road one night, and I think there was genuine concern on the part of those of his advisors who were truly pro-*Humanae Vitae* that he was working too hard. As he makes clear, there may have been other concerns by anti-*Humanae Vitae* forces at the Abbey and University. I heartily recommend his autobiography. You will get to know Father Marx as a person and leader, and you will gain an unequaled insight into the abortion industry.

As a result of these events at St. John's, he founded Human Life International in 1980 to continue the work he had begun at the Human Life Center, and in 1981 he moved to Washington, D.C. to develop it fully and to fight abortion all around the world. For this work he was twice branded as "Public Enemy Number 1" by Planned Parenthood. For that same work Pope John Paul II called him an "Apostle for life," and that may be the only time a Pope has called someone an Apostle since the death of the last of the Twelve. I visited him three times in the last half dozen years of his life, and I regard it a privilege to have walked on the same path with him. He went to his eternal reward on March 20, 2010.

Joseph Cardinal Bernardin (1928 – 1996)

When we arrived in Cincinnati in June of 1972, the front entrances to some Catholic churches were draped in black mourning cloths for the beloved Archbishop Karl Alter, and in November, Bishop Joseph L. Bernardin was appointed as Archbishop of Cincinnati where he served until he was appointed as the Archbishop of Chicago in 1982. In the latter part of 1973, we began making the case for the archdiocese to fund our new organization, enabling us to have some full-time staff. We made the same approach to the Archdiocese of St. Paul-Minneapolis where we had started the League. The outcome was joint funding for two years to develop a truly national organization, and for that I remain ever grateful. Since he was considered a liberal by many who follow such things, I think some were surprised. I was not at all bashful about giving him due credit for our existence, and he may have enjoyed whatever "conservative" good press I gave him.

Support for our efforts in Cincinnati was different from his support for our national effort. When we started to teach NFP in 1972, we had full classes, sometimes up to 35 couples. At a Sunday-afternoon course about 100 miles north, we had almost 100 couples. Those were the good old days, but then the moral theology at the seminary declined in value. As indicated previously, when Archbishop Bernardin criticized at length the new Paulist Press book, *Human Sexuality: New Directions in American Catholic Thought* in 1977, I wondered why he was so upset since it seemed to me that its bad theology was about par for the course at his own seminary.

A real test case arose in 1978. A young teacher, Thomas Ruwe, at Our Lady of the Angels Catholic high school for girls in Cincinnati was told by some of his students that one of the teachers, a religious sister, was telling them that masturbation was okay, and she was backed by the principal, a member of the same religious congregation. Mr. Ruwe, still believing full Catholic teaching on morality despite having recently graduated from a nominally Catholic university in Cincinnati, was concerned. He talked with priests who guided him through the appropriate channels to challenge erroneous teaching in a Catholic school, and eventually his complaint reached Archbishop Bernardin who responded with a 14-page document about teaching sexuality. He also told the principal that she could not fire Mr. Ruwe because of this theological dispute. In the spring, the principal sent him a notice of non-renewal despite the directions received from the archbishop.

Mr. Ruwe was appalled by this, and so were some of us who read about it in the daily paper. With the support of his attorney, he filed for an archdiocesan due process hearing, and at length had his hearing. The principal responded in writing to his complaint by alleging he was let go because of pedagogical shortcomings such as addressing the students by their first names and putting a foot on a chair as he spoke. With such obviously false excuses, the principal didn't bother to appear at the hearing, so in any normal judicial setting Mr. Ruwe would have won his case by reason of default.

In this case, however, the archdiocesan authorities sided with the principal. They agreed with Mr. Ruwe that he had not been disemployed because of the alleged classroom shortcomings. They further agreed that he had been dismissed because of the theological dispute. Then they offered the flimsy excuse that he wasn't really *fired* because all teachers have only one-year contracts, but they knew that no one would believe that rationale so they played their real trump card. They alleged that even if the employee had employment rights, the employer-principal had a prior right to form around herself a group of people with whom she felt comfortable. In short, they affirmed as a working policy of the Archdiocese of Cincinnati that the employer has the right of universal discrimination. If he or she feels uncomfortable with someone who is too short or too tall, too skinny or too fat, black or brown or white, or an orthodox Catholic, the archdiocesan employer is entitled to fire such a person. To add irony to insult, this happened at the same time that Archbishop Bernardin was leading the U.S. bishops' effort to boycott an east coast clothing manufacturer that was claiming a similar but less inclusive right of discrimination for its managers.

Considering all that Catholics have heard about social justice, an observant person would think that there would have been a huge cry of protest and support from Mr. Ruwe's fellow Catholic-school teachers all throughout the city if not all throughout the archdiocese, but there wasn't a peep. One might have even dreamed that the unionized public school teachers would have raised a cry of protest, but there wasn't a word. As in Salina, I took up his cause, but this time only via correspondence. I wrote to Archbishop Bernardin imploring him to overrule the unjust decision and penalty enacted against a teacher whose only grave fault was his Catholic orthodoxy. I reminded him of his own order that the principal had disobeyed. The archbishop would do nothing. One can only guess at the reasons for such pusillanimous shrinking from due discipline, so I will hazard mine. I think it was because he did not want to upset the apple cart in his relations with the Sisters and their religious order. If so, his strategy failed. Neither the principal nor the teacher returned the next fall. In fact, the school closed six years later.

This was not the first time I had reason to question his enforcement of proper discipline. In the mid-Seventies, a neighbor told Sheila that she had a tubal ligation at Good Samaritan Hospital. Since this was contrary to the Catholic Hospital Directives that were supposed to govern such matters, we talked to Catholic medical persons who assured us that anyone involved with sterilization at a Catholic hospital would lose his or her job. We reported the sterilization at this Catholic hospital to its chaplain. He denied that it could have happened and said we had no way to prove it. Our friend promptly gave us a copy of the medical papers that listed the doctor's name and the specific form of tubal ligation that he had performed; she said she would sue if she ever became pregnant. We took this to the archbishop who told us that he would take care of it. That was the last we ever heard of it. True, we have no proof that he did nothing, but there was something about the whole situation that didn't feel right. I should have diplomatically pursued it further, but there was something in the way he said he would take care of it that led me to think that any further action on my part would be counterproductive to our other pro-chastity efforts. I count that as a mistake on my part.

Because of his handling of the Ruwe situation, I lost respect for Archbishop Bernardin and essentially had no further contact with him in Cincinnati. Four years later, however, when he was Archbishop of Chicago, I asked him to review my manuscript for a little booklet titled *Birth Control and Christian Discipleship* that was intended for Protestants and Catholics who think like Protestants. He offered several helpful suggestions which were duly incorporated to improve the text.

Bishop James T. McHugh (1932 – 2000)

The national organization of American bishops, currently called the USCCB or United States Conference of Catholic Bishops, has its headquarters in Washington, D.C., and in the Seventies the director of its Family Life Office was then-Monsignor James T. McHugh. We began corresponding in 1972, and, despite a few bumps in the road, over the years we developed a good working relationship. In 1978 he endorsed the CCL plan for providing nationwide services and mailed his endorsement to every American bishop heading up a diocese. It called for 6,000 teaching couples (TC) spread throughout the United States—at least one TC in every populated rural county and sufficiently more in urban areas. Msgr. McHugh gave a ringing endorsement of the program we had developed and the level of service we wanted to provide, but I am not aware that it did us any good. Bishops are independent, and it is quite possible that lots of them pay as much attention to letters from their Washington bureaucracies as some pastors and associates pay to envelopes from their diocesan headquarters. I recall one priest telling me he never opened any letter he received from the chancery office. He would store it in a desk drawer, and if he received a follow-up phone call, he would manage to stall a bit while he found and read it.

Monsignor McHugh had problems right in the US Bishops' headquarters. As we were having an after-hours drink in his office one day, he said, "John, I may be the only guy in this building who accepts *Humanae Vitae*." He understood well the problems that we and the other players in the NFP movement were having around the country, and he stayed in touch with what he called the major players. His favorite time to call me was noontime, usually just after I had taken a big bite out of my sandwich. We could discuss differences of opinions and approaches, and if I would more or less apologize for getting a bit strong in my pleadings, he would assure me that I was quite mild compared to some of the other players.

Probably because of his education in sociology and family life, Bishop McHugh shared our interest in breastfeeding, and in this he seemed to be unique, or at least very rare, among the bishops of the Eighties. In May 1995, when Pope John Paul II and the Royal Society of England co-hosted a conference on breastfeeding in Rome, Bishop McHugh was chosen to introduce the Pope and his message. It was at this conference that John Paul II endorsed the recommendations of the World Health Organization and UNICEF that mothers should breastfeed their babies for at least two years.

I think Bishop McHugh understood what ecological breastfeeding is all about and appreciated the way we had integrated it into our NFP program. He probably also realized that ecological breastfeeding or something very close to it was the only way a mother could maintain a milk supply for two years or more. I wish that when he returned from Rome he had insisted that ecological breastfeeding needed to be included in every NFP program as an important form of natural family planning.

In 1985 we had some significant differences that are described in the next chapter. In 1989 he was consecrated as Bishop of Newark, New Jersey, and in 1998 he was appointed as coadjutor bishop of the Diocese of Rockville Centre, New York, becoming the Ordinary in January, 2000. To our great loss he contracted cancer about that time and died on December 10, 2000, less than a month shy of age 69. The great irony of his early death is that he was probably the most "fit" bishop in the country, taking long Sunday afternoon bicycle rides in the countryside when he was in Camden. Even with his new responsibilities as bishop, we kept open communications, and in 1998 he celebrated Mass at the CCL office for a group of priests who were attending a seminar. (He was in town for the national convention of the Knights of Columbus.) After Mass, he asked me if I knew why he had celebrated Mass for us. I said I thought it was just to be a nice guy and perhaps to see our office. No, he said. "I wanted these priests to see that you have friends in high places." The Knights gave him a commemorative medal, and some years after his death, Theresa Notare, his right hand staffer at the Diocesan Development Program, gave that medal to me. On December 13, 2008, Franciscan University of Steubenville honored Sheila and me with honorary doctorates in ethics at the winter graduation. At dinner Theresa told Sheila and me a story about Bishop McHugh. She said he had a high regard for all the players in the NFP movement, but he said I was a bit different. "Kippley is a man of the Church." I couldn't ask for anything more.

Monsignor John B. Seli

The former director of the Family Life Center in Pittsburgh, Msgr. John B. Seli, went to Washington, D.C. in 1974 to found the Natural Family

Planning Federation. It was a good idea, and Dr. Claude Lanctot told me that he asked Msgr. Seli to work with me in getting it established. I was not contacted, however, until the Federation had already been established and he had on his Board of Directors three dedicated providers of the Ovulation Method—Kay Ek and Drs. Hanna Klaus and John Brennan—but no providers of the Sympto-Thermal Method or teachers of Ecological Breastfeeding. At the meeting I attended in 1974, the Federation had already developed an attractive logo that showed symbols of people sitting at a round table, symbolic of open discussion and equality. I was not informed before the meeting about voting procedures, so I was disappointed to learn that while I was allowed to speak, only the Board members could vote. That didn't seem fair to me if this was to be a true federation of NFP providers. Further, the Federation soon began to develop its own program in Texas. That was contrary to the action of any federation I had imagined. A federation of car dealers does not open its own dealership. If it learns of a town that wants a dealership, it would notify its members and let them compete fairly for the business.

The Federation was founded on the financial expectation that it would soon be receiving funds via federal Title X (Title Ten) birth control programming. With such anticipation, it had rented office space on K Street, famous for its high priced real estate and generally inhabited by lobbyists. Then it hired as its executive director a former worker for Planned Parenthood. While I am all for employing converts, I thought it was going too far to employ as the first well-paid person in the NFP movement someone who had previously earned his living by promoting the contraceptive way of life. This was now one year after the infamous Court decision, *Roe vs. Wade,* that dissolved all state laws against abortion. I think that the former PP gentleman was appalled by PP's abortion work and thus had resigned.

Doctor Claude Lanctot's vision was for a representative American NFP federation that would then take part in an international federation. The idea was good, but the Federation started by Msgr. Seli had three strikes against it. Its Board did not represent the diversity in the American NFP movement; it acted as a competitor instead of a federation; and it was founded on unrealistic financial expectations. The Title X money was not available to NFP organizations, and the Federation folded.

Claude Lanctot, M.D.

Doctor Claude Lanctot was the organizational man of the NFP movement. My first contact with him may have been at Father Marx's NFP conferences in 1972 or 1973, and we were certainly in contact in 1974. As previously indicated, he had come from Quebec to Connecticut in 1964 for a medical residency, and ten years later he was trying to get NFP organizations around the States and around the world to be in meaningful contact with each other.

For this purpose he organized the International Federation for Family Life Promotion (IFFLP). I don't know where he found the money, but in 1977 the IFFLP held its first international meeting in Cali, Colombia. The organization paid my expenses, and it was a real privilege to associate with NFP leaders from around the world. I remember in particular having my picture taken with Drs. John and Evelyn Billings. Some of the talks could be somewhat tedious, so one afternoon I stole away a bit early to do some shopping for Sheila and the girls and also for the women in the office. The second international meeting was scheduled for 1979 in Hong Kong. Once again, the IFFLP was willing to pick up my expenses, but by this time I realized that such meetings are no fun unless you are prepared to spend a bunch of your own money on special meals and souvenirs. Since I didn't have any spare funds, I asked Dr. Prem to represent CCL, and he was happy to do so. Although he never complained, I imagine he was less than happy when he lost his wallet to a pickpocket.

To be self-sustaining, a federation has to be supported by its member organizations or be a completely volunteer operation. The Federation's members, unfortunately, ran on survival budgets so they didn't have funds for the Federation. For some years Claude managed to put together sufficient support from outside sources, but eventually the IFFLP ran out of funds and folded.

What I remember about Claude is that he unselfishly tried to help NFP organizations accomplish their mission better by knowing what others were doing, and he almost always had a big smile. He was personally in favor of what he had helped to introduce in Connecticut, the cross-checking method taught by couples to other couples, but he always spoke diplomatically about the mucus-only systems. While he appreciated the efforts of mucus-only promoters in less developed countries, he thought that those peoples would eventually want the cross-checking system.

Thomas W. Hilgers, M.D.

In 1985 Dr. Thomas W. Hilgers started his own program, the Pope Paul VI Institute, to teach a variant of the Ovulation Method that he called the Creighton Model (CrM). In his version, women would use a different system for observing and recording the external mucus signs. Along with his method of observation and recording, he also invented a new way to evaluate unintended (surprise) pregnancies. If an unintended pregnancy occurred as a result of the marriage act on a day the woman had marked as a mucus day or on a day when she had not made the observations according to his rules, or had in any way not followed his rules, he did not include it among the unintended pregnancies. Instead, he labeled it as occurring from "pregnancy achieving behavior."

This contrasts with the other NFP systems which count not-following-the-rules pregnancies as unintended. There is a certain logic in the Hilgers' system, but the rest of us in the NFP movement think that if we are to be credible to the world outside the NFP movement, we need to evaluate pregnancies according to the same norms that are applied to the unnatural methods of birth control. The result is that the Hilgers' effectiveness statistics appear to be better than they would be if they were evaluated by the same standards used by the rest of the NFP movement. Fortunately, a study by Joanne Doud that reported a very high user-effectiveness (96.2%) according to the Hilgers system also included evaluations by the couples themselves (*International Review of Natural Family Planning*, Spring, 1985). Counting the pregnancies that the couples themselves regarded as unplanned, the user-effectiveness rate dropped to 67%. The IRNFP published my short analysis on this matter in its Winter 1985 issue.

In the late Nineties, Dr. Hilgers published a paper that at first glance had the appearance of having appeared in a medical journal, but upon closer examination no journal was cited. It purported to be a study of three different NFP methods—the CrM, the Billings Ovulation Method, and the CCL version of the STM. By applying his own criteria to his ideas about the other programs, his own program came out as much better. The quality of the paper was such that advocates of the Billings Ovulation Method boycotted the next year's annual meeting of mucus-only teachers in protest. I corresponded with Dr. Hilgers for several rounds, pointing out his misunderstandings of our program, some of which could have been avoided by asking us or by the simple expedient of reading our published materials available at any bookstore.

In the early part of the first decade of the 21st century, Dr. Hilgers changed the name of his program to the Creighton Model FertilityCare™ System which indicates the area in which he offers a valuable service. While all too many ob-gyn doctors have switched to immoral high-tech methods such as *in vitro* fertilization, Tom retained tried and true methods and made further advances that are morally acceptable. In doing so he has rendered a great service to couples suffering from female infertility. With regard to his system for couples of normal fertility, however, I regard his systematic NFP program as both expensive and deficient. It does not teach how to cross-check the mucus sign with the temperature sign, or how to make and evaluate observations of the cervix, and it does not teach ecological breastfeeding. It is a case of paying more and getting much less.

Theresa Notare, PhD

One of the most influential people in the NFP movement was Bishop James T. McHugh's right hand staffer for years. Theresa Notare met then-Msgr. McHugh in June of 1984 when she was 27 and a religious studies teacher in a Catholic high school. As a member of the Holy See's Permanent Observer Mission to the United Nations, Msgr. McHugh was preparing for the U.N. Mexico City Population Conference, and he needed someone to assist him in his New Jersey office. Father Manuel Cruz, a friend of Notare, lived with McHugh and told him he had a friend who needed a summer job.

That was Theresa Notare's introduction to the Diocesan Development Program (DDP) for NFP, an effort founded by Terence Cardinal Cooke in 1981 due to his participation in the 1980 Synod on the Family that took place in Rome. After the Synod, Cardinal Cooke contacted Msgr. McHugh to work with him to design a pastoral plan for diocesan NFP ministry. McHugh consulted with a number of people and worked especially with Mary Catherine Martin to create the Diocesan Development Plan for Natural Family Planning (DDP/NFP).

When Theresa met Msgr. McHugh, she was on her way to a Master of Arts program at the Graduate Theological Union in Berkeley, California. From Berkeley, Theresa went to Rome for further study on the Catholic Church's involvement in the ecumenical movement at the University of St. Thomas Aquinas (The Angelicum). Once her course work was complete, Bishop McHugh (now auxiliary bishop for Newark), asked her to work full time for the DDP while she completed her MA thesis.

Theresa had never heard of Natural Family Planning until she met the future Bishop McHugh. She came from a pious Catholic family and knew that her parents used the Rhythm Method, but most of the recent information about NFP was new to her when she began to study it. In terms of Catholic teaching, she knew what the Church believed and taught but not "why." At first she was struck by the beauty of the teachings and mystified as to why at age 27 she had never heard of them. More importantly, the question of "Can these teachings be lived well in the lives of couples?" began to haunt her.

Theresa told me that "the lights went on" (a McHugh saying) for her after constant contact with NFP couples. She found that these couples were joyous and candid in an honest and non-offensive way about their married lives and how God was a part of it. That's when she realized that NFP is a pure gift for couples because it can help them grow in holiness together in the Lord.

In 1987 Notare began to work for the NFP office full time. From 1987-1990, Bishop McHugh began to increase her responsibilities from secretary to special assistant. In 1990 when Bishop McHugh was to be installed as bishop of the Diocese of Camden, New Jersey, he asked Theresa to move with the NFP office to Washington, DC. He promised that she could work on a doctoral program at the Catholic University of America part time while working for him full time, and she accepted the offer and earned her PhD in theology in 2008. As of this writing, Dr. Notare is the Assistant Director of the NFP Program of the U.S. Catholic Conference of Bishops. In that job she serves both the U. S. bishops and their diocesan NFP staffs and also seeks to support the wider NFP community in the States. Considering that in 2010 less than five percent of fertile-age Catholic married couples use NFP and that only a half dozen dioceses have seen fit to make NFP instruction a required part of marriage preparation, it is indeed a challenging position.

Ralph McInerny (1929-2010)

This congenial expert on Thomistic philosophy entered my life when we were both students at the St. Paul Seminary in Minnesota. He was a year ahead of me and was a good friend of my roommate with whom he shared a great interest in classical music. After we both left the seminary, he went on to earn his doctorate in philosophy in 1955. By day he taught philosophy at the University of Notre Dame, and by night he used his fantastic imagination to write fiction including the Father Dowling mysteries, some of which were made into the television series that ran from January 1989 through May 1991. At the end of the day, after he had completed his professional and family responsibilities he would go down the basement and write his whodunits. He said it was such a change from his day job that fatigue never affected him.

Our next meeting occurred in 1987. The occasion was a California conference that is memorable for two things. A priest who is neither a philosopher nor a moral theologian lectured about the papal Theology of the Body and the theology of St. Thomas, and he met heavy criticism from the philosophers in attendance. I did not understand the talk or the questions, so on our way back to our lodging, I asked Ralph what the fuss was all about, and he remarked simply that the speaker didn't know what he was talking about. What stands out most about that San Rafael conference, however, is the discussion that took place after a talk by one of the nation's leading Thomistic philosophers. As the discussion focused on some fine point in the writing of St. Thomas, Ralph rose from the audience and with his big smile said to the speaker who was a great friend of his, "On this point, my friend, you are uncharacteristically wrong." "Uncharacteristically wrong." What a beautiful way to offer a point of criticism. I have never forgotten his congenial ability to express his convictions this way, all in the service of the truth.

Ralph knew much about a lot of people, but he didn't gossip When I asked about a former classmate, he replied that the gentleman had been ordained, encountered some difficulties, was no longer serving in the active ministry, and had been directed to live with his mother. He had answered my question, and the very way he did it implied very charitably that the subject was not one for further discussion.

Sheila and I owe a special debt of gratitude to Ralph for the first honor we received. As Ralph and I talked at the San Rafael conference, I shared with him our firsthand experience in the battle to sustain the teaching of *Humanae Vitae* and to provide the practical help of natural family planning. Three years later the Wethersfield Institute invited us to New York to receive an Award for Outstanding Achievement on September 28, 1990. Ralph was on their Board, and we are sure he was responsible for the award.

We are also quite sure that he was significantly responsible for the second award given to us. In the mid-Nineties, the Fellowship of Catholic

Scholars developed the Patrick A. Cardinal O'Boyle Award to honor people for activities beyond the world of academia. It was also known as the "swinging in the wind" award. Cardinal O'Boyle was the Archbishop of Washington, D.C. who was faced with massive dissent among his priests in the summer of 1968 after the issuance of *Humanae Vitae*. He responded by suspending a group of the most vociferous, and then he waited for other bishops to take similar action. He was left very much alone, swinging in the wind so to speak, without support from his fellow bishops. Mother Angelica was the first recipient of this award in 1995, and on September 21, 1996, the Fellowship awarded it to Sheila and me "for their contribution to Catholic Family Life." Providentially, that was within weeks of the 25th anniversary of the first NFP course we taught in the St. Paul suburb of Shoreview.

Ralph McInerny was the Michael P. Grace Professor of Medieval Studies and professor of philosophy at Notre Dame and was the director of the Jacques Maritain Center from 1979 to 2006. He authored two dozen scholarly books and over eighty novels including the well-known Father Dowling series. This true Renaissance man died on January 29, 2010, and is missed by many. It was a privilege to know him.

Church Renovations

In my opinion, what has passed for church renovations has sometimes been a clear example of injustice to parishioners both past and present, and that sort of injustice brought me to crossing swords with some of the parish leadership at our home parish in the Westwood community of Cincinnati. The grade school principal at St. Catharine's parish (and that's not a misspelling) asked me to be a candidate for parish council, so I found myself once again in a situation of potential conflict. Our lovable and orthodox pastor died very suddenly from some sort of infection and, apparently, from the consequences of its treatment, and a new pastor was duly appointed. Though he was not a young man, this was his first pastorate; for the previous seven years, he had been involved in archdiocesan administration, chiefly as a very pleasant, affable, and smiling fund raiser. He arrived at St. Catharine's in 1981 and four years later began a church renovation project.

Built in 1923 of Indiana limestone and in the architectural style of 12th century Norman Gothic, the church was beautiful both inside and out. In 1985 it underwent an exterior renovation with no visible changes to the building itself, just cleaning, repair, and some pleasant landscaping. Our new pastor then decided that it needed an interior renovation, and this raised some issues on the parish council. Some members spoke well in opposition or at least they argued well in favor of a plan that would have to be approved by the council. Somehow, the pastor agreed. However, as the plans proceeded and the proposed changes were seen as radical, the conflict within the council grew. The pastor solved the problem by dismissing some of the council members, appointing new members, and then appointing a building commission.

The conflict that had been pretty much confined to the council now increased outside the confines of that body. I saw that some of the dismissed council members were really hurt, and that's what got me involved. I became the de facto leader of the loyal opposition, and a handful of us formed a team to educate the parish. I would write a reply to the gratuitous assertions we were receiving, and we would stand on the city sidewalk and hand the fliers both to the walkers and to car drivers as they passed over the sidewalk.

The pastor had some public meetings in the church itself, and speakers were allowed to voice their opinions. In one small meeting, not in church, some members of the opposition truly exploded and used language that said much more about their frustration than about the pastor or his project, and that was truly unfortunate. He was, after all, still our priest and pastor. He also began to give reasons for the proposed changes, and that was definitely helpful to the loyal opposition. For example, he wanted to extend the sanctuary area into the pews. Then the pews in the front part of the church would be placed on either side of the extended sanctuary at a 90 degree angle to the rest of the pews so that the pew sitters on either side of the sanctuary would be looking at each other. The reason given for this was that it would bring about greater love and unity between those who thus saw each other in that way at Sunday Mass. This was truly absurd, and my team distributed a flier to challenge this assumption. Since there was some experience in other churches with that arrangement, we asked for documented evidence that it had the desired effect. More importantly, most families could relate in a negative way to the idea. We knew from experience that there is nothing about sitting around the dinner table that automatically generates love, peace and harmony, and I knew of a Cincinnati rectory where the two priests did not eat dinner together because of underlying conflicts.

The loyal opposition also held a packed meeting at the Westwood Town Hall, and we allowed both sides to speak.

The net result was that the pastor announced that he would hold an election and abide by the results. If he was confident that the parish was with him, he was shocked by the results. The number of votes in favor of the pastor's proposed renovation roughly equaled the number of members on his revised parish council and building commission. It was a total rejection by the parish as a whole, thus showing that perhaps the council members and building commissioners were clearly out-of-touch with the rest of the parish. Or perhaps they accurately sensed the situation and persuaded the pastor to have the vote as a strategic and non-embarrassing way to back away from a clearly unacceptable proposal. At any rate, the pastor had his architect draw up a less controversial plan. The new proposal was, in my opinion, a huge waste of money, but it was not so horribly bad from an architectural standpoint that I would publicly oppose it.

On May 11, 1989 our pastor died unexpectedly. Considering that he was ordained in 1956, the same year as my seminary classmates, he was only about 59 or 60. We were informed that he had been wearing a pacemaker for some time, and that he died that evening while watching television. We heard indirectly that some of the pastor's friends and supporters then called me a priest-killer, but no one ever said anything to us directly. When the new pastor was appointed, I introduced myself, and the best way to put it is that his remarks were not welcoming, and we left the parish.

After a few years in our new parish, the pastor announced a renovation plan. He assured the parish that it would not involve any major changes. The communion rail would remain, and the tabernacle would remain where it was. Unfortunately, the proposed costs for his minor renovation reached a certain point that made it a "major" renovation, and that brought in the diocesan liturgical experts, so we were told. They insisted that he had to take down the communion rail, and I'm not sure what other changes were mandated. I made a few low-key efforts to oppose it, but I was not going to engage in the public opposition of a few years back. We just switched parishes once again.

By the time of the first renovation conflict, our older children were out of grade school, so it was very easy to switch to another parish where we did not feel any animosity directed towards us. That's one of the great advantages of our neighborhood. From our 1890's house, there are four Catholic churches within two miles and another four parishes within four miles.

The renovation controversy was repeated many times throughout the States during the Seventies, Eighties and Nineties. Resources were wasted, parishes were divided, and pastoral efforts were misdirected. In the meantime, the Catholic birth rate plummeted, vocations to the priesthood dropped seriously, Catholic schools were closed for lack of students and finances, and then the parishes themselves were closed or consolidated. The dissenters and the liturgical "experts" have left their marks, but who will be around a hundred years or even fifty years from now to notice? That's a book for someone else to write.

10. CCL 1981-2001

Dioceses and NFP Programs

On November 18, 1965 Pope Paul VI, on behalf of the world's bishops at Vatican Council II, issued *Apostolicam Actuositatem* better known as the *Decree on the Apostolate on the Laity*. It's really a beautiful document. In my copy that I obtained in 1966 while in Santa Clara, I have many passages underlined. For example, I have this passage circled with a broad yellow marking pen:

> Indeed, if the needs of cities and rural areas are to be met, laymen should not limit their cooperation to the parochial or diocesan boundaries but strive to extend it to interparochial, interdiocesan, national, and international fields, the more so because the daily increase in population mobility, the growth of mutual bonds, and the ease of communication no longer allow any sector of society to remain closed in upon itself (n.10.3).

Wow! What an endorsement of what we would start some six years later. A few sections later, I underlined this with yellow marker and in blue pencil:

> In the present circumstances, it is quite necessary that, in the area of lay activity, the united and organized form of the apostolate be strengthened. In fact, only the close pooling of resources is capable of fully achieving all the aims of the modern apostolate and firmly protecting its interests (18.4).

Sheila and I certainly modeled our NFP program after such common sense direction. A real clincher came two paragraphs later:

> Among these associations, those which promote and encourage a closer harmony between the everyday life of the members and their faith must be given primary consideration (19.2).

What could be more in need of harmony between everyday life and the Faith than married love and sexuality? Another passage that I double underlined should have been on a plaque hanging in every diocesan NFP office.

Yet the scattering of energies must be avoided. This waste occurs when new associations and projects are promoted without a sufficient reason, or if antiquated associations or methods are retained beyond their period of usefulness (19.4).

The program we developed mirrored what the bishops taught when in Council. What we experienced in many dioceses did not reflect what we had hoped for. We thought that our Triple Strand approach would find favor in dioceses because of its completeness. Instead, we experienced rejection on the basis of each part of the Triple Strand.

Rejections

1. An early rejection was based on our explicit support of *Humanae Vitae*. A couple in the Diocese of Kalamazoo wanted me to establish CCL in that diocese, but they were concerned about the priest who was in charge of NFP services. The priest had been brought to Kalamazoo in 1973 to establish the office of Marriage and Family Ministry. One fine summer day in 1975 when he was visiting his religious headquarters in Dayton, he dropped down for a visit. As we talked in my third-floor office, our topics rather quickly shifted from methods to morality. It became more and more questionable to me whether he believed the teaching of *Humanae Vitae*. Eventually, I thought the question could no longer be avoided. I told him that he sounded just like archdissenter Fr. Charles Curran, and I asked him whether he really accepted the teaching of the encyclical that marital contraception is a grave moral evil. He never gave me a straight answer so I wondered out loud how someone who didn't believe this teaching could head up a diocesan NFP effort. The NFP priest replied that he had discussed this matter with his bishop and that he could do a good job regardless of his personal beliefs.

That fall the couple invited me to meet with the bishop, so up to Benton Harbor I went, and then to the chancery office in Kalamazoo. Around the table were the bishop, the priest, the couple, and myself. When I could see that all was lost, I thought I might as well go for broke. So I said to the bishop something like this: "Your Excellency, when your NFP priest and I talked down in Cincinnati, he spoke as if he did not believe the teaching of *Humanae Vitae,* and I wonder about the feasibility of having a non-believer as head of your NFP program." Then I turned to the priest and said, "Father, if I have in any way misinterpreted your remarks, please correct me here and now." There was a very long silence. Everyone in the room knew I had not misinterpreted the NFP director. Finally, the bishop rather awkwardly cleared his throat and said something to this effect: "Mr. Kippley, you have made some serious statements. Father and I will have to discuss this matter." Some days later the NFP priest wrote me. A dissenter would remain in charge of the diocesan NFP program.

At an NFP program in Pittsburgh a few years later, I overheard some women who had attended a session taught by this same priest. The women couldn't understand why he seemed so opposed to teaching morality in NFP courses. As long as we were with CCL, we had no teachers in the Diocese of Kalamazoo.

This raises the issue of what a diocesan-approved NFP program should be. Should it just teach fertility awareness and say nothing about morality? Should it include morality but say nothing about the reasons for accepting the teaching of the Church? Should it transmit Catholic teaching that NFP is not simply Catholic birth control and that couples need a sufficiently serious reason to postpone pregnancy beyond the limits of breastfeeding infertility? Should it teach ecological breastfeeding as a form of NFP? Should it place the entire teaching of NFP in the context of Christian discipleship? Is it necessary that the NFP director and teachers themselves accept the teaching of *Humanae Vitae* as true and live by it according to their state in life? The experience in Kalamazoo and elsewhere demonstrated that these are realistic questions and that it is wrong to assume that all dioceses will respond in what we think is simply a matter of commonsense Catholicism.

2. Another early rejection was based on our advocacy of ecological breastfeeding. We recruited an enthusiastic couple in Columbus, Ohio and early in their teacher training they contacted the diocesan NFP-related person. He was opposed to our advocacy of ecological breastfeeding and told them that if they wanted any cooperation from his office they would have to become certified in his diocesan program. Wanting to teach and not engage in fruitless fights, they went with his program.

3. The most common reason for rejection was that we taught the full Sympto-Thermal Method (STM) instead of an NFP system favored by the diocesan NFP person. Usually the NFP director was an advocate of a mucus-only method, but sometimes difficulties would come from the diocesan NFP person who was trained by a different organization teaching the STM. As we shall see, rejection didn't necessarily mean that the diocese told parishes not to cooperate, but when the diocesan NFP person would prefer not to have you around, your efforts are made less effective.

A Happy Event

The happiest and most hopeful event in my recollection of the Eighties, aside from our CCL biannual conventions, occurred in the fall of 1986. Mount St. Mary's Seminary in Emmitsburg, MD, the oldest (founded in 1808) and one of the largest seminaries in the United States hosted a weekend conference on natural family planning. We were now at *Humanae Vitae* + 18, and seminaries were generally in deplorable shape, but that was definitely not the case at the Mount. After night prayers were concluded, there was no rushed exit but only a very slow trickle of the men going back to their rooms. It was evident from their participation in the conference that they were truly interested in what the various NFP presenters were saying. They had come to learn, not to scoff or argue. Father Robert V. Zylla, OSC, and his fellow theology teachers had done their job well. Fr. Zylla went to his eternal reward on July 29, 2009 at the age of 82.

The Diocesan Development Plan

By 1980 there were two national NFP programs teaching the cross-checking STM, several national programs teaching a mucus-only system, and many small programs. There were no common standards, and there was a need for some sort of orderly approach to this service. Thus, in 1981 Msgr. James T. McHugh worked with Terence Cardinal Cooke, the Archbishop of New York, to develop a diocesan plan for natural family planning that became known as the Diocesan Development Plan or DDP. The DDP then encouraged each diocese to develop its own NFP plan or to use one or more of the national programs. The practical result was that many dioceses sought to develop their own plans. Typically the diocese would hire a woman to be the NFP director, and typically she would model the program around the particular method she used. This was frequently a system that relied almost exclusively upon the external observations of cervical mucus. Our CCL teachers were usually unavailable for the NFP-director jobs because they were full-time at-home moms with husbands working full-time jobs away from home. Finally, the NFP director would, all too typically, obstruct the development of other programs in her or his area of jurisdiction.

As long as Sheila and I were associated with CCL, we never asked a diocese to make CCL its exclusive NFP provider. I would have liked that status, but I was against it in principle because then such exclusionary policies could be used against us. We sought only a level playing field. My conviction was that it was a waste of time and money for a diocesan NFP director to attempt to duplicate what we had already done and were offering to dioceses for free. Such duplication of effort was precisely warned against in Vatican II's *Decree on the Laity* quoted earlier. What diocesan NFP directors should be doing is something that only they can do—visit their diocesan priests individually and in small groups to help them grow in faith regarding *Humanae Vitae* and encourage them to require their engaged and married couples to attend a good NFP course.

A level playing field seemed to be feared by some of the diocesan NFP directors, and sometimes the effort of the NFP director to make her (and sometimes his) particular program the "official" program of the diocese became almost humorous in its exclusivity. A sympathetic priest once shared with us a letter his bishop had sent to every priest in the diocese telling them that the director's program was the only one to use and therefore not to use the CCL program anymore. Fortunately, the letter included all the propaganda points put out in favor of her program—she must have drafted it for the bishop's signature. That enabled me to respond point by point to the bishop. Shortly thereafter, the bishop issued another letter rescinding the previous one and saying that priests could again use our program.

By 1985 it became clear that something was needed beyond the individual diocesan programs. The quality of some programs was such that the program of Diocese A would not be accepted by adjacent Diocese B, so diocesan NFP coordinators requested an instrument they could use to evaluate teachers who had received different kinds of training. In 1985 the DDP held a national meeting at which Msgr. McHugh announced the development of national standards.

He also announced the development of a standardized NFP client education project. It sounded like an organizational duplicate of the program Sheila and I had developed. As I recall, there would be a uniform teacher-training system and a uniform teaching system with all teachers using the same text, slides and teaching notes. On this I went toe-to-toe with Msgr. McHugh. I accused him of simply duplicating what we had already done, and I said it would probably kill us. He acknowledged it would hurt us in the short run but said it would be good for us in the long run. He assigned the project to a committee of NFP program people, and I was relieved, figuring that such a committee wouldn't be able to agree. They did manage to put together a curriculum, but Msgr. McHugh eventually killed the project because he realized the great practical difficulties of getting all the dioceses to use one approach or system to teach natural family planning.

The DDP Standards were discussed further in 1987 and were published in 1990. A revised version was published in 2000.

I wish I could say that the publication of the Standards both solved the problems of quality control and created a level playing field. From my perspective, the Standards were too heavy on paperwork while being light on doctrine and said nothing about ecological breastfeeding. When you are conducting a research study, lots of paperwork is essential; but when you have volunteers teaching a tested method in a uniform way, unnecessary paperwork makes busy work for bureaucrats but provides a disincentive to volunteers. They, after all, volunteered to teach, not to become minor bureaucrats and record keepers, and they are intelligent enough to know that record keeping above a certain basic level is unnecessary. Further, the paperwork standards provided another excuse for exclusion.

Generally the exclusionary effort was not quite as obvious as the ones described previously, but it was there. In another memorable case, the NFP director was trained in a competitive NFP program. We had a great volunteer promoter in that diocese, and she wrote excellent bulletin announcements that were being read by the priests, inserted in parish bulletins, and drawing couples to the CCL courses. The NFP director then alleged that the priests were finding it confusing to receive items directly from the CCL promoter, so she made a policy that all such announcements had to go through her office. For unexplained reasons, they were greatly delayed in getting through her office and were reaching the parishes too late for inclusion in bulletins before the course started.

Efforts to get around this policy resulted in the only truly nasty letter I ever received from a bishop. He appeared to adopt the management theory that he had to back his employee against any outside complaints, the same sort of erroneous theory some bishops seemed to use when they heard complaints of sexual abuse by one of their priests. I blacked out everything in the bishop's letter that could give any hint of its author and sent it to one of the most kindly priests in this country, Father John F. Harvey, OSFS, the courageous founder of Courage, an apostolate to help men with same-sex attraction to be chaste. He was shocked at its tone and replied in his dignified way that such a letter should never have been sent.

I hope that some day someone will write a history of the NFP movement during the 40 years after *Humanae Vitae*, and I certainly hope that author will have access to the CCL files. I trust the author will find humorous a number of letters I wrote to bishops but never sent. With a sense of history, I filed them with NOT SENT in large handwritten letters. When something was really going wrong and there was nothing I could do about it, I found it psychologically helpful to write about it for the historical record and then not send the letter. Once I had expressed my frustration by typing the letter, it was much easier to move on.

The biggest obstacle to our apostolate was the lack of faith on the part of many priests and not a few bishops. An in-the-know Chicago chancery priest told me in the Seventies that maybe only half of the American bishops were solidly behind the teaching of *Humanae Vitae*. Others accepted it but didn't see any need to do anything practical about teaching its doctrine. I would rank diocesan NFP directors as the second biggest challenge to our apostolate. For example, when Archbishop Joseph L. Bernardin of Cincinnati brought a proposal to the bishops of Ohio for them to adopt CCL as a preferred but not exclusive provider, it was defeated. He told me that it was okay with the bishops but was turned down by the family life directors.

On the other hand, a good number of dioceses were wonderfully cooperative. The Diocese of Peoria stands out in a special way because of Betty Gilmore, the director of social services, who treated us in a thoroughly professional way. She was accustomed to having contracts with service providers, so she presented us with a three-year service agreement, to which I added only that we would continue to serve to the best of our ability after the term of the contract. She arranged for me to accompany Bishop Edward W. O'Rourke at a series of deanery meetings. He talked, I talked, and then we fielded questions. Some of his priests had absolutely no qualms about directly opposing the teaching of *Humanae Vitae*, and I think this was very hard on him, the bishop known as "the friend of the poor." Too many of his priests had been educated on the principles of the dissenters and were not about to change their minds.

We had great relationships and enthusiastic diocesan support particularly in the American heartland—Fargo, Sioux Falls, St. Paul-Minneapolis, Peoria, Omaha, Denver, Cincinnati, Covington KY, Lafayette LA, and also in that eastern outpost of orthodoxy, Arlington VA. And if the diocesan support was not exactly enthusiastic, it was at least permissive and enabled CCL to have great chapters in Chicago, Dubuque, Hot Springs, Tulsa, Phoenix, and Steubenville, and I am sure I am forgetting some. Amazingly, we were able to certify teaching couples in every state in the Union. Tom and Olivia McFadden brought CCL to Ireland and England in the mid-Seventies. One Irish priest compared it with the Legion of Mary. That was Ireland's gift to the States, he said, and our League was the States' gift in return to the Emerald Isle.

In 1989, The NCCB Bishops' Committee for Pastoral Research and Practices published *Faithful to Each Other Forever*, a book on preparation for marriage. In this document, they urged that every engaged couple should be required to attend a full NFP course—not just a couple hours sandwiched into a pre-Cana day—as a normal part of preparation for marriage. Twenty-two years later, only six dioceses have inaugurated that practice. In a 2006 document on NFP (*Married Love and the Gift of* Life) and in a 2009 document on marriage (*Marriage: Love and Life in the Divine* Plan), both issued by the entire body of American bishops, an NFP requirement for marriage preparation was not mentioned. In short, the American bishops were urged by some of their own to create a market for NFP services, and as a whole they have failed to do so.

Reflection on the Middle Years

The in-fighting and exclusionary policies of some diocesan personnel certainly didn't help the CCL apostolate and probably harmed it. But the steady 15 percent decrease in new-couples-taught each year during the Eighties and into the Nineties was part of something much larger than any organization or the entire NFP movement. It was the gradual acceptance of the sexual revolution by the Catholic laity and many of their priests—in effect becoming liberal Protestants and seculars in matters of sexuality. In 1995 the federal National Family Growth Survey (NFGS) found that among those who called themselves Catholic and were doing anything about birth control, only three percent were using any form of natural family planning. In the 16 years since that survey, there has been no indication that matters have improved, and unfortunately there's a good indication that the reality has gotten worse.

The latest version of the NFGS was released on May 26, 2010. An analysis by Professor Richard Fehring, who teaches nursing at Marquette

University, is posted at the USCCB website dealing with natural family planning. His analysis shows that only 1.1 percent of the self-identified Catholic women in the study reported they were using any form of NFP. (That's one point one percent, not eleven percent.) To be sure, there are problems with these numbers. They do not include those who are pregnant at the time of the survey; they do not include those who are using ecological breastfeeding for baby spacing; and they do not include those who are not doing anything to postpone the next pregnancy. The most important analysis from a moral perspective is the percentage of Catholic married couples who are using unnatural forms of birth control. No matter how we try to adjust the NFGS figures, I think there is no way to avoid the conclusion that at least 90% of fertile married couples are using unnatural forms of birth control. The 2010 figures point out the tremendous failure of the Church in this country to teach and to convince its people of the need to practice marital chastity.

Within the NFP movement, we have become accustomed to repeat the saying of Mother Teresa of Calcutta to the effect that we are called to continued effort but not necessarily to success. That, however, does not excuse us from trying to do better. For example, if we had a North American NFP organization, we could lobby the bishops to follow through on what their *Faithful to Each Other Forever* had urged in 1989—that every engaged couple should be required to attend a full course of NFP instruction, not just a couple of hours sandwiched into a pre-Cana day or weekend.

I still think that with the right kind of instruction, at least 25% of newly married couples will start their marriages without contraception—either accepting pregnancy right away or using systematic NFP to postpone pregnancy if they have a sufficiently serious reason to do so. Further, I think that with the right kind of supporting ecclesial environment, that number will increase gradually so that by their tenth anniversaries, about two-thirds of them will be living according to the truths taught by *Humanae Vitae*.

That isn't going to happen without effort by the responsible parties in the Church. Catholic bishops and priests need to work together to make sure that truly and fully Catholic teaching about love, marriage and sexuality is conveyed in Catholic schools at every level from grade school through college. They need to make sure it is part of what people hear every year from the pulpit and read in their parish bulletins. A full course on NFP needs to become just as much a part of preparation for marriage as the rehearsal is a part of preparation for the wedding ceremony.

I doubt that an NFP course that teaches just fertility awareness will have any significant effects regarding marital chastity. With that limited form of instruction, some couples who learn the abortifacient properties of hormonal birth control drugs may switch to contraceptive barrier methods during the fertile time. Some nature-oriented couples may eschew contraceptive devices as well as the drugs; but without spiritual motivation to be chaste, such couples will probably practice mutual masturbation or marital sodomy during the fertile time. It's vitally important for couples to have the right kind of instruction that not only offers complete method-related instruction but also places it in the context of Christian discipleship. For more on the right kind of instruction, see Chapter 20 on the program of NFP International.

11. Some of My Mistakes

This and the subsequent chapters that deal with the separation of Sheila and me from the Couple to Couple League have been the most difficult to start and may be the most difficult to read, at least for some. These chapters will describe what I believe are injustices, misbehaviors, and mistakes—including my own. Writing the previous chapters was tedious at times, but it was almost fun at other times as my research and focused memory brought back things from the past. That research led me to renew some contacts with some people such as Father Randall Blackall whom I hadn't been in contact with for over 30 years, and to intensify my contacts with others such as the Schambers with whom we have exchanged Christmas cards but have not seen in person for more than 40 years. Some chapters forced me to collect research that we did not have on hand, and that was beneficial.

This part of the memoirs is different. It is about painful experiences and it has been an unrelieved pain to put them down on paper. The financial results of this book, if any, will never equal what I could have earned for the same hours bagging groceries. To be sure, there was tremendous pain in the Regina experience, but with the hindsight of more than 40 years, I can see, or at least imagine, something of divine providence in that experience as I noted in that chapter. Suffering that is seen as having a purpose becomes relatively easy to accept, and even joyful in hindsight. With the benefit of hindsight, I can see that every time a door closed in the years chronicled in the previous chapters of these memoirs and also in my premarital years, another door opened to a better opportunity to serve.

With that in mind, I have tried to see if some good has come out of the events related in this part of the book. We have done a few things that perhaps we could not have done if we were still with CCL such as posting our online manual that the poor can download for free and for which we have received some gracious thanks from couples who said they were financially hard pressed. CCL's abandonment of ecological breastfeeding (EBF) as a form of natural family planning led us and others to place added emphasis on it, and as of this writing, there is a previously unexpressed level of interest in EBF as a form of NFP. But by and large, we are still hoping to see some good outcomes that seem commensurate with the difficulties we have endured since the beginning of 2001.

Looking ahead, perhaps these memoirs might be read by some *Humanae Vitae* believers who may come to a new realization of the importance of the social justice teaching of the Catholic Church. Perhaps some of those who do so much talking about social justice may come to see that it is a social injustice not to require every engaged couple to attend the right kind of NFP course, as described in Chapter 21, as a normal part of preparation for marriage. To paraphrase *Romans* 10, how are people going to practice chaste NFP unless they believe, and how are they going to believe unless they hear the complete teaching, and how are they going to hear unless they are required to participate in the right kind of NFP course?

Mistakes of Special Significance

Some of my mistakes concern finances, and some of these dealt with our teaching manual, *The Art of Natural Family Planning*. In 1991 we brought to the Board the concept of revising the manual to include the *Practical Application Booklet* and the *Home Study Guide,* both of which we had written as supplements to the teaching manual. Since this would increase the cost and the selling price of the new manual, we all agreed that the royalties to the Kippleys would be kept at an average of the last five years, without bothering to determine what those years were. We all assumed that the new manual would be published in two or three years. The reality was that it was published five years later, and by that time everyone on the Board (and also the business manager) had forgotten about the 1991 decisions. If I had remembered that decision, I would not have made some of the mistakes that follow.

1. My first and huge mistake was to copyright the Fourth Edition of *The Art of Natural Family Planning* in the name of the Couple to Couple League. All of the previous editions were copyrighted in the names of John and Sheila Kippley, and we should have done the same thing with the Fourth Edition. When I was typing the copyright page, I deliberately made the change in the mistaken and silly hope that this might lead other NFP teachers and organizations to use this text. I don't recall even discussing this with Sheila since I didn't think it made any real difference. What counts is the publishing contract, and that would be the same no matter who held the copyright. I made this change solely for the benefit of CCL, and that decision would come back to haunt us.

2. My second big mistake occurred when I started to receive social security. The Social Security law at the time required SS recipients who were under 70 to pay back to the government one dollar for every two dollars earned over $15,000 per year, with the base rising each year. I found this irritating especially since the money would be going to the Clinton anti-life administration. I thought CCL could use that money a lot better than the

government, so I slashed my own salary from $44,000 to $15,000 per year. As a result, I was the lowest paid salaried employee in the CCL organization, and on an hourly basis, my rate was about the same or lower than some of the part-timers. The savings to CCL for the years 1996-1999 was $119,360 assuming that my salary would not have increased during those years. In addition, CCL saved an additional $9,130 in Social Security and Health Insurance taxes. Thus our gifts to CCL that are reflected in my W-2 forms in 1996-1999 totaled $128,470.

In making such gifts, Sheila and I assumed that when we parted from the scene, our successors would carry on the program that we had started and had been directing all these years. Invalid assumptions can cause you grief.

There's a lesson to be learned. If you as an employee want to give money to your organization, don't do it as we did. In some cases you might be able to help your organization's cash flow by taking part of your salary as deferred income. I am advised that you will not pay any taxes on that until you start to draw it out. If at that point you want to make it a permanent gift, you can tell your employer that he can take whatever amount you state as a gift from you and reduce your deferred income account accordingly. The advantage of that process is obvious. If the management goes in a direction you oppose, you can withdraw your funds as regular income. Do all of this with the advice of a competent accountant and/or lawyer. Put it in writing and have it approved by the Board and entered into the official Minutes of the Board meeting. You might build into the process the provision that the company will have to bear any legal costs you incur if the company does not pay you your deferred income according to your written agreement. Alternatively, perhaps you could structure your help to your organization as a loan to be repaid at a certain time or at certain events such as your separation from the organization.

Do not assume that everything will remain the same as you get older and you want others to share or take your responsibilities. The only assumption you can afford to make is that something might go wrong. Then you can be relieved when everything happens as it should.

3. My third huge mistake was to defer, beginning in 1997, some of the royalties we earned on *The Art of Natural Family Planning*. The CCL organization was having more cash flow problems than we were having personally since at this time we had only one child at home and he was being homeschooled. In doing this I made three more mistakes. First, I did this only informally. We had a small staff, and when I wanted to defer a royalty payment, I would just tell our business manager to defer that payment. At other times, we would take it, and at other times we might gift it. It was our hope and our plan that royalties would form a helpful portion of our income once we retired. Sweet dreams. Thus it did not appear on the CCL balance sheet as a liability titled "Deferred royalties." The second mistake in

deferring the royalty payments was that I did not set up some obligatory process for the payment. For example, if we had made a contract that the organization would have to remit all the deferred royalties upon our retirement or disemployment, some of the problems we had would have been avoided or greatly reduced. My third mistake was that we did not build into the process that the organization would have to bear the legal costs of both parties in the event that we would have to litigate in order to gain the return of our deferred royalties.

The lesson here is the same as above. Don't make the same mistakes we made. We assumed that the same goodwill that led us to make these gifts and deferrals would be mutual when we needed the funds. It never occurred to us that our relationship with the Board would sour and that our donated funds could be used to finance litigation against us. Assume that things will change. Assume that the worst might happen. Assume that someone may use his or her corporate power against you. Make sure that you have clear terms about any loans or deferrals. Invest a few hundred dollars to have your own lawyer, not the company lawyer, draw up the terms in such a way as to protect you. After all, you are under no obligation to defer income, make loans, or make gifts to your organization. Of course, in writing this I am assuming that you are not overpaid and are more than fulfilling your responsibilities.

4. My next huge mistake was to resign abruptly from my job as Executive Director. To be sure, several times the Board had discussed the hiring of a new ED, and once we offered the position to someone who probably would have done a great job, but we couldn't meet his financial needs. I did not like the management aspects of the job. One of the part-timers got under my skin with her repeated requests for more pay. She had already looked around for another job and then realized how good she had it at CCL with our flexible hours for part-timers, but she kept it up. I should have pointed out to her that her rate was about the same or higher than my own. Or I should have told her that her requests were upsetting me to the point that one of us would have to go. But I didn't. I simply demoted myself.

Identities

This chapter starts the account of various things that led to our separation from CCL at the end of 2003 and the founding of NFP International in 2004. We are not happy with the treatment we received for our last three-and-a-half years with CCL, but I see no need to identify by name those whose behaviors I believe were faulty. They may all be proud of their behaviors, but I think that at least some of their family members might find some of them embarrassing. Thus we refer to CCL's staffers during this time simply as "staffer." All Executive Directors are referred to as ED; every Chairman of the Board during this time is called the CM; every Board member during that time is referred to as BM.

Two Executive Directors

After deciding to resign from the ED position, I contacted a former staffer who had resigned a year or so before to work with his wife in their family business. He was interested, so I hired him. As the Chairman of the Board would remind me later, I didn't follow the proper procedures in doing this.

This would turn out to be a huge mistake. The new ED was installed on April 1, 1999. April Fools Day and I was the fool. After a little more than two years, this ED abruptly resigned effective at the end of 2001 to move with his wife and family to another state. I wanted to return to the job of ED until we were able to hire someone from the ranks of CCL teachers. Unfortunately, one of our staff had alerted someone whose résumé looked good but who had absolutely no experience within the CCL organization. Sheila and I opposed hiring someone outside the organization, but we were overruled.

5. My next big mistake was that I accepted the responsibility for the search without corresponding help from an experienced human resources person. I had no experience in conducting such a search, and thus I missed a big clue that should have been pursued. When I was conducting a phone interview with a person who had a responsible position in an organization that had previously employed the ED candidate, that person told me nice things about him but also said that he needed supervision. Since everyone needs some sort of supervision, I didn't follow up on that, and that was unfortunate. The CCL Chairman pushed very hard for the hiring of this person instead of limiting our search to current CCL teachers or promoters.

6. The new ED started in early January, 2002. Within a month, Sheila and I started to have grave doubts about what was happening, so we changed our Will. Previously the Board had operated with economic conservatism and with the clear realization that what happened at the CCL office affected our teachers and promoters around the country. Sheila and I sensed that this might be changing. My mistake was to tell the Board that we had changed our Will, hoping that this might cause them some second thoughts. If it did, I am not aware of any beneficial effects. The lesson is obvious. If you sense that there is a changed attitude on the Board or see actions that run contrary to your better judgment, and if you think the organization might not use your funds wisely, change your Will and donations, but don't make my mistake. Don't tell the Board or try to make an issue of it since that may just aggravate the situation.

Other mistakes will follow, as you shall see, and they won't all be mine.

12. The Whistleblower

This chapter and the next contain many details and unpleasantries that can make difficult reading, but they are an important part of the story. I want to note at the outset that the people about whose performance I complain were people of good character. Unfortunately, good personal character is no guarantee of freedom from job-related mistakes.

Quality control is an issue in almost every organization, and NFP organizations are no exceptions. One of the chief functions of CCL as Sheila and I had formed it was to train volunteer teachers to teach student couples. Much of this was quite straightforward, simply the application of the standard rules in various situations. Thus a significant part of our teacher training was the application of the rules to a wide variety of charts, and for ease of quality control, every test corrector had an answer sheet. Still, the correction of these exercises required attention to detail, and some people are much more adept at that sort of thing than others.

Teacher Training

Sheila had long been involved in teacher training, and she has a great eye for detail. Changes in personnel created an issue of quality control. This chapter is primarily about her efforts to maintain good quality control and the whistleblower treatment she received for such efforts.

Test correction can be tedious, and errors do not necessarily reflect on a person's innate abilities. A person whose native intelligence was more oriented to creative writing became heavily involved in test correction, and he started making mistakes, mostly not catching mistakes made by the candidate teachers, but sometimes making some new ones in his corrections. In fact, in her test corrections, Sheila discovered three applicant teaching couples who had corrected this staffer's comments or corrections. Sheila would complain to me, but after April 1, 1999 I was no longer the Executive Director and could do nothing about the situation. I suggested that she should make copies of these mistakes, and she began to do so later in 1999. She would take the mistakes to the ED. He would agree with Sheila, and for a while he regularly reviewed the staffer's work. However, the problem continued.

The continuing problem was discussed at a Board meeting in mid-2000. The Board was ready to disemploy this staffer, but when Sheila saw the pain on the face of the ED, she intervened with the hope that with a little more guidance the staffer could overcome his problem with mistakes. Unfortunately, that didn't happen. In September 2001 the ED resigned to take a job in another state, and before leaving he told the staffer that he should find a new job effective at least by June 30, 2002. We thought that was an excessive notice for a notice of termination, but we didn't fight it, content that at least that particular problem was being solved.

A new ED was installed the first week of January 2002, and within less than a month he rescinded what we thought had been a notice of termination. It turned out that far from being a written notice of termination, the former ED had merely cautioned the staffer that he would no longer be around as ED to protect him. As a result, on February 5, Sheila wrote the new ED a seven-page letter objecting to that decision; five of those pages were simply a record of the staffer's mistakes.

As will be indicated in the next chapter, we had some welcome absences from these Cincinnati conflicts in February and March, but other conflicts developed in March and late April, and the teacher training conflicts resurfaced in May.

On May 13, the ED assured me by email that the test corrector was "fully qualified to train teaching couples" and that he "is the fastest test corrector in the office." We hadn't questioned these abilities. The issue we had raised was that this experienced and fast worker was making too many mistakes despite having an answer sheet.

On May 16, the ED emailed Sheila and me a strongly worded message dealing with her whistle-blowing, alleging that she was unfairly trying to get the test corrector fired. The ED also opined about what a valuable employee this person was.

As indicated above, at my request, Sheila had been documenting the test-correction mistakes. Amazingly, no one at the CCL office ever asked to see the documentation, and neither Sheila nor I was sufficiently assertive to insist that the ED sit down with her to review the documentation. Sheila never felt comfortable with this ED because he never once invited her into his office to talk. Yes, the ED had seen a description of the mistakes as noted above, but he had not viewed the actual data.

As a result of these emails, Sheila felt ostracized by the staff, so she began to pick up and drop off her work in the early morning hours to avoid meeting those who made her uncomfortable. She didn't know it at the time, but she was starting to get the standard whistleblower treatment.

Our primary concern at that point was to get the ED to do what needed to be done to improve the staffer's performance, not terminate his employment. But most importantly, we asked for the evidence of his charges against us. So I replied on May 25:

> In your email letter of May 16, you made some extremely strong charges against Sheila and myself. You accused us of pursuing "a

campaign to get [the staffer] fired" and supporting this alleged campaign "with untrue and misleading allegations." You continued with four more similar phrases: "complete disregarding (sic) for the evidence to the contrary," 'false and demeaning information," "unjustified complaints," and "inaccurate information."

Given that barrage of accusations, I think that ordinary folks would say that you are accusing us of lying in order to get [the staffer's] employment terminated.

It took a while, but on August 22 he apologized to Sheila, saying he had never intended to accuse her of lying.

The problem was less with his language than with his management. If he had been a sufficiently good manager, he would have asked to see the evidence that Sheila had compiled, and he would have seen the mistakes for himself. Further, he would have told the staffer in charge of teacher training to devise a way that the routine correction of tests could be done by clerical staffers using an answer sheet. In that way the test corrector could devote his attention strictly to helping candidates see the problems with their answers. That's what was already being done with the Home Study Course reviews, and Sheila was doing most of the correspondence with the students. It could have and should have been done that way with the candidate teachers. The man making too many mistakes certainly knew the material backwards and forwards. I think the system was simply too routine and that good management could have worked around that problem. I don't think the faulty management was by any means exclusively the fault of the ED, but when you wear that hat, the buck stops there.

The irony of this whole situation is that Sheila had saved the test-corrector's job in mid-2000 as previously indicated in this chapter. It had then been suggested that he be given other jobs, such as webmaster. Unfortunately, Sheila found that his work with the website also was poor. Yet two Executive Directors and another staffer said we were out to fire him, and we were told over and over again how valuable he was as an employee. To skip ahead about a year, in May of 2003 we were looking for an interim ED, and Sheila suggested this test corrector for that position, but he declined. I mention this to illustrate that there was not one iota of personal animosity towards this test corrector, simply a desire to have an improved level of quality. To skip further ahead, the next Executive Director after a month in office reported to the CCL Board of Directors: "After a month of assessment, I believe that Sheila Kippley's concerns of a Quality Control (QC) problem at CCL Central are accurate." In the morning of October 17, 2003 he came to our home and told me, "Sheila is right. This man makes mistakes." About a year later, the test corrector was no longer with CCL.

The Basic Spanish Manual

Some of those involved with teaching less educated Hispanics in the States thought that these folks needed a simpler method of instruction, and so they developed the "Basic Spanish Manual." Unfortunately, they did not see fit to notify all the members of the Board. The basic Spanish manual was used out in the field for two years before we were informed about it just before a Board meeting. On May 11, 2000 Sheila wrote to the current ED: "I am totally surprised by this blue manual used for the past two years, and I have never seen it until now. It began when John was in charge." We were the founders of this organization, we attended all staff and teacher-training meetings at this point, and yet no one had told us about this experiment.

Without getting into details, the basic Spanish manual was a constant source of concern to us, and reviewing it took many hours of staff time and staff meetings. The Teacher Training Committee met six times (Dec. 3, 5, 10, 20, 21 of 2001 and January 10, 2002). Each meeting lasted three hours except for the last meeting. Most of the text was re-written. During these meetings Sheila suggested that the Lactational Amenorrhea Method be added to the basic Spanish manual. This method is taught worldwide and has been shown to be clinically 98% to 99% effective. The immediate answer from the person in charge of the CCL Spanish program was "no." All the staff members present were silent on this issue.

On Monday, February 25, 2002, Sheila and I spent all day reviewing the revised text. We found items that had been agreed upon by the committee but were not implemented, and we also found other things that none of us had detected the first time. At these staff meetings, the English translations of the ten charts were not available for review. Much later, at the second final review, Sheila saw the charts for the first time and discovered that all charts had a "3rd dry day" application. What does a couple do if they cannot meet that 3rd dry day application? A few charts had to be changed.

The ED and the chairman of the Board did not want us to review the final Spanish text. We fought and fought to look at the final product because of our concern for quality control. Our first review was with the Spanish text. We asked that some changes be made, mostly for better teaching and clarity. After the corrections were made, we reviewed those sections before it was finally ready to go to press. Fortunately, in that final review Sheila spotted an error in which the Spanish manual stated that cultural-nursing mothers were completely infertile during the first eight weeks after childbirth. This eight-week postpartum effectiveness rate applies *only* to *exclusively* breastfeeding mothers. The erroneous statement could have led to unintended pregnancies, so we were grateful that Sheila caught this error before the basic Spanish manual went to press.

A Frustrated Chapter

The Archdiocese of St. Louis granted $3,000 to the St. Louis chapter to train a Spanish-speaking teaching couple. The CCL chapter followed the recommendations by the Spanish staffer to recruit such a teacher. When they found a willing couple, the staffer wanted this St. Louis couple to fly to Yakima, Washington for training. They had small children and this was not possible. Then the St. Louis chapter wanted to send the couple to Cincinnati for two weekends to be trained, but the staffer said he could not do that.

A St. Louis priest had two couples lined up who wanted to learn NFP in Spanish. The staffer was asked to teach these couples. He said they should come to the English class and have an interpreter. The St. Louis chapter thought this would be unfair to the English attendees. The class with an interpreter took 3.5 hours to teach (instead of the usual two hours) and some of the teaching had to be left out. In frustration, a person involved with the Spanish program in St. Louis wrote to the staffer:

> You said we need to do the ground work. We have attempted to do so. Much effort has gone into this work with little result. We do, however, have a pastor who is very supportive. His mother was an NFP-Billings teacher years ago. He is on board and willing to work directly with us at his bilingual parish.
>
> St. Louis seems to be a small fish in the big sea. Obviously, with the lower percentage of Hispanics here as compared to the East and West Coasts, we shouldn't expect much attention from an already taxed employee. That is too bad, especially since the archbishop's NFP designate is waiting for news about how we are progressing and spending our diocesan funds for Hispanics. Considering our troubled past with this designate, it would have been a good opportunity to work with her on a positive venture.

In the end, the chapter was unable to have a Spanish-speaking couple trained by CCL headquarters and returned the $3,000 to the archdiocese.

A Non-published Translation

Sheila's book, *Breastfeeding and Natural Child Spacing*, was translated into Spanish, then reviewed by a staff member page-by-page, and then reviewed again by a staffer's wife page-by-page, and then reviewed again by the same staff member page-by-page. When Sheila was told this by the staffer's secretary, she was surprised to learn of the translation and its many reviews. In October 2001 the cover was picked, the number of copies to be published was decided, and the book was ready to go to press. Two years passed and the Spanish *Breastfeeding and Natural Child Spacing* was never published. This was an expensive translation with no publication results.

Beyond Improvement?

The *New Corinthians Curriculum* (NCC) was a program developed for parents and teachers to teach children the virtues with a special emphasis on the virtue of chastity. A staff person claimed that he was receiving calls from parents concerned about the sex education being taught in the schools their children attended. This staffer made what the Board thought was a good case for us to develop a good chastity education program, and so we authorized the project. As a result, funds were allocated, two staffers were placed in charge of developing this program, a curriculum professional was engaged, and it was promoted by the Couple to Couple League. I was not its author, but I did review the text prior to publication with a view to not changing anything I really didn't have to change. In other words, if I felt something could have been better worded, I let it go unless I felt it was serious.

When it was published in 1996, it was probably the best chastity education program available, at least text-wise. But it was not without its problems. The educational consultant had designed it so that the classroom teacher would have to do some personal preparation work to teach each session, and this contrasted with many educational texts that told the teacher just what to do, thus requiring minimal preparation. From an analysis given to the Board of Directors in 2002, Sheila found that the sales were down and that 66% of the institutions did not reorder.

Since it dealt with sexuality, it was criticized by some who believed that sexuality education, no matter how well done and how orthodox, should not be taught in any manner in the schools. That, however, didn't mean that their comments were without value. At a June 2001 conference honoring the work of Fr. Paul Marx, Sheila and I met with one of the NCC critics, Lisa Marie Contini, and with Edward Szymkowiak of STOPP, an anti-Planned Parenthood organization associated with the American Life League. We were surprised to learn that Mr. Szymkowiak had written me to express his concerns about the *New Corinthians* program and mailed his letter to the CCL office. He found it difficult to understand why I never received his letter, and I shared his puzzlement. Sheila and I listened to their areas of concern and agreed with them. That summer I made the simple changes the critics requested, but that was not the end of the story.

More than three years later, on September 25, 2004 at the Fellowship of Catholic Scholars conference in Pittsburgh, Sheila attended a session on sex education. A variety of programs were discussed and found inadequate, including *New Corinthians*. A man from the audience asked the speakers what was wrong with *New Corinthians*. The speakers said they did not have their critique with them and could not answer his question at the time. The man was furious because, he said, this was John Kippley's program and in essence the critics were attacking John Kippley. Sheila finally raised her hand, introduced herself and informed the audience that we were no longer with the Couple to Couple League. She added that I had met with the critics, agreed with them, and made the necessary changes to *New Corinthian*. But, she said, as far as she knew, CCL had not made any of those changes.

In an email dated October 1, 2001 the Executive Director explained that the head person of *New Corinthians* said that what I suggested would "result in a substantial change for *New Corinthians*. Some may be good but many are not necessary and will change the pedagogy of the program." Also the program would then have to be resubmitted for the imprimatur, the two staff persons would no longer be involved as editor and project director, the program would need a new field test, and it would cost several thousands of dollars for the new plates and layout.

Since I was associated with this program, even though I had little to do with its formation and development, I felt I should explain what happened as above. A look at the CCL website in May 2010 showed that this program is no longer available. Apparently the demand was not that great. If the program had been selling well, I think CCL would have continued to publish and promote this program.

The Whistleblower Experience

Time magazine's Persons of the Year Award for 2002 were "The Whistleblowers," three women who risked health and sanity to tackle problems in their institutions. These three women experienced persecution, times of constant crying, and fought against an all-male network. They had to show they did nothing wrong and worried about losing their jobs in their attempts to correct problems in their respective organizations. When an interviewer asked if these women have ever been thanked, they laughed. Sheila's experience was similar. What hurt the most were attacks on her integrity and reputation. Sheila wanted to quit work at CCL four times during the year 2002, but each time I talked her out of it.

For more than four years Sheila struggled to remedy the problem of mistakes in teacher training. Instead of thanks, she not only received the treatment related above, but she also got a classic runaround treatment. As we prepared for a showdown at the Board meeting in November 2002, the ED and another staffer looked for mistakes made by Sheila. They did not provide us with a single documented misapplication of the rules or erroneous counseling. Instead they resorted to a list of nine ridiculous or unsubstantiated accusations that the ED used against her at the Board meeting. Although we had given the ED a copy of our charges against him to be reviewed at that fateful Board meeting, Sheila was given no such previous notice about these accusations. (There's more on this in the next two chapters.)

Sheila would not wish her experience on anyone. As Frederic Whitehurst, a whistleblower who blew his career on the truth, said: "When you do what they call blowing the whistle in this country, they pull your guts out about 30 yards down the road and stomp on them." (*The Cincinnati Enquirer*, September 28, 2002). Sheila suffered the effects of whistle-blowing. After 23 years of employment and 31 years of volunteer work for the League, she was often reduced to tears and then cried so much that tears were no longer produced. This was not a noble moment in the history of the Couple to Couple League.

13. More on Quality Issues

In the previous chapter, I mentioned a showdown at the November, 2002 Board meeting. Well before the meeting, I had presented the Board with "Management Issues," my case for the demotion (not his firing) of the ED for serious shortcomings in his exercise of management. (More on that in the next chapter.) The Chairman had rightly insisted that we give a copy to the ED, which we did, and we expected him to reply to that document. Instead, he took us by surprise by not responding to my critique and instead focused on criticizing Sheila. For whatever reasons, the Chairman apparently saw no reason for him to let us see his case.

Simply Erroneous to Silly

Accordingly, the ED told the Board that 1) Sheila's "grounds were not true" and that a "number of things were not true;" 2) She based her whistle-blowing "on what somebody said;" 3) Sheila made an error with the Clinical Experience Rule; 4) One never-specified letter of Sheila's was harsh; 5) One letter "implied fornication;" 6) Ten years ago she did some never-specified thing that was deserving of criticism, 7) Her handling of a Vietnamese couple's file was inadequate, 8) She unnecessarily added "serious" to one essay question, and 9) "last week two staff members said [she] told them [she] was against rapid growth."

Regarding the #1 and #2 criticisms, Sheila had first hand experience with all the facts and copied them. All the facts in her teacher-training criticisms were based on what she personally saw in the teacher-training files, not hearsay. Interestingly, there was no case by case argument against what she presented, just negative generalities.

Regarding #3, Sheila was not told what her "error" was with this rule. She always followed the book, frequently with direct quotation and page number. It should be noted here that none of the criticisms against Sheila at this Board meeting should ever have been brought forth at a Board meeting. If the head of Teacher Training had a problem with Sheila's performance in any respect, he should have notified her and explained why.

Regarding #4, no one, including Sheila, knew what letter the ED was talking about.

Regarding #5, the letter supposedly implying fornication was not available at the Board meeting. Sheila later received the letter from the ED on February 21, 2003. There was nothing in that letter to suggest fornication. The accusation was totally erroneous. In this case Sheila should have been defended by CCL and not criticized. Her letter to the ED explains the situation. The bold italics words were in the letter.

> You said the Diocesan Family Life Director and the deacon preparing [the engaged lady] for marriage felt my letter implied she was using the Pill for contraception. ***Nowhere in that letter did I say or infer the Pill was being used for a contraceptive purpose.*** In fact, I went out of my way to imply a medical reason, referring her to an NFP-only physician and the book *Fertility, Cycles and Nutrition.*
>
> You say "I'm sorry this became an issue." I agree with you. However you were the one who made it an issue by bringing it to the Board meeting last November.
>
> Sheila

The ED offered no apology and simply said: "Evidently the Director of Family Life and the deacon misinterpreted your letter."

Regarding #6, it is simply silly to make an unspecified accusation if you are serious. On the other hand, in the development of an overall negative impression, non-factual negative generalities are useful.

Regarding #7, the complaining couple wanted Sheila to state that they had completed the Home Study Course. It was obvious to Sheila that they had not done the reading and had not learned the method. No wonder, the man and woman each had two jobs! They called Sheila at the office and then called her twice at her home to put pressure on her. She encouraged them to read at least one part of the manual, Part 1 minus Chapter 13. Their interpreted charts showed no knowledge of the method or having read the manual. The ED also complained to a Board member about this file. When the latter asked for a copy of the file, she never received it. If someone had a problem with this case, the ED should have asked Sheila about it. Regardless, it was not a Board matter.

Regarding #8, test correctors were asked to make sure serious sin was implied by candidate teaching couples when answering this particular essay question about masturbation. Sheila had inserted the word "serious" in a candidate's response. It may have been redundant, but it was certainly not a Board matter.

Regarding #9, it was erroneous on two counts. First, Sheila certainly was not against rapid growth. Secondly, she had been exchanging her completed work for new work before normal working hours, so she hadn't been chatting with staff members for some time. She would have loved to have these two unnamed witnesses come forward so she could challenge their alleged statement.

At the beginning of his criticism of Sheila at this November Board meeting, the ED apologized for the presentation he was about to give and said he was embarrassed for the founders because of what he was going to say. Once we heard his allegations, we felt *he* was the one who should have been embarrassed by such a presentation. However, in that forum in which we had no opportunity to provide an evidence-based reply, his approach worked. He simply ignored my criticisms of his work, dismissed Sheila's criticisms of teacher-training mistakes, and created a cloud of doubt about Sheila's work and credibility.

One does not have to look far for a reason to create suspicion about Sheila. At this meeting she had given to each Board member a list of 12 areas, as follows, where she was concerned about CCL as a teaching organization. It was a call for reform.

Basic Spanish manual
The Art of Natural Family Planning
Test correcting and chart interpretation
Counseling
Teacher training
Hispanic program
Sex and the Marriage Covenant
Ecological breastfeeding
Family Foundations
In-House
Website
Physician and clergy seminars.

The priest who took the Board minutes wanted to add both the ED's criticisms and my "Management Issues" as attachments to the Minutes for the November 2002 Board meeting. I was willing to do so if the ED also added his remarks. He refused to do so and the Chairman at that time supported him. As the priest said:

> I guess I was mistaken about attachments being added on. I think that having such documentation is important for the record keeper, even if it wasn't all discussed. Written records are the only way to trace certain things. I would propose that John's Management Issues and [the ED's] written responses be added to the file of the Board Meeting even if not made part of the official minutes. The joys of being a recording secretary!!

Opposed to Change?

One of the ridiculous things Sheila and I heard while we were still with CCL and since our departure is that we were opposed to change. In our 32 years with CCL, those initials came to have a second meaning—the Constant Change League. We were never opposed to change as such. On the other hand, there are some things that could not be changed without changing the character of the organization, namely the Triple Strand approach to NFP instruction. And there are other changes that cannot be made at any particular time because of the restrictions of manpower and money.

On Thursday mornings the CCL staff met for informal reports, coffee and pastries. One morning Sheila happened to see a notice by the ED posted on a public bulletin board for anyone to read. Disturbed by the second and third sentences, she copied it. Dated October 31, 2002, it read:

> Regarding the upcoming Board of Directors meeting, [the CM] and I realize that the problem is simpler than we initially thought. John and Sheila's vision is for 2040, and the Board's is for 2020. Unlike 2040, 2020 calls for massive expansion. ***The Kippleys are not comfortable with rapid growth—they are attempting to put the brakes on.*** [Emphasis added.] We need a clear discussion to diffuse the confusion. [The CM] believes the BOD needs to acknowledge to the Kippleys that they have not been given an adequate opportunity to express their concerns about the 2020 vision. Let John and Sheila tell the BOD what they think, bring their views back to the staff, and get the whole staff involved.

The statement that we were "not comfortable with rapid growth" and wanted "to put the brakes on" simply was not true. In the early years of CCL, I had busted my butt working for growth, and we experienced more growth during those years than at any time since.

Another ridiculous thing we heard was an accusation that we would not change any of the slides in the teaching program. That was a figment of someone's imagination. My thinking was that the classroom teaching program should be reviewed every five years followed by the appropriate changes. I had engineered one such review about the time when we started to use the Fourth Edition of *The Art of Natural Family Planning*. I had given every teacher the opportunity to suggest changes, slide by slide, and I was amazed at the diversity of opinion about many of the slides with totally contradictory advice being given. I had no taste for another such experience; that could wait for another ED.

Related to the desire for changes in the teaching program was the wishful thinking that such changes would draw more couples. The reality is that in the 21st century Western culture, almost nobody comes to classes that teach chaste and generous NFP unless they are prodded by a diocesan or parish requirement to do so. When they register, they don't know what to expect.

Is Quality Control Uncharitable?

After we resigned as employees in November 2002, I was allowed to come back as the interim Executive Director at the very end of April 2003 while a search was underway for a new Executive Director. Sheila was allowed to come back part-time. The staff was pushing for the publication of the

English translation of the Spanish teaching notes. Sheila was interested in reviewing the English version, so I arranged to give her a copy.

She found significant teaching problems in this text. There were incomplete sentences that could cause misunderstandings and unintended pregnancies. There were statements about Phase 3 that lacked a cross-check by the temperature sign or a cross-check by the mucus sign. Five times the teaching notes stated that infertility began or fertility ended as soon as the cervix became low, closed or firm. The "absence of menstruation" was missing where needed when explaining the "nearly zero" and "less than one percent" effectiveness rate for the natural infertility of ecological breastfeeding during the first six months. The wording "evening of" for the start of post-ovulation infertility was missing in the instruction during the first four classes. It was finally mentioned in the fifth class. Sheila brought these teaching problems to my attention, and I put a temporary stop to the use of the English version of the Spanish teaching notes.

I also put a temporary stop to the use of the Spanish teaching notes by the CCL Spanish teachers, and that brought us some heavy criticism. A staffer had been developing this program for several years, and the Spanish Teaching Notes had been reviewed by four staff persons. When I asked the head of Teacher Training if he had reviewed the Teaching Notes, he replied, "yes."

Neither Sheila nor I had seen the final product after we asked for changes in the Spanish Teaching Notes and the Slides. It must also be noted that these notes and slides were aimed for a less educated audience and thus there was an even greater need for accuracy and clarity.

At a coffee break with all the staff present, the issue of getting the English version of the Spanish Teaching Notes out in the field came up. The staff said we needed this now. Sheila and I explained that some changes had to be made first. The head of the Spanish program then publicly accused Sheila of being uncharitable. Sheila had to explain that exercising quality control is not a matter of being uncharitable. There was a need to improve the teaching content before the Teaching Notes and Slides became available. I would add that the real offense against charity is putting materials out to the public before they are ready for use.

Incidentally, the same mistake made in the Spanish basic manual as it went to press occurred again in printed form to CCL Board members. In a December 2003 report, the head of the CCL Spanish program wrote:

> If you are unable to follow all seven standards of ecological breastfeeding, it becomes very important to be monitoring for signs of return of fertility beginning 56 days after childbirth.

The 56-day recommendation applies only to those mothers doing exclusive breastfeeding. It does not apply to mothers doing cultural nursing.

They should be watching for signs of returning fertility beginning three weeks postpartum, not waiting until eight weeks.

A New Executive Director in 2003 and Continuing Problems

The first of September 2003, CCL had a new Executive Director. His first action was to meet with the entire staff, including ourselves, and assure everyone that there would be no changes for at least one month, but Sheila and I were unemployed within a few days. On the ED's first day at the CCL office, Sheila presented him with files where mistakes had been made by a staffer. One candidate teaching couple was approved by the staffer for certification as a CCL teaching couple although this couple had made several serious mistakes on their final exam, including the incorrect labeling of Peak Day, mistakes not caught by the test corrector.

After one year, the new ED stated that "for the last year quality control has been my primary focus" (Autumn 2004 edition of the *In-House* Memo). Yet, four of the issues of *Family Foundations* following that statement had incorrect chart interpretations. (*Family Foundations* is a bi-monthly magazine for CCL members.)

What Is Plagiarism?

One of those wrong chart interpretations was interesting because it involved what most people would call plagiarism. What exactly is plagiarism? As defined by the *Random House Compact Unabridged Dictionary*, plagiarism is "the unauthorized use of or close imitation of the language and thoughts of another author and the misrepresentation of them as one's own original work." As recommended in *The Wanderer* by a reader in the column written by James Fitzpatrick ("Focusing on Plagiarism," July 13, 2008), "every phrase of borrowed work, whether taken word-for-word or not, should be cited."

When Sheila notified CCL of a chart-interpretation mistake in the January-February 2005 issue of *Family Foundations*, the mistake was admitted by email (February 6, 2005). Two days later we are told that "the article that ran in the Jan-Feb issue is an old one written by John." At first we thought that CCL was blaming me for the mistake, but that impression was soon corrected by CCL. In the Table of Contents, the credit for the article was given to the supposed author, a CCL staffer, but his name was not associated with the article itself, and CCL later told us that he had nothing to do with it. As a result of this incident, I asked that "CCL not reprint any articles by the Kippleys and/or their children." On February 20, 2005, I wrote the following to a CCL Board member:

> The publication of the CyCLe article and charts in the January-February 2005 issue was massive plagiarism. Everyone admits that it was copied—inaccurately—from my article in the July-August 2000 issue. Further, not only was a chart copied

incorrectly, but my article was modified to give the impression that it was current.

   a) In my article, I started this way: "My wife, Sheila, reviews most of the charts that come to the office as part of the CCL Home Study Course..."

   The anonymous author wrote: "We receive quite a few charts at the CCL Central office from couples taking the CCL Home Study Course..."

   b) In paragraph 3, I wrote "This year, the Jubilee Year 2000, is the 70th anniversary of the landmark encyclical of Pope Pius XI, Casti Connubii, dated December 31, 1930.

   The anonymous author wrote, "In this year of 2005, we will mark the 75th anniversary of the landmark encyclical..."

In a real world publishing organization, such plagiarism would be grounds for dismissal or at least severe sanction. In the new CCL, what will happen? Will this even be noted in the employees' evaluation file? Will there be any sort of penalty? Any reduction of bonuses? Or will the main criticism be that the whistle-blower shared her concerns and what was happening (not in a broadcast way but only with a very few) and that her whistle-blowing perhaps caused a slight distraction around the office?

   This incident serves as a good example of why we cannot accept a gag rule. Instead of being incensed over the plagiarism and the inaccuracies in copying the charts, you are upset that Sheila would tell someone else what has been happening. What if we had signed onto a gag rule? Would we be forbidden from mentioning plagiarism and mistake-making to anyone other than Board members and staff?

   I trust that [the Executive Director] will apologize for the plagiarism as well as for the mistakes in copying. ...As soon as this whole matter came to light, he should have told us the issue in which my article appeared, apologized for the plagiarism, and explained the whole matter... The facts remain that one or more persons at Central engaged in plagiarism, made errors in that unethical activity, and then initially attributed the mistake-containing article to me. In any real-world organization that would call for some apologies" (email Feb. 20, 2005 to a Board member).

On February 21, I was told of CCL's perspective. Basically, CCL's position was "anything [John Kippley] wrote as ED for CCL is the property of CCL—the same standard that applies to any article written by any former employee. It is not plagiarism for an organization to use its own property…no apology is due you."

The matter came up again two years later, and I was told by a Board member on April 30, 2007:

> I do respectfully disagree that the matter presented "plagiarism" *in the legal sense*. [Emphasis added.] There was a personal apology to you from [the ED]—and an explanation. Here's a copy that [the ED] sent to you on June 8, 2005: "Regarding this email and the other one you sent, [the staffer] did not plagiarize your article. We ran the article and inadvertently left [his] name on the table of contents since he usually writes that column. [He] had absolutely nothing to do with it, so I will apologize for that mistake. It was merely an oversight and not an intent on anyone's part [to] plagiarize."

Thus the new management would apologize for mistakenly attributing the article to someone who didn't write it, but it refused to apologize for the use of my words without proper credit, treating it strictly as a legal issue. Yes, I believe they are correct about their legal right in this matter, so it was not plagiarism in the legal sense. However, in the areas of journalism, academia, and professional writing, the use of another person's writing without credit is considered plagiarism, a violation of professional ethics, regardless of copyright ownership.

The New *Art of Natural Family Planning* by CCL

In November 2007, we received the new CCL manual titled *The Art of Natural Family Planning: Student Guide*. Sheila immediately checked the information pertaining to breastfeeding infertility. She found a mistake on two pages of the manual concerning exclusive breastfeeding. On page 161 the CCL manual stated:

> Some studies show that 97% of mothers who exclusively breastfeed can be assured of postpartum infertility for at least six months.

And on page 254, the CCL manual says this about exclusive breastfeeding: "highly infertile during the first six months postpartum."

The missing requirement is the absence of menstruation in both statements. Also, studies show an effectiveness rate of at least 98% according to the Bellagio international breastfeeding experts, but that 1% difference is immaterial. What matters is that the breastfeeding amenorrhea requirement was completely missing from the text.

CCL admitted this mistake but refused to insert a corrections sheet. This mistake, of course, could have led to an unintended pregnancy. I phoned the CCL Executive Director about this mistake and the need to insert a correction sheet inside their manual. He said he had other priorities. I offered to write the corrections sheet for him. I was turned down. We were told at a later date, December 11, 2008, that with the next printing of the manual the mistake would be corrected. We believe that this error should have been corrected immediately with a corrections sheet inserted into the manual.

A Consistent Problem

Later we heard from a few others who were also concerned about quality control. As one CCL teacher wrote,

> I suppose that I too have been a "whistle-blower." Whenever a new page was to be inserted into our notes, I've reported some of the mistakes to central. I guess that makes me 'nit picky'. I feel that accuracy is of utmost importance if we want couples who are confident in using the sympto-thermal method" (October 8, 2004).

Another CCL teacher said:

> We teach in Spanish. We used the 'short' manual once, but with heavy doses of slides from the regular course. We decided that this new program is incomplete and stopped using it altogether (November 13, 2004).

When CCL went to the quick two-weekend teacher-training seminars, we heard of problems with the NFP teaching out in the field done by those couples trained in the weekend seminars. The "seminar" teachers needed to be mentored for their first series of classes, and some needed mentoring for their second series of classes. As an older teacher said, "When we went through the correspondence testing, we finished knowing all the material well and knew how to interpret charts. We were definitely ready to teach. These 'seminar' couples are not as ready to teach and interpret."

Quality Control of the Mouth

With regard to writing and speaking, a most important factor of quality control is accuracy of facts, and we would have liked this quality as it pertained to us. At 8:15 a.m. on March 25, 2003 (7:15 the caller's time) our phone rang. It was a former Board member who hadn't slept well the night before. She was troubled by what she had heard about me the day before. She asked Sheila if it was true, "Does John have Alzheimer's or dementia?" Those terms are medical diagnoses, and to make such statements about a person goes beyond idle negative gossip. To say such things erroneously about someone who is still involved in active, public intellectual life is serious. The source was a CCL staffer who should have known better as a Christian not to spread his negative thoughts; he had told someone that I had dementia. His statement about me was, fortunately, completely false. Seven years later in 2010 I am actively playing golf, taking long bike rides, and writing articles and a book. In fact, on February 27, 2010 a health-care article I wrote for Matt Abbott, a blogger, was carried by USAToday.com. I thank God every day for my good health. By the way, this employee suffered no consequences for his statements.

I started the previous chapter with the general statement that quality control needs to be a universal concern. We have illustrated sufficient examples to show that not only did CCL have some quality control issues but also showed a reluctance to admit mistakes. We no longer read CCL materials. We hope the quality control problem has been fixed.

The only significance of this issue is that it illustrates the atmosphere that had developed at the CCL headquarters office. A staffer could make such a comment to someone outside the office without any evidence and apparently without fear of any consequences. I submit that in any normal situation, such a situation would have seen the calumniator looking for a new job. In this case, the only consequence was that eventually the person had to apologize to me face to face.

Do I have a memory problem? I certainly do, and I've had it for a long time. I had a very hard time memorizing Latin and Greek declensions and conjugations, and trying to memorize the key points of what various philosophers had taught over 25 centuries was like trying to memorize nonsense syllables. My most embarrassing loss of memory occurred not too long before I met Sheila. In my search for a wife, I had lots of first dates, deciding that this one and that one wasn't to be my lifelong partner in life, and I am sure that other party frequently reached the same conclusion even before I did. One night the numbers caught up with me. I was with a first date at a party and needed to introduce her to others, and I couldn't remember her name. A complete blank. I couldn't fake it, so I had to ask her for her own name. Talk about embarrassing! But that's why I can still remember it—the event but not her name—almost 50 years later. The good effect was that I decided to put that matter in the hands of the Lord, and in the not too distant future I met Sheila.

14. 2002: Our Last Full Year with CCL

When we incorporated CCL in 1974, Sheila and I asked three other people to share the leadership on the Board of Directors—Dr. Paul Busam from Cincinnati, Father Don McCarthy from Cincinnati, and Roger Carter from St. Paul. We kept the Board at five members for 21 years. At our spring 1995 meeting we elected to the Board a gentleman who had been extremely generous to CCL and had considerable business acumen. At the spring 1999 meeting we elected three more members to the Board—another doctor, a priest, and another generous businessman. Sheila and I had deliberately put ourselves in a minority position on the Board from the beginning, and with these and future additions our influence was proportionately less. As a general rule, based on our experience and that of others, we would advise anyone with a similar organization to keep the Board of Directors small, and some advisors suggest a limit of three. Better yet, get legal advice on how to set up your organization so that if your larger Board turns against you, it can be dissolved. Some experienced folks were astonished that we had not arranged matters in that way.

Changes in Leadership

Dr. Paul Busam was chosen as the Chairman of the Board and held that position for 25 years. In August, 1999 he resigned as Chairman while remaining on the Board as a voting member, and a new chairman was elected. At the June meeting in 2001, the chairman of two years announced that he would be leaving the Board in June 2002 but desired to resign from the chairmanship immediately. The rest of the Board reluctantly accepted his resignation as Chairman and elected a new chairman. As previously indicated, late in 2001 when the ED had resigned, the new CM promoted the hiring of a person outside the organization as the new ED.

The new Executive Director, as of January 2002, was certainly a likable gentleman, and I think he shared the normal human inclination of wanting to be liked by his fellow workers, especially the five gentlemen with whom he shared second-floor offices. Sometimes, however, the desire to be liked can cloud a manager's analysis of employee-related problems and hamper his ability to take effective and beneficial action. He also wore rose-colored glasses as he estimated future income that would be available for new projects.

February 2002

It seemed to us in late 2001 that the chairman of the board did not want us around CCL. He had been quite insistent that I should not continue as an interim ED until we could find a permanent ED from within the ranks of CCL teachers and promoters, and thus he had championed the hiring of the new executive director. Still, the CM was the one to whom I had to bring my complaints about the ED, since he was the only one who had direct control over the activities of the Executive Director..

We had a Board meeting on February 9 to welcome the new ED, introduce ourselves, and discuss our vision. An underlying problem described in Chapter 12 had been creating tension for two years, and this meeting did nothing to dispel it.

March 2002

Early in March, the new ED faced another challenge—bullying behavior by one of CCL's key employees. On March 6, 2002 when I was working in the library, a staffer entered, screamed at me in a very loud voice with some sort of criticism, slammed a file folder on my table, and then left, slamming the door for maximum effect. The object of his displeasure was a teacher-training file I had placed on his desk early that morning before he had arrived. Attached to the file was a note from Sheila dealing with a quality-control issue. One of the women who helped with the teacher-training files had asked Sheila for help in having all file comments initialed by the reviewer who made them. Sheila had simply reaffirmed this request in her note to the staffer who found this quite objectionable. My only role in the matter was to place the file on his desk as was our usual routine. I reported this outbreak to the ED who later told me that the staffer had offered to resign. The ED didn't accept that offer, and by March 15 the matter was resolved.

This was not the first time that staffer had exhibited his temper. At least twice before he had yelled at me in a very derogatory way, and one time he criticized one of CCL's secretaries so loudly and publicly that she walked to her car, fully expecting to resign. I followed her out and begged her to stay. In one of his verbal blowups against me, there was a threat of resignation, and I told him to go home and talk with his wife about it. In almost any other organization, he would have been fired after the second bout, but I had a great reluctance to fire anyone. First, it was hard to find anyone who shared our beliefs who would also be willing to work in the CCL apostolate. This staffer was dedicated to the NFP apostolate and was quite willing to work within our low salary scale. In fact, in our pre-employment interview, when I asked him how much salary he needed, his request was too low. I told him he could not make ends meet on that amount and raised it ten percent. Second, I had this weird idea that it is better to deal with someone whose faults you know than to bring in someone else whose faults you will get to know later. For reasons I have never asked about, this staffer told me that after the first time his wife met me, she told him that I would fire him. She was wrong, but not for any lack of adequate reasons.

Growing Tension

One of the areas of conflict and tension was the production of a basic manual in Spanish. Sheila and I had some very real reservations on quality control issues, but the ED and the Chairman were in a hurry to get it published. We were supposed to review it and give it our approval. This may sound very simple, but I noted in my day-book for February 27, 2002: "The conflict and stress regarding the project that was generated in the week of Feb. 25-27 [2002] caused me so much physical pain that if it were a continuing thing it would either kill me or I would quickly quit." The next day we had an all-morning meeting with the ED on this issue.

On March 6, after the blowup described above, I felt real tension resulting from the ED's early non-action on the matter. Also in March and April, I was working on revisions for *Sex and the Marriage Covenant* (SMC), and these led to disagreements with the ED. In fact, after the Archdiocese of Cincinnati had granted its *Imprimatur* to SMC, the ED asked the Archdiocese to withdraw it, which they did. They made it very clear that the withdrawal was based solely on the fact they did not want to enter a dispute between an author and the publisher.

We had a couple of welcome breaks from all of this. In the third week of March we drove to visit Jennifer and her family in Scarsdale for a couple days. A clergy conference the first week of April provided more of a break from the conflict, but I restarted my work on *Sex and the Marriage Covenant* the second week of April. The third week in April we traveled to Gaming, Austria to visit Christopher who was working there for a year of postgraduate experience.

In the meantime, the ED had contacted Msgr. William Smith, a leading moral theologian, about certain issues in SMC. Then he erroneously interpreted the theologian's comments as saying that I was teaching "false doctrine." When I contacted Msgr. Smith by phone the evening of April 28th, he assured me that he did not agree with me on three points, but he also assured me that he had not used that language. Controversy on SMC continued in the first two weeks of May, and on Friday, May 10, I noted in my day-book "chest pains in morning from ED-related stress. Mowed lawn in afternoon." On May 14th I saw a cardiologist, and two days later a stress test showed I had no heart problems, just an ED and CM problem.

June 2002 Board Meeting

The main concern of this Board meeting on June 2 and 3 was the budget that I thought relied far too much on wishful thinking. Two of my first three efforts to reduce the overall budget passed, and two of my three efforts to reduce spending related to the *New Corinthians* curriculum also passed. I still thought that even the amended version was an unrealistic budget, but the feeling was so optimistic that I was the only person to vote against its adoption.

A significant non-budget item was a slightly revised edition of my book, *Sex and the Marriage Covenant*. I had added a section on marital rape based largely on Father Ed Bayer's book, *Rape within Marriage: A Moral Analysis Delayed*. Our new ED had some serious reservations on this, and we had gone through a frustrating exchange of emails, as a result of which I had made some revisions to clarify matters, and the Board approved it 6 – 1. In the end, as Sheila and I felt more isolated in the organization, we persuaded the Board to let us take it to Ignatius Press which accepted and published it in 2005, thus giving us a friendly publisher.

Father's Day Weekend

What seemed a minor item at the time was the Board decision to fund the employment of an International Field Director but only after the development of a complete job description. In addition, there was a consensus that the Chairman and the Vice-Chairman would write this job description. Due to a misunderstanding on this point, a staffer thought he should be composing it. Shortly before our regular five o'clock closing time in the afternoon of June 14, 2002, the Friday before Father's Day, that staffer came to my cubicle and asked if I had a minute. "Sure, c,mon in, but it will have to be quick since I'm expecting Sheila here at five." He then began berating me for something that was going on between him and a Board member. As indicated above, the Board had decided to create the position of Director of International Development, and it had appointed two Board members to write the job description. Apparently this was not communicated to this staffer because he thought it was his right or responsibility to write it. Earlier that Friday afternoon, this staffer had offered me his opinion on the matter, and I had been basically non-responsive because the matter was out of my hands. As the staffer started to berate me, I told him that I didn't have to take that anymore, and I got up and started to put some materials in my backpack, thus turning my back on him. Suddenly, he was right behind me, yelling at the top of his lungs, and so close that I felt his breath on the back of my neck. I had the good sense not to challenge him. He was younger, taller, and stronger. After two or three minutes, it was all over. He backed up. I wished him a happy Father's Day, and we went our separate ways.

Both the staffer and I recognized that this could have consequences, and so each of us wrote a Memorandum for Record in which we described what happened. While I felt no fear at the time, I began to realize that it could have been much worse. The first thing I did was to make a blotter report at the local police station. That's a report that doesn't become public unless there is a subsequent criminal act possibly related to the event reported. For me, it was a way of making sure that if something violent happened to me in a mysterious way, the police would know where to start looking. As I told the staffer some months later, my reason for not making a public report was that I did not want to embarrass his family, and he thanked me for that consideration.

When I reported this to the ED, he refused to do anything about it. He could have fired him, which he certainly deserved, or he could have required an apology. He did neither, and in such inaction, he demonstrated that he was unqualified for that job. At the time the concept of "going postal" was still in the news, and it certainly weighed on me. I grew to fear what might happen if the staffer and I had a big disagreement. In the case at hand, his disagreement was with another Board member so I was essentially out of the loop. But as a result of the blowup and the ED's refusal to take any remedial action, I feared going into the office unless there were others around. One night Sheila and I drove to the office to drop off some completed teacher-training files and to pick up some new ones. (Sheila was doing her work at home at the time.) When we saw a light in the staffer's office, we feared to go into the building and returned home without making the exchange of files.

The staffer told another staff member what had happened, and when I explained it to the latter staffer from my perspective, he said that our two stories matched. When I told him about my fears, he said I shouldn't be afraid because I was in the best condition of any 70-year-old he knew. Actually, I was 71, and I already knew that at that age a person heals more slowly from any sort of injury. I was not going to willingly put myself in the position of having to try to protect myself physically from someone who was younger, taller, and stronger, especially if that person were additionally strengthened by enragement. The second staff member then tried to set up a reconciliation meeting. I agreed but insisted that our meeting had to be in a public restaurant where I thought the potentially angry staffer would feel constrained, but the latter refused any such meeting.

About a year later, after we had a new Chairman and I was the interim ED, the staffer finally apologized. He had told one of his sons what had happened, and his son told him he had to apologize. The young man's reasoning was that if you accidentally step on somebody's shoes in an elevator you apologize, and "what you did, dad, was deliberate." After the apology, we shook hands again.

Convention 2002, Shawnee Oklahoma, June 23-26

Just one week later, on Friday, June 21, Sheila and I went to a Diocesan Development NFP conference in Milwaukee where Sheila gave a well-received talk on ecological breastfeeding. From there we flew to Oklahoma City, where someone drove us to the CCL Conference in Shawnee. The talks at the convention went well except that three of the speakers chose to elaborate on the same biblical text, Ephesians 5:21. One of them said almost nothing on the assigned topic.

The most prominent guest was Archbishop Karl Josef Romer of the Pontifical Council for the Family in the Vatican. We had invited our friend Alfonso Cardinal López Trujillo, President of the Council, but he was unable to come so he sent Archbishop Romer as his substitute. From our perspective, the most significant thing he did at the convention was to request a small meeting of its leadership and teaching couples. Also, very significantly, those in charge of putting this meeting together did not invite us to attend. Fortunately, we got word of it via the grapevine and secured an invitation.

One of the first things Archbishop Romer did was to inquire about the origins of CCL. When he learned that the founders were present but had not been introduced to him, he recognized that something was not right. He then reflected upon his 37 years in Brazil where he said they had seen many promising apostolates rise and then fall as the successors of their founders forgot or abandoned the charisms of the founders. I think that he was sounding a warning to the then-current leadership, but it turned out to be of no avail.

It did, however, have at least one lasting effect. Sheila and I had never thought about what we brought to the founding of the Couple to Couple League in terms of "founders' charisms," but Archbishop Romer caused us to think about it. It didn't require much reflection, for we were very much aware of what we had brought to the League and why we had founded it. The three principal charisms were very easy to identify.

1. The first was ecological breastfeeding as a specific form of natural family planning. This charism was not an advocacy of breastfeeding in general; that was the charism of La Leche League. Rather, it had to do with the science, the research, and the advocacy of a pattern of nursing and baby care so distinctly different from typical Westernized patterns of breastfeeding that we had to give it a distinct name—ecological breastfeeding—to separate it from those other patterns of breastfeeding that have little or no effect on the return of fertility. At the time of the founding of CCL we had already done the research that demonstrated that ecological breastfeeding delayed the return of the first postpartum menstruation for an average of 14.5 months among American mothers. The pattern of frequent suckling is what we now call the "Seven Standards of ecological breastfeeding."

2. The second charism was the covenant theology as a way of explaining Catholic teaching against unnatural forms of birth control. It is very simple to understand and can be summarized in 17 words: "Sexual intercourse is intended by God to be at least implicitly a renewal of the marriage

covenant." I had started to use this "renewal of the marriage covenant" concept in my Santa Clara evangelization efforts and had first put it into print in 1967. Later, Pope John Paul II incorporated it into his 1994 *Letter to Families*. The charism was not just a general upholding of *Humanae Vitae* but a very specific way to defend and explain it. It is so simple that people grasp it almost intuitively, saying "That makes sense. Why haven't I heard that before?"

3. The third charism was an open-minded approach to systematic NFP that taught all the common signs of fertility and infertility and provided a variety of rules to enable couples to choose the options that would entail the least amount of abstinence. We were very much influenced and reaffirmed in this by Dr. Konald A. Prem, our chief medical advisor and mentor.

For some years we had been calling this the Triple Strand approach to natural family planning, but Archbishop Romer's talk led us to describe this more clearly in terms of the charisms on which we founded the League. Unfortunately, all three of these charisms were jettisoned by CCL's new management starting in 2004 and made crystal clear in its highly publicized "Extreme Makeover" announced on December 12, 2007. More on this in Chapter 19.

July through October

Back at the office after the convention, I had another job to do. The ED and staff had proposed the allocation of funds for two part-time counselors at the home office, but the proposal was defeated at the early-June Board meeting. I thought the claims of excessive time being spent on counseling were exaggerated, so I volunteered to handle all the counseling calls to determine the actual amount of time consumed in such activity. On July 1, I had 4 e-mails and 3 phone counseling calls for a total of 1 hour and 18 minutes. On July 2, apparently I spent 30 minutes on one e-mail and one letter. July 3 brought no counseling requests. July 4 was a holiday and July 5 was declared a paid holiday by the ED because the staff had worked so hard. In the second week of July, I had 33 requests that took 6 hours and 6 minutes. In the next week, I handled 24 requests in 7.28 hours. The last week in July required 7.77 hours. This is the sort of analysis that should have been made before the budget request, but the times might have been more extended. It was well known that some of those who took the counseling calls talked a lot. At any rate, there was no reasonable basis for the budget request; all the issue required was better management of time.

The tensions continued between us and the CM and ED. My day-book notes that on the night of Sunday, July 21, I received a call from a very unhappy CM that left me depressed for the next two days.

In early August, I was in contact with Fr. Joseph Fessio, S.J., about *Sex and the Marriage Covenant*, and eventually he agreed to have Ignatius Press publish it. In mid-August I started to write my reservations about the ED's management. In some ways this was also an indirect criticism of the CM because every Wednesday morning the CM would call the ED and they would talk for about an hour. It seemed as if the real Executive Director was the CM.

It was still my responsibility to review every certification file. If I felt the Candidate Teaching Couple still showed a weakness, I would buck the file back to the teacher trainer for additional work. The file of the ED and his wife arrived on my desk in mid-August, and I felt I could not certify them. They were technically ready, but I felt that the ED's management performance was such that he would soon be gone and might be alienated. That decision on my part caused additional tension between me and the CM. The month of August was filled with disputation, and I continued to work on a document I was now calling "Management Issues."

"Management Issues"

By early September, I had completed my description of the management by the ED. On September 4, I sent to the Board Members a letter which called for 1) the firing of the anger-challenged staffer for his behavior on June 14 for which there had been no apology and 2) the demotion but not the firing of the ED. I also stated that the retention of the staffer "is tantamount to requesting my resignation" and that the retention of the ED in that role "is tantamount to requesting Sheila's resignation." We clearly put our jobs on the line because we could no longer tolerate the conditions of fear and runaround that had become our lot. I also enclosed, and later sent to the ED, my 12-page "Management Issues" starting with this paragraph:

> This document illustrates why I have come to the conclusion that CCL's current Executive Director, [X], is seriously inadequate for the demands of this position.

"Management Issues" (MI) contained six sections with multiple sub-sections. The first was titled "Serious inadequacy in handling controversy," and the first subsection was "Accusations against Sheila Kippley." As indicated previously, Sheila had been an unwelcome whistleblower regarding mistakes made by teacher trainers and in a Spanish-language project. The document concluded with a summary of the matters that we believed demonstrated that the ED was inadequate for the job. We requested the Board to reaffirm the Charisms and Convictions we brought to the League and to allow us to exercise leadership once again.

I did not criticize the ED's character. He was a nice guy with a big smile. To the best of my knowledge, he was a man of fine character. The problem was that his performance as a manager was inadequate, and that was his primary job. He would probably have excelled in the role of a regional field director.

We tried to get a special meeting of the Board to consider "Management Issues," but that couldn't be scheduled. Thus it would be discussed at the regular Board meeting in early November. The chairman wanted the ED to have a copy so that he could respond. We had hoped he would respond in writing so that we in turn could offer a rebuttal as is normal in disputed matters, but that did not happen.

Board Meeting, November 3 and 4

The meeting formally opened at 2:10 Sunday afternoon. Under "Old Business" I moved for the acceptance of the revisions I had made to *Sex and the Marriage Covenant*, and that was unanimously accepted. Then I proposed the demotion of the Executive Director who then left the room at 3:00. At 5:00 the ED returned and had the floor to respond to the criticisms in "Management Issues" and to criticize Sheila. With breaks for dinner and prayer, that discussion continued until 8:55 p.m. at which time the ED, Sheila, and I were excused from the meeting. The rest of Board discussed the matter and called all of us back into the room to vote. The vote on demotion was Yes-2 and No-7. The rest of Board added, "It is the consensus of the Board that this vote is not a full endorsement of [X] as Executive Director. There are areas of improvement that continue to need to be addressed."

The bottom line: The ED was retained and we were out as employees. The meeting was adjourned at 10:40 p.m. Not one Board member said anything to us as they left for evening prayer in the chapel. We felt so alienated that we went straight to our room. We felt absolutely betrayed and crushed. Sheila cried most of night and had little if any sleep.

The next morning we continued to feel completely alienated. After a couple of items which Sheila and I opposed, I raised the issue of replacing the CM as the Board chairman because I believed he was hostile to me and Sheila. By consensus, the item was withdrawn from the agenda.

Not included in the Minutes was the conversation in which a Board member suggested some sort of six-figure financial separation package for us. I told him that we were not interested in such a package and that all we wanted was the payment of royalties on our works published by CCL. No one had a problem with that.

When Sheila was driving on the way home that afternoon, the lack of sleep had its effect and she dozed at the wheel and started to veer off the road. My yell woke her up, and she got us back on the road safely.

Lessons to Be Learned

The old proverb "old too soon but smart too late" certainly applies. I have no regrets about presenting our concerns to the rest of the Board in my 12-page 'Management Issues." It was, however, absolutely stupid to put our own jobs on the line. That was my first mistake. We thought it would have some influence in our favor, but we failed to see that it offered an opportunity for a certain member or members of the Board to get rid of us as employees without having to do something really messy such as directly firing us. We could have resigned at any time. It also presented the Board with a very unwelcome "him or us" dilemma that, in practice, militated against us. In the weeks after the meeting, some Board members made it clear that they did not regard their vote as wanting us out. We should have kept the issues entirely separate and left the consequences up to their imaginations. On the other hand, we felt we had to do something. We were part-time hourly employees, and thus we had to work a certain number of hours each week for health-insurance coverage. But we could not continue to work under the conditions of fear and whistleblower treatment. We were in a difficult situation.

Second, I should not have been so hasty in turning down a six-figure retirement package. The person who initiated the offer added something to the effect that they didn't want to be reading about this separation in the pages of *The Wanderer*, and I told him that we didn't want to see that sort of thing either. Whether they would have insisted on some sort of gag rule that would seek to prevent us even from speaking about the separation and writing our memoirs will never be known. I foolishly turned down the offer without any effort at a negotiated settlement. I told the Board I thought that such a package would set a bad precedent. We didn't think that was a wise use of donated funds; all we wanted was the payment of royalties on what was making money for CCL, some of which was already in a contract. Once again, I was thinking of what would be good for CCL instead of what would be good for us.

Third, in the months and weeks preceding the Board meeting, we had enjoyed a dialogue with a Board member who seemed to agree with us about the ED. When the tally showed that even that person voted against us, the knife was twisted. The lesson is this: unless a person is willing to give you a definite promise, preferably in writing, don't count on that person's support. Even then, don't be a hundred percent certain of a person's support, especially if that person will be involved in discussions that exclude you and has to make a decision without hearing your response.

Those are the evident mistakes we made. The Board members also made a big mistake. We had written that the retention of the Executive Director would be tantamount to an invitation to us to resign as employees. If some members of the Board did not want to invite us to resign, as they indicated later, they should have said so at the meeting. As it was, on Sunday night after the verdict was delivered, no one said anything, and the meeting was quickly adjourned.

At the Monday morning meeting, one of the members said that this meant that we were not to be involved at all in the day-to-day activities of the League. Later that was clarified to mean that we could still be involved with special projects, but by then it was too late because we had already officially resigned as employees.

Closing up

When we got home, there was an email from a long-time CCL Teaching Couple expressing their concern about the Thanksgiving fund appeal in which the ED had written about "a new approach for promoting NFP." I replied two days later, letting him know what happened. That same day we received an email from another Teaching Couple who wondered how the Board meeting went. They were concerned because the ED had emailed all the Teaching Couples asking for special prayers for the Board meeting, something that had not been done previously. I replied the next day as I had done with the first couple and sent copies of my replies to the Board members.

We wrote the ED and asked that our contractual royalties on *The Art of Natural Family Planning* be started effective November 4, the first day after the Board's decision that effectively asked for our resignations. We had been deferring the royalties as a favor to CCL, but now we needed the income. That request was granted.

The word was getting out. On November 13 we received an urgent appeal from another long-time teaching couple thanking us for what we had done and urging us not to leave the NFP apostolate.

On November 14, I called a BM. We had read in the Minutes that she had been appointed to deal with us regarding the publications we had authored. She said that she did not think the Board excluded us from day-to-day work.

I phoned again the next day to urge her to do what she could to prevent the hiring of new staff in the light of a bigger than usual first-quarter deficit and a big drop-off in teaching. She reiterated her opinion that the Board did not deny us regular work despite statements by one of the members that we were not to be involved in the day-to-day activities of the League but could still do special projects. I told her for the second or third time that denying us day-to-day work was effectively forcing us to resign because of health insurance. As hourly employees, in order to have health insurance coverage, we needed to have 20 hours of billable work each week. The only way for us to maintain our coverage was to resign and pick up Medicare and Archdiocesan "retiree" insurance coverage.

On Wednesday, November 21, on the advice of an attorney, Sheila and I hand delivered our one-sentence letters of resignation to the ED, effective November 30. He signed one copy each, noting he had received them. We wrote to the chairman and a BM about our letters of resignation, noting that the computer, fax and desk that Sheila had been using would soon be picked up by CCL personnel. The Board member replied, saying she hoped we would stay on the Board and that at times she felt like resigning, and at other times staying on to fight for some issues.

In the meantime, a dispute developed over what should be included in the Minutes as indicated in Chapter 13. There seemed to be a fear that telling what happened would be detrimental to the best interests of the League.

On Monday, November 25, the BM wrote us an encouraging message giving six reasons why she thought we should remain on the Board. I replied the next day with a full five-page letter that took me all day to write. It started this way:

> I thank you for your email letter of November 25. I appreciate your first paragraph in which you offer some reasons for Sheila and me staying on the Board. I would certainly agree that "the Board needs the perspective of the founders." As we see it, however, the Board actions of November 3-4 and the non-actions since then constitute a powerful statement that this perspective is regarded as no longer important or needed.
>
> Please consider what happened. The founders detailed their complaints in a 12-page document. We put our own jobs on the line. Could we have expressed our perspective any more clearly and forcefully? The result? The CM proposed to lock Sheila and me out of any relevant discussion. No one expressed any outrage. No one thought it improper to require us to spend two full days, including driving over 700 miles, to be present simply to approve the Minutes of the last meeting and to schedule the next meeting, and then to be locked out. The only way I could get us into the discussions at all was to go along with the idea of locking us out of the key discussion. The Board accepted, de facto, [a staffer's] intimidation of me, thus asking me to resign. The board accepted [the ED's] attacks on Sheila and decided to keep him at the expense of asking Sheila to resign.

The rest of December was spent on odds and ends. We ran up some legal bills by having our attorney involved with the negotiation of new contracts on our publications. But for the most part we were involved in household projects.

At the end of the month or early in January we received a three-page document dated 12/29/02 with this heading: "Kippley Recognition and Retention Committee Request for Five Resolutions." Given the language, I think it was drafted by the CCL attorney. It contained four resolutions dealing with health insurance, a consultancy contract, special projects, royalties, and lastly a non-compete and non-criticize clause. If the first four resolutions had been adopted and kept, the last clause would have been superfluous.

December 29th was a pleasant-weather Sunday, and we biked a couple of eight-mile rounds at Miami-Whitewater Park, We spend the last two days of the year finishing up a patch and paint project all around the house, a tennis clinic with Christopher on Monday, and New Year's Eve with friends. It was a pleasant end to a tumultuous year.

15. 2003: Our Last Year on the Board

The year 2003 started with Sheila writing a 12-page, double-spaced letter dealing with quality control issues. It was addressed to CCL Teachers, Promoters, and other friends, but it was never sent. It offered some commentary on the November Board meeting, but for the most part it described the quality issues that she had been observing and dealing with for more than four years. By the end of the month I had reworked it somewhat to put it over my signature, but the revised letter was also never sent. "Not sent" letters were not time wasted. They enabled us to clarify our own thoughts and also had the psychological effect of getting certain things off our minds by getting them onto paper.

Sheila and I continued to be serious about our responsibilities as Board members. We still hoped that we could do something to rectify what we thought was a big mistake by the Board at its November 2002 meeting. We participated in a telephone Board meeting on January 5 that was mostly about some additions to the Minutes of the meeting on November 3-4, 2002.

On January 30, the Board Chairman reminded me that if, as a Board member, I needed information from any CCL Staff members I was to funnel my requests through him. I replied with several requests and a criticism of the ED for spending too much time on an NFP chatroom. The CM replied on February 3 that he had noticed this too and had taken care of it. On February 6, a Board member proposed that the Board "do a serious and fair evaluation of [the ED's] performance as Executive Director."

On March 1, a former Board CM and I met with the CM at a restaurant in Columbus for three and a half hours. The most concrete result was that the CM asked me to bring to the next meeting a publishing contract we thought was fair, so we spent some more money on legal fees for our attorney to draw up something fair to all parties. A teleconference was scheduled for March 6, and that same day I sent several proposals to all Board members, some for discussion and resolution that day and some for a meeting around March 23. The first five proposals had to do with quality control; the next eight had to do with publications, royalties and personal freedom; the last had to do with CCL personnel. The last section had to do with my personal agenda, and I wrote with great naiveté as follows:

> Some of you have asked what I would like to do. As I have indicated to some of you, I would like to be reinstated as executive director. I would like to hold that office long enough to

complete a Policies and Procedures manual, the Employee Handbook, adequate job descriptions, perhaps some other systems, and do what I can to develop a uniformly good work ethic. I would like then to participate in the search for a new ED among CCL's experienced teachers and promoters. I would consider this a service to the League.

I would then like to retire peacefully and be appointed as Chairman of the Board in order to oversee the transition. With a knowledgeable, prudent ED and a hard-working work force to promote, I would also like to fill the roles that have been mentioned by [two Board members]—writing, speaking, friend raising, and fund raising. The two roles of Chairman of the Board and spokesman are not necessarily linked. Lastly, I would like to assist in the formation of a national NFP association that could serve to promote to the Church and State and the Media the common interests of all those who are working to sustain the teaching of *Humanae Vitae* and to provide the practical help of instruction in chaste NFP.

Late in March a BM wrote a six-page letter that amply expressed the conviction that the ED was seriously lacking in the leadership qualities needed for the position of ED in CCL.

What is clear to me today without reservation is that [the ED] needs to be replaced immediately. We need to put JFK in as chairman of the board and temporary CEO to protect the charisms and convictions of CCLI. We need to immediately codify policies and procedures with the founder couple leading the actions since they know the primary purpose for CCLI intimately. As one priest friend of ours remarked, just let the founders be a major part of the scene until they don't want to be—why do all these organizations feel they need to remove them before they need to be?

Since the document is undated, I don't know if it was sent before or after the teleconference meeting on March 23. Since it does not have any of the usual email trappings, it apparently was a Word document. Thus I don't know if it was sent to everyone on the Board or just to us for possible editing. About five months previously, the writer had voted to retain the ED. What caused the change of opinion? From the same document:

"In recent weeks I have been in a more difficult conversation with [the ED] (email of course). [Two Board members], I have not relished the difficulty of the discussions and emails; however, it has given me a clarity and definition that has been missing in the past."

At the March 23 teleconference, three important votes were taken. First, a Board member moved that the Board would have a special meeting on April 26 to evaluate formally the job performance of the ED. It passed unanimously.

The second item was a motion made by me that "all Candidate Teaching Couples shall submit at least two personal charts that they have interpreted. The last one of these shall be properly interpreted without correction by CCL Staffers," and it passed 5-2. It was an effort to remedy a weakness we saw in the current teacher-training process.

The third item was a motion that "the Couple to Couple League shall negotiate 'good faith' contracts on *The Art of Natural Family Planning, Breastfeeding and Natural Child Spacing* and *Sex and the Marriage Covenant* and the *Rosary* booklet if CCL continues to publish these last two works." Passed unanimously.

The day after the March 23 teleconference, the CM asked for the names of some couples we mentioned as examples of improper training and/or improper certification. I talked about this with a Board member and noted on my printout, "No reply sent per advice of [BM]." The Board was becoming divided.

April 26, 2003

The meeting to evaluate the performance of the ED started at 8:15 Saturday morning, April 26. A BM offered a generally supportive evaluation. Another BM offered a critical evaluation and concluded that he should be removed as the ED. Sheila offered criticism based on issues related to quality control. I offered examples that I thought showed a lack of sufficient prudence for that position. A BM moved the termination of the employment of the ED. After considerable discussion, it passed 5-2-1 (5 Yes votes; 2 No votes; 1 abstention). I was sitting near a BM and asked immediately after the vote, "Should we change that vote to demotion instead of termination?" and the answer was no. I should have made that an official motion, but such wishful thinking simply indicates the superiority of hindsight. This man had many good personality traits, and he might have made an excellent field representative. Two Board members (one the CM) resigned immediately from the Board and left the meeting. I moved that a BM fill out the term as chairman, and that passed. I was appointed as interim ED with no authority to hire or fire or make any new policy without Board approval. The meeting ended at 2:00 p.m., and new CM phoned the ED to convey the decision to terminate his employment.

The Aftermath

The new CM came to the CCL office Monday morning, April 28th, to explain things to the staff. She and I met with the patience-challenged staffer who had confronted me, and she handled that very well. He realized that such behavior would not be tolerated at all anymore, and our meeting ended with us shaking hands, even though there was no apology. A similar meeting with the person who had started the Alzheimer's rumor ended with an apology and a handshake. Two more staffers also apologized, one for trash-talk about us and the other for, in his own words, betrayal. The latter handed me a pile of paperwork to illustrate what he meant, but I never looked at it since I was interested only in the future, not the past.

We received ample criticism for our decision, and since I was back in as the ED, much of it was directed at me. To some of CCL's good teachers, promoters, and supporters, it appeared to be a completely unjustifiable power grab. Since they didn't know what happened behind the scenes, that was understandable, but even so, the language of some stretched the envelope, so to speak. It became obvious that a standard criticism was circulating via email. Not a few wrote that they didn't know any of the facts, but they did know that we were wrong. One accused us of appearing to be agents of Satan.

The problem was that the staff was completely unaware of the events that had led us to resign as employees the previous November or the events since then. At a staff meeting we discussed full disclosure, but when I started to talk about what would be disclosed, the patience-challenged staffer quickly sided with those in favor of no disclosure.

There was also some definite support from some staffers. One wrote me a message on May 2nd in which he noted:

> Just a word about [the former ED]. I enjoyed working for him, but I did not enjoy his management style. I found him to be a poor communicator. Did not start meetings or prayer on time. Spent too much time on the NFP list. Did not complete tasks that the field directors gave him.
>
> I think he made three major mistakes when he came on Board as E.D. 1. He argued with you about "SMC." 2. He did not allow you to continue to help make decisions about CCL. 3. He never fostered good working relationships with all of the board members. I will leave my comments to these thoughts. Thanks.

I suggested that we try to re-employ the former ED as a field representative, and several of us had a meeting with him on June 9. The CM ran our meeting in a style that seemed to be overly aggressive for an interview, and I later apologized to him that I didn't intervene on his behalf for a gentler approach. His decision to decline the offer was wise for a reason none of us contemplated at the time: the concept of regional field directors would be dropped in the near future.

When I met with the test corrector person who had been making too many mistakes, he asked why I didn't like him. I told him that he was both a likeable person and that I did like him, and I tried to make clear that criticisms of his work were not personal but were simply part of professional responsibility. We also discussed the time I had walked into his office and he had quickly hidden the book he was reading. I should have challenged him right then and there, but I had immediately resorted to my non-confrontation style of poor management. The result had been that he was left feeling guilty while I was left feeling angry that he was doing his personal reading on donors' time. When we had another meeting with the teacher training staff about a dispute among themselves and in which I explained that differences of opinion are normal and not necessarily bad, he said it was the best meeting they ever had.

June 8-9, 2003

The new Board had its first meeting on Sunday and Monday, the 8th and 9th of June 2003, starting at 2:10 p.m. A teacher from Louisiana came to express his concern. He would have liked to attend the meeting, but we met with him ahead of time to listen to his concerns and offer our reply.

The first item of new business was an allegation that I had acted improperly as a Board member. Specifically, it was alleged that after the events of the November 2002 meeting I had tried to get some donors to stop giving to CCL. Sheila replied that I had told her that in our conversations with others about the CCL conflict we had to be very careful not to suggest that they stop donating. She carried the day, and the allegation was dropped. I may have told one big donor, who had written a favorable letter mentioned earlier, that he might try to use his influence on our behalf, but I had not told him to stop donating. He had called me, and Sheila's recollection is that he asked us if he should stop contributing, and I had told him that would be up to him.

One Board member told Sheila and me that he had come to the meeting prepared to vote me off the Board. Sheila replied that if I was on a campaign to have CCL members stop their donations, there would be at least one email to prove it, and the Board member agreed.

The substance of the meeting was the budget, and quite a meeting it was. The business manager had been asked to work up various options. He favored the one in which I would have worked as the ED for a dollar-a-year (as I had volunteered to do) and which would grant the terms of a package agreement dealing with royalties and copyrights on the books we had written, but that one was not selected. Eventually we ended up with a balanced budget that was based on at least one misunderstanding, but it was not the unrealistic budget passed a year previously.

Significantly, the Board approved the payment of $101,995 of deferred royalties on *The Art of Natural Family Planning* to be paid over 10 years without interest. It also approved royalty contracts similar to that on *The Art of NFP* for *Breastfeeding and Natural Child Spacing, Birth Control and*

Christian Discipleship, The Seven Day Bible Rosary and both editions of *Marriage Is for Keeps*.

Looking at the possibility that the Kippleys might be completely separated from CCL, the Board also approved the transfer of all of these publications to another publisher of the authors' choice, and the payment of the deferred royalties over five years at the interest rate earned by the CCL investment account. Less than nine months later, most of these promises were abrogated.

Back at the office, we continued to deal with some unpleasant results of the April 26th decision to relieve an employee of his job as ED, but these were more among some of the staff members than from CCL teachers and promoters.

August 4, 2003

The next Board meeting was a three-hour teleconference on the evening of August 4th. There was more discussion about the copyright ownership of *The Art of Natural Family Planning*. The outcome was significant. The Board voted 3-0, with the Kippleys abstaining, that CCL keep the copyright and pay the deferred royalties of approximately $145,000 to the Kippleys over a ten-year period. In the agreement at the June 8-9 meeting, the amount was less because in that agreement the copyright would be owned by the Kippleys as it was in the previous editions. This was the second Board meeting at which the Board agreed to pay the deferred royalties. [Differing back royalty numbers on pages 173-175 are from the records. Sometimes the figures included the copyright value; sometimes only the back royalties.]

The other major issue was the process to be used to hire the new Executive Director. We already had one candidate whose qualifications looked good, but the Board felt in fairness to other teachers and promoters we needed to advertise the opening in the *In-House* going out in early August.

In late August, the Board hired CCL's new Executive Director. He started on Tuesday, September 2, the day after Labor Day. He held his first staff meeting that day and assured all of us that there would be no changes in the first month.

The misunderstandings and mistakes started immediately. Sheila had noticed earlier the weekly working plan of a staffer, and it appeared he really didn't have enough work to keep him busy. So on Wednesday Sheila told the ED that since the staffer apparently didn't have enough work and he was salaried while she was hourly, he might as well work on the Home Study files that she would normally have taken home. She loved that sort of work and was thinking only of CCL's financial situation. Unfortunately, the new ED misunderstood the reasons and thought she didn't like that work and thus didn't want to do it anymore. I volunteered to stay around the office for two or three months, and he said that two or three weeks would be fine. I understood that to mean he didn't want me around, so I would just await his call.

The call never came for either one of us. We had both put ourselves on an hourly basis, and that meant we didn't get paid unless we were given work to do. Thus the new ED effectively caused us to become unemployed as of September 3, his second day on the job.

It would later be said erroneously that we retired. We never retired from the League as employees after we came back to employment right after the Board meeting of April 26th. We believe that the proper way to describe what happened to us is to say that the ED disemployed us, that is, that he caused us to become unemployed. He didn't fire us and we didn't resign. To skip ahead, sometime after the Board meeting of December 7-8, we were discussing with the ED things that had happened, and he told us that sometime in October he had realized his mistake about the Home Study work but by then, he said, "it was too late."

September 7-8. 2003

Our next Board meeting was held on Sunday and Monday, the 7th and 8th of September, 2003, at the Holiday Inn on the Riverfront in Covington, just across the bridge from Cincinnati. After Old Business, the Chairman "brought up the matter of the back royalties and wondered whether this information should be released to the TCs [Teaching Couples]," but there was no vote at the end of the discussion. The rest of the first day was spent mostly on internal documents that were being revised.

On Monday, the CCL outside accountant was present along with two attorneys (I would have too much to do with them in the next two years) to discuss matters relevant to the deferred royalties and copyright of *The Art of Natural Family Planning*. At the end of the presentation and discussion, a BM moved that CCL purchase the copyright for *The Art of Natural Family Planning* for $43,138. The only two Board members who could vote voted in favor. The Chairman doesn't vote, and the Kippleys abstained. Then the BM moved that CCL agree to pay $101,195 in back royalties over a period of ten years to the Kippleys. Approved as before with the Kippleys abstaining. This was the third Board meeting that approved the payment of the deferred royalties.

There were also other votes dealing with *The Art* and other publications that were passed. Two staffers made presentations dealing with the Hispanic apostolate and the Diocesan Development Program.

November 5, 2003

The Board had another teleconference meeting the evening of Wednesday, November 5, 2003. The first item was to table everything that the Board had agreed to on September 8 regarding publications authored by Sheila and me until a later date when a firm proposal would be presented. Sheila and I obviously didn't understand what was going on, for the Minutes say the vote was unanimous.

The rest of the meeting had to do with two documents, "Charisms and Convictions" and the Constitution on which several of us had been spending lots of time.

The December agenda was listed: Budget, Spanish Development, Hour for the ED, and Christmas party. It would be changed significantly.

November 24, 2003

This teleconference meeting of the Board on November 24, 2003 dealt with a review of the Bylaws, but first it was noted that one person who had been invited to join the Board would probably not do so. We penciled into our Minutes, but it was not in the final version, that a CCL employee had visited him and apparently had discouraged him from joining the Board. One BM resigned because of increased personal responsibilities.

The rest of the meeting dealt tediously with fine tuning of the bylaws.

December 7-8, 2003

This was our last Board meeting. At least from our perspective, it was an important meeting. It was also an unusual meeting from the perspective of attendance. Three staff members had been invited, and four of the nine Board members were first-time participants. If CCL becomes a much stronger organization, some will undoubtedly think that was due to this meeting that led the founders to resign from the Board and get out of the way. If CCL fades or becomes just another "Catholic birth control" organization, that may also be attributed to this meeting and the loss of whatever perspectives the founders might have continued to contribute. Either way, from the perspective of anyone doing any historical work on this subject 10 or 25 or 50 years from now, what happened at this meeting is important. We do not have the Minutes, but we do have the chairman's printed PowerPoint presentation.

The chairman prepared well for this meeting, and on December 5th she sent me a copy of the 62-frame PowerPoint presentation she was going to make. It was clear that she wanted to get the business of publications, copyrights, and royalties settled, and that was good, but her approach initially shattered us. I was so upset that I called our attorney at his home. There was nothing he could do, but I needed someone to talk with. Of course we do not know her intentions, but it seemed to us that she was painting us as rip-off artists at this meeting that would be attended by four new Board members. She had invited us to respond, and so we did.

In my preparation, I asked CCL's administrative secretary to check the donation records. When I was in the office, I had access to them, but never checked them because I did not want to become prejudiced one way or the other. So I asked only for the total amount of the contributions ever donated by the second-floor non-secretarial staff as a group and the total ever donated by all the current members of the Board as a group.

The chairman took the Board through some of the history on the issue and included quotes from the CCL lawyer dealing with copyright law. They cited a case in which the plaintiff didn't have a written contract and still won his case; I never understood its relevance to our situation where we had a written contract. When litigation started some time later, that case was never mentioned. Some of her statements were simply erroneous, and others were accurate. She finished with her ideas about our future role in the League and offered a royalty proposal that we would have to sign that very day.

Since it seemed to me that the thrust of her presentation made it look as if we had been taking financial advantage of the League in an improper way, I thought the issue of royalties needed to be put into the context of our overall financial relationship to the League. I noted that it is standard in the publishing industry for authors to receive royalties, and I had set my initial salary low in the hopes that it would be offset somewhat by royalty income. I had hoped that eventually I could work as a dollar-a-year man and live just on royalties, but that remained a pipe dream. The chairman had asked why we had deferred royalties on *The Art of Natural Family Planning,* so I told the Board it was very simple. It seemed to us that the cash flow problems of the League were worse than our own. We assumed that we would be able to work for CCL as long as we were physically able, and the payment of the deferred royalties would supplement our Social Security income once we retired.

I explained that I had voluntarily reduced my salary from 1996 through June 2002, and I estimated that saved CCL $160,874.

I stated that the deferred royalties amounted to $145,133.

I noted that we had made direct cash gifts to CCL worth $38,015

I had donated my time from May through September 2003, and that saved CCL $16,500.

The total of those four amounts is $360,522. We were seeking the return only of the deferred royalties, and we were quite willing to have this sum paid to us over a five or ten year period.

Then I noted that the gifts of the non-secretarial staffers not including the ED because of his recent employment. Their ever-donated-total was $6,560.

The ever-donated-total for all the current Board members was $57,000.

If the total deferred royalties were paid, the balance of our charitable giving to the League would be $215,389. I asked if that sounded as if we were trying to rip off the League.

Another question that had been raised was this: why were we calling for the deferred royalties now? I explained that we had grown wary of the previous ED's attitude towards CCL's savings in the bank; the budget he had proposed was based on wishful thinking, and our assumption of continued employment was a false assumption.

Another important question was this: why did we want to own the copyright to the Fourth Edition of *The Art of Natural Family Planning* and continue to own the copyrights to *Sex and the Marriage Covenant* and *Breastfeeding and Natural Child Spacing*? I responded that the chairman had expressed her opinion that if we owned the copyright to *The Art*, we could do almost anything we wanted including non-publication, so if that is her idea of copyright ownership, we fear that she may think that CCL can do almost anything it pleases with the book including non-publication.

At the end of that portion of the meeting, we were asked to leave the meeting, so we went home. We returned the next morning, and the second day of the meetings started with a statement by the vice-Chairman. He said that the Board wanted to do three things.
 1. Protect CCL.
 2. Treat the founders with respect; they are an asset; the Board needs to define their role.
 3. And they hoped to resolve the issues out of court.

But there was not one word of apology for the treatment we had received the day before.

 1. On the surface it would appear they protected CCL very well. As evidenced by their 2007 version of the manual, anyone can see that CCL owns the copyright and the title of the book.
 However, the process of dealing with CCL on these issues has cost us over $75,000 in legal fees, and it would have been higher but one of our attorneys let us do some of the time-consuming work. I would not be at all surprised if CCL's total legal bill was much higher than ours. When the final agreement was reached, it was a settlement, meaning that neither party got all it had hoped for.
 2. Regarding treatment with respect, I suppose that depends on what you mean by respect.
 3. Yes, we did settle out of court, but there was lots of litigation. We had to sue CCL for breach of contract regarding *The Art of Natural Family Planning*. Then CCL countersued, alleging that Sheila's 2005 book, *Breastfeeding and Catholic Motherhood*, violated the non-compete clause of the publishing contract on *Breastfeeding and Natural Child Spacing*. Then there was mediation with a paid mediator, and later there was a less formal mediation with just the interested parties and their lawyers.

We worked cordially and constructively with the rest of the Board that day of December 8, 2003. The Board appointed a BM to negotiate the issues with us. At the end of the day, the Chairman told the Board that if John can work with me, I can certainly work with him, and then she gave me a hug. As she did so, I was asking myself, what kind of a Judas hug is this?

On December 9th we wrote very brief letters of resignation. The issue of quality control had not been addressed, and we did not want to be on the defending end of a lawsuit alleging improper teacher training. Not one person on the Board had offered a single word of support; there was not one word of thanks for the current bank balance that was its size largely because of our gifts to the organization. We were tired of fruitless fighting. Still hopeful of some sort of working relationship with CCL, I even wrote in my letter that this was a friendly departure, knowing that they would use that to reply to inquiries. Before taking a brief vacation, I emailed the Chairman as follows:

> Dear [CM],
> This is to inform you that Sheila and I hereby resign from the Board of Directors of the Couple to Couple League, International, Inc. effective the close of the meeting of the Board the afternoon of December 8, 2003.
> I want to assure the members of the Board that this is a friendly departure. When we return from our brief trip to California, we will submit hard copy letters of resignation.
> **I am giving you this immediate notice so that you can appoint someone else to author the Minutes while the details of the Board meeting are still fresh in the memories of all.** This immediate notice will also facilitate planning for the Convention, deletion of our names from all stationery, the convention ad, etc. I will be sending a check to CCL for the $41.00 that we committed to the program ad.
> We hope to have a long-time professional relationship with the League, but at this time we think it is best for us to resign from our permanent membership in the CCL Board of Directors.
> We look forward to the meeting with [a BM] at which time we hope to negotiate a cordial and professional settlement of matters entrusted to him for negotiation.
> Oremus pro invicem.
> Sincerely,
> Signed: John F. Kippley
> P.S. I am sending this letter by email so that you can address the Minutes situation immediately. I am also sending an email copy to [the ED], and I hope you or he will send our decision to the other members of the Board and inform the CCL staff.

The Chairman replied cordially on the same day, and she suggested a party in Cincinnati and at the convention for "celebrating your years with CCL." Under the circumstances, we didn't feel like celebrating. In addition, she asked CCL volunteers to write thank-you notes to us for our years of service. We asked the editor of *Family Foundations* not to publish them, and she agreed not to do so. However, I surmise she was overruled because some of them were published, thus giving the impression we had retired in the normal sense of that term.

Returning home from California, we wrote longer letters of resignation dated December 30th. One of the criticisms leveled at us on Pearl Harbor Day was that we didn't offer sufficient explanations for decisions we made, so we trust that after reading these letters the Board members understood the reasons very well. Sheila's is first, but I am not including her seven-page attachment "Problem Areas within CCL" that described those problems in some detail. Some or most of those problems have already been mentioned. In the two letters that follow, especially mine, there is a considerable amount of repetition of what has already been stated in this and previous chapters. The avoidance of names entailed the use of bracketed descriptions that sometimes becomes awkward. The arithmetic error on the next-to-last page of my letter was in the original.

December 30, 2003

Dear Board Members,

This is an explanation of my resignation from the CCL Board of Directors. The continuing problem of quality in teacher training and related areas is my first reason for resigning from the CCL Board. The attachment titled "Problem Areas within CCL" describes some of the problems. Please read those pages.

The second reason for my resignation is the treatment John and I have received from the staff and the lack of tangible support from the Board. During the [previous CM-ED] administration, the treatment I received from the ED, a Board member (now an ex-Board member), and several staff employees (one is now an ex-employee) caused me great pain over an extended period of time. I believe that John and I did nothing wrong before, during, or after the dismissal of [the ED]. After his dismissal, some CCL members wrote some very ugly ***public*** statements about us. To the best of my knowledge, not one staff employee or Board member wrote one public sentence in our defense.

On the Sunday of December 7, 2003, twelve people heard a very strong anti-Kippley presentation. We were described basically as crooks, ripping off CCL, and giving the appearances of "impropriety and wrongdoing." I believe that such charges are unjustified. However, twelve persons heard that presentation, but no one said anything in our defense. There was complete silence. Would you like to work with people who thought you were the person characterized by the Chairman on December 7th?

The [CM] reinforced the view that the staff is hostile toward us, but she only guesses why. We have not been given facts or reasons for their negativity.

I feel I can no longer represent CCL due to the lack of support from the staff and from the Board when we needed it the most. As an author for and as a founder of CCL, I can no longer be legally responsible for anything CCL, or a CCL representative, says, does, writes, counsels or teaches. Therefore I reaffirm my resignation offered on December 9th.

I thank you in advance for any work you do to improve the work of the League.

Sincerely,
Sheila Kippley

Subject: Reasons for Resignation from the CCL
Board of Directors
To: Members of the CCL Board of Directors
From: John F. Kippley
Date: December 30, 2003

Dear Members of the Board,

As indicated in the letter that we sent by email on December 9th to [the CM], Sheila and I resigned from the CCL Board of Directors effective the end of the Board meeting on December 8, 2003. This also includes our resignation from the Board of Directors of the Foundation for the Family.

As you will recall, one of the allegations that [the CM] lodged against us on December 7th was that we have failed to give adequate explanations for past decisions. We think her undocumented allegation is erroneous, but to relieve her of the opportunity to make a similar charge against us with regard to our resignations, we will explain the primary reasons for our decision. It is our hope that our explanations will stimulate the Board to take the actions necessary to improve some operations and to avoid some mistakes in the future.

First, however, I want to thank each one of you for your interest in the work of the Couple to Couple League, your willingness to serve on the CCL Board of Directors, and your desire to promote the work of the League as a vehicle for promoting and teaching marital chastity. I also want to apologize, especially to the new members, that the first meeting of the new Board was marked by the confrontation that occurred toward the end of business on December 7th. I had hoped that the issues that arose from the Board meeting of November 3rd and 4th, 2002 would be resolved prior to the gathering of the new Board, but quite obviously that did not happen. It is very possible that I will never see some of you again, so I want to thank you for your contributions to the work of the League, past, present, and future.

The number One reason for my resignation from the Board is the issue of quality control at CCL Headquarters. For three years [actually four] Sheila tried to improve the quality of teacher training, but what was the response? She received the classic whistle-blower treatment that made it psychologically impossible for her to continue. As a result, she put her job on the line in November 2002. [The CM's] Board chose to do nothing to improve the situation. The bottom line is that she was psychologically isolated and then effectively fired for repeatedly calling attention to the mistakes being made in teacher training and in the review of home study charts.

In this document, I use the phrase "effectively fired" in the disemployment of Sheila and myself. Please understand that in order to conserve funds for CCL, Sheila was never on salary, and I put myself on an hourly basis after I moved out of the office on April 1, 1999. Hourly employees need to put in 30 hours a week [actually 20] to qualify for fully employer-paid health insurance. That means that they need steady work. Denying work to a part-time worker is to effectively fire that person even if such denial of work does not come with a letter of termination. Taking us out of the day-to-day work of the League meant that we could no longer count on the required number of hours. Therefore we were effectively forced to resign in order to pick up the insurance coverage as retirees. This is a good illustration of the law of unintended consequences.

Sheila returned to work in May of 2003 after the previous Executive Director and previous chairman of the Board had left. She found that mistakes were still being made. After a month on the job, [the new ED] confirmed that this was still true. We explained at the Board meeting on December 7th that written directives are not sufficient because there have been mistakes in test correction even when the correct answers were already specified in writing.

After [the new ED] was hired, Sheila happened to see [a staffer's] weekly working plan. Based on her experience with test correction and file reviews, it appeared to her that he had scheduled less than a half-day's work each day. Therefore she turned over the home study reviews for [him] to do. She did this *only* out of consideration for CCL's finances. She figured that CCL ought not to be paying her, even at a lesser hourly rate, if the full-time salaried staff did not have enough to do. Unfortunately, [the ED] misunderstood this at first, and by the time he understood, [the CM] had imposed her theory that Board members could not be employees and vice versa. Therefore Sheila was excluded from test correction and final file reviews as well as from home study reviews, and thus she was effectively fired once again.

It appears that [the new ED] has taken upon himself the responsibility for the final file reviews. Is he good at this? Does he find the mistakes that Sheila would find? We do not know. He may be as good or better than Sheila, but we have no way of knowing. When I turned that job over to [a former ED in 1999], I kept reviewing his work for some time until I was satisfied that he was doing it well. I had wanted to bring [the new ED] in as a "management trainee," giving him some time in each major function at CCL Headquarters so that he would know how to do each job. That would have entailed my continuing to work as the volunteer interim ED. In that way Sheila and I could have viewed the quality of [the new ED's] work regarding teacher training. The chairman, however, would have none of that.

Problems in quality control are not limited to teacher training and home study chart reviews. On December 7th, [the CM] accused us of thinking that we are the only ones who know how to do things. While that is not true, the history of the Hispanic program demonstrates that Sheila *does* find mistakes that others do not. The teaching notes and slides for the basic program were written by [a Spanish staffer]. They were reviewed by [the ED] and three staffers, and it still contained mistakes. Some of the mistakes could easily lead to unintended pregnancies. You have in your notebook for the Board meeting December 7 and 8 the list of corrections that [this staffer] made, based on corrections made mostly by Sheila plus some more by [a BM]. [The staffer] listed five pages of corrections, and even then he didn't have it right. He still had a serious mistake dealing with postpartum infertility. The outcome of this is that those who made the mistakes and/or failed to see the mistakes are firmly entrenched in the current CCL bureaucracy while the person who found the mistakes was effectively fired. I submit that getting rid of the whistle-blower is a completely unsatisfactory solution to the quality-control problems at CCL Headquarters.

Nor are the problems with the Hispanic program limited to the above. The program, including both the Basic Manual and the Basic teaching notes, has nothing against immoral sexual activities during the fertile time. The value of describing all the Phase 1 rules but only one Phase 3 rule certainly needs further consideration. The production of a complete English translation of the [Spanish] Basic Manual should have been completed prior to its publication according to established Board policy but has yet to be accomplished.

There are still other problems with quality.
Under the leadership of [a former CM], the CCL Board decided to avoid relationships with multi-level marketing (MLM) organizations. He said he had seen a marriage break up over the financial aspects of an MLM. Now *Family Foundations* is

carrying advertising for them. I believe that CCL should suspend all such advertising pending a review and definition of advertising policy.

When I was in the office and was counseling someone regarding the possible use of a transdermal progesterone supplement, I carefully pointed out the abortifacient potential of an abrupt withdrawal of the supplement. In doing this I was simply drawing attention to what Dr. John Lee has pointed out in his writings. I considered the use of this hormonal supplement as the last thing that non-doctors could discuss after other supplements had been tried and found to offer no help. Now *Family Foundations* is carrying ads for progesterone supplements. Do we know if those running the ads are treating this supplement with equal caution regarding its abortifacient potential? Again, I believe that CCL should suspend all such ads pending a review and definition of advertising policy, including proof that such caution is being used. (I have been informed that the hormone supplement ads have been suspended following my complaint shortly before Christmas.)

I have heard remarks about a possible brochure dealing with Depo-Provera, remarks that make me wonder what the current CCL staff is saying about it. Does anybody know how to detect, with certainty, either breakthrough ovulation or the earliest return of fertility after the discontinuation of Depo? Can we warn about the abortifacient properties of this drug for its users and then infer that a woman coming off Depo can ignore its abortifacient potential? For the repentant person who is coming off Depo, can we rightly recommend anything except total abstinence until the standard off-the-pill rule applies? The reason I never wrote a brochure about Depo or made special mention of it in *The Art* is that I simply did not and do not know the answers to the questions I am asking. I am not aware of any statements by well-informed moral theologians about the difficult situation of stopping Depo and being chaste and respectful of human life. But if CCL's staffers are going to be recommending anything except total abstinence, then it is certainly the responsibility of the Board to make sure that what is said is morally sound.

As we indicated in our "Charisms and Convictions" document, we believe that quality is more important than quantity. When we were in charge of CCL, we believed that quality was our most important product. We think it is unfair to teachers, users, and donors to countenance a reduction in quality, especially in teacher training and teaching materials. We believe that failure to maintain high standards in teacher training will result in unplanned pregnancies and eventually in litigation. We believe that effectively firing the whistle-blower is no way to maintain high standards. Therefore, since our efforts at maintaining quality have thus far resulted only in the effective firing of Sheila the whistle-blower, I have resigned. I cannot be held responsible for anything that CCL and/or its agents say, do, write, counsel or teach under the present circumstances.

I am also concerned about the quality of CCL's leadership. No one can reasonably question [the CM's] dedication to the CCL apostolate and to her job as chairman, but the same could have been said about her predecessor. Dedication, however, is no guarantee of prudence. I think it is highly inappropriate for the chairman to impose her personal theory on employment as she has done. Employment theories and practices are matters for Board policy, and even when a new policy or practice is established, it is customary to apply a "grandfather" clause to current employees who would be adversely affected. Some of her proposals of December 7th, if accepted by the Board, would have led to litigation. I do not understand the prudence and wisdom of her portrayal of me in the light of the available facts. I think CCL would be well served by a three-person management committee that would have to review any proposed actions, including statements, of the chairman that could affect relationships with others, regardless of who the chairman is.

The Number Two reason for my resignation is the lack of support from other members of the Board and the staff.

In her efforts to maintain quality during 2002, Sheila felt no support from [the CM's] Board of Directors as a whole. At its meeting on November 3, 2002, when the Board voted to retain [the ED], it *de facto* voted to do nothing to support her and to invite her resignation as an employee.

[The CM's] Board was well informed that I felt intimidated by [a staffer] on June 14, 2002. As I indicated at the Board meeting on December 7, 2003, I feared to go to the office lest I have a disagreement with [him] that might lead to his taking physical action against me. It appeared to me that this was a grossly unjust situation. I proposed that [the CM's] Board terminate the employment of [this staffer] and laid my job on the line. At the meeting of November 3-4 2002, [the CM] said that he would not entertain a motion to fire [the staffer]. No one on the Board objected. On November 4, I was further told by a former chairman that I could have nothing to do with the day to day activities of the League. He later denied saying such a thing, and I believed him when he said later that he had no intention of firing me. But that's what I heard on November 4 and based my actions upon. By doing nothing to ensure that I could feel safe at the office, [the CM's] Board effectively fired me.

In early 2003, [a staffer] decided that I was suffering from early Alzheimer's disease or dementia, and he shared his thoughts with a priest. Fortunately, the priest was sufficiently shocked by [this staffer's] evaluation that he notified someone who notified us. What can you say about someone who is trying to exercise oversight that would be worse? If detraction that is untrue constitutes calumny, does not the promulgation of [the staffer's] opinion constitute calumny? In any normal business situation, such an allegation would be grounds for dismissal. [The staffer] later explained to me that he thought I was mentally off because he had heard of my fears of [the patience-challenged staffer] whom he described as sweet. He could have asked me for the reasons for my fears, but he chose not to do so. As part of the conditions for coming in as "interim executive director," I was not allowed to terminate the employment of anybody.

After the termination of the employment of [the ED], CCL received a number of letters of criticism. Sheila and I were sometimes the special objects of criticism. To the best of our knowledge, no one said or wrote one word to the critics to defend us. [The CM] drafted a complimentary letter in response to one teaching couple who had inferred that we were doing the work of the evil one, but she did not send it to them. I believe that other Board members could have said some things to defend us that would be well within the limits of the severance agreement.

At the Board meeting on December 7, 2003, Sheila and I were subjected to a negative commentary by the Chairman. As you heard, she portrayed me as a rip-off artist. She made much of the board decision in 1991 related to a ceiling on the royalties from sales of *The Art of Natural Family Planning*. She gave two interpretations but completely omitted a third interpretation, the only one that I believe is relevant in the context. I apologize for forgetting about the 1991 Board action, but it has not been applicable for the following reasons. By way of review, here is the wording of the relevant paragraph in the Minutes of November 11, 1991. "The CCL manual will be revised incorporating the Practical Application Booklet. Proposed publication goal: the 25th anniversary of *Humanae Vitae*—July 25, 1993. Royalties to the Kippleys will continue, but they will receive nothing above the average of the amount of royalties received in the last 5 years."

The phrase "received in the last 5 years" is ambiguous, but I think that the context supports my view that it meant the five years prior to the publication of the revised edition. The 1991 Board action was taken in the light of a future edition of *The Art of NFP* that would be larger and more expensive. The increased retail price would result in increased royalties. Thus the royalties on the new edition (the 4th edition) were to be limited to the average of the "last 5 years." In context, those would be the five years immediately prior to its publication in 1996. However, I began to donate royalties on the Third Edition starting in FY 1994 and deferred royalties on the 4th edition. Therefore we received no royalties from sales of the Fourth Edition until after the Board meeting of November 2002.

The 1991 Board action must also be understood in the light of CCL's situation at the time. For ten years starting in 1981, CCL had witnessed a steady decrease in the number of new couples taught. It averaged a negative 15% per year. In 1980, CCL had taught 9094 new couples; in FY 1991, CCL taught 3727 couples in classes and another 302 via the Home Study Course, only 44% of the 1980 total. We were thinking in terms of survival. Thus, Sheila and I gladly assented to the royalty cap despite the fact that we had originally set my salary low with the hopes that royalties would supplement our overall income. (My salary started at $18,500 in 1974 and finally reached $44,000 in 1995. There was never a "raise," just cost-of-living adjustments.)

The 1991 decision was made under the assumption that I would be receiving a full-time ED salary. That has not applied since January 1996 when I started my salary reductions.

Fortunately, the Chairman indicated to me prior to the December 7th meeting the general gist of her timeline, and I was thus able to offer some data in response. Using figures I obtained from CCL Headquarters, I was able to show at the Board meeting that Sheila and I have made the following charitable contributions to CCL: $38,015 in cash, $160,874 in reduced salary from January 1996 through June 2002, another donation of <u>office</u> time this past summer valued at $16,500 and $145,133 in deferred royalties. (This does not include the time I spent at Home in September and October helping [the CM] with the Constitution and bylaws.) Excluding the deferred royalties, the sum of our charitable contributions has been $215,389. Including the deferred royalties increases that amount to $360,522. Since the Board meeting, I have found that we also donated royalties from the third Edition in fiscal years 1994-1997 as follows: $2361 (27% of total) in FY 94; $5884 (74%) in FY 95; $7680 (100%) in FY 96, and $1096 (100%) in the first half of FY 97, for a total of $16,941 [$17,021]. This amount is <u>not</u> included in the $145,133 of deferred royalties we are claiming. To clarify, the deferral of royalties on *The Art* started on January 1, 1996. The $145,133 includes $1412 in royalties from the Third Edition sales after that date, but it does not include royalties donated prior to calendar 1996. Therefore the total of our charitable contributions to CCL is the $360,522 plus the $16,941 which equals $377,463. The Chairman had access to this same data in the same way that I did—phone calls to [two CCL staffers]. She chose not to use it and instead wrote in her slide presentation (slide on "Why the animosity from the Staff") that "There have been appearances of impropriety & wrongdoing." I was not aware of such appearances, but if that is the case, then it seems that the staff should be fully informed about the realities.

You heard the Chairman, and you heard my response. I am not saying that anyone agrees with the Chairman. What I am saying, however, is that there has not been a word of apology from the Chairman, nor did any other Board member offer a word of support prior to my making a few phone calls on December 27.

It belabors the obvious, but I will state it anyway. When your financial gifts (not counting the deferred royalties) to the organization amount to working for free for about five years, when you are then portrayed as a rip-off artist by the Chairman, and finally when you do not sense immediate support from other members of the Board, what basis remains for an organizational relationship? To be sure, Sheila and I could have retained our lifetime membership on the Board; we could have continued to come to Board meetings wondering how many thought evil of us; we could have continued to fight. But we are tired of the fighting of the last two years. It is emotionally draining, and it distracts us from the positive things we hope to accomplish.

A good number of the letters criticizing the firing of [the ED] emphasized that CCL has to be more than legal. It has to be fair and just. If only the writers had know[n] how well their comments resonated with this reader and writer. I believe that [the ED] was treated fairly and justly. I believe that he had demonstrated that he was not a sufficiently good manager.

Sheila and I believe that CCL is an apostolate that is spiritual at its core. We believe that CCL has been under God's special protection because we as an organization were promoting and teaching the divine truth about human love when few others were willing to do so. We believe that we were treated unjustly during the [previous CM and ED] administration, and we believe that we have been treated unjustly by the [new CM and new ED] administration. I believe that the unilateral effective termination of Sheila's work under this administration was unjust. I believe that the portrayal as rip-off artists that we received from the

Chairman at the Board meeting on December 7th was unjustified. The silence of the rest of the Board until I made some phone calls three weeks later was seriously troubling. Sheila and I agree with those other critics that CCL has to be more than merely legal, that it has to be just and fair. When we shared with a couple of friends the treatment we received at the November 2002 meeting, one of them wondered whether an organization that treats its founders in this way has much of a future. We think it's a good question.

    I regret that our exclusion from the day-to-day activities of the League excludes you from receiving the perspective of working-staff Board members regarding the quality of work taking place at CCL Headquarters. I am reminded of the story of a priest who was about to be consecrated a bishop. One of his fellow priests wished him good luck, telling him that he would no longer hear the unvarnished and unfiltered truth.

    Seven pages ought to satisfy the desire that we give reasons for our decisions to resign from the CCL Board of Directors. For those reasons, I reaffirm my December 8th resignation from the Board of Directors of the Couple to Couple League, International, Inc. and the Foundation for the Family, Inc. We are unhappy about resigning. We are at peace with our decision, but we are in protest at the conditions that have occasioned it.

Sincerely,
Signed: John F. Kippley, Co-founder

16. 2004: CCL Reneges on Its Agreements

During the first full week of January, 2004 I worked on changes for *Sex and the Marriage Covenant* to be published by Ignatius Press. On Saturday, January 10th, we met with the member of the CCL Board appointed to negotiate with us about contracts and royalties on our publications. Thinking it might be a long day, he had scheduled the last available return flight, but the day went so pleasantly that he was happy to be able to catch an earlier flight. He told us he could not guarantee that the Board would accept what we had worked up, but we had high hopes that the Board would see that it made good sense to pay royalties on our publications that were making good profits for the League.

Shortly after our meeting, I wrote [this BM] that CCL could make a 70% gross profit on sales of *The Art of Natural Family Planning* if Ignatius Press was the publisher. CCL would have to purchase only 2,000 copies at a time instead of investing in a much larger order as they had been doing. The idea did not resonate with the Board.

I continued to work on *Sex and the Marriage Covenant,* and on March 19th mailed the signed contract to Nellie Boldrick at Ignatius Press. Exactly a week later I sent her the printed and CD versions of the manuscript. The new edition of SMC was published 18 months later, after more than three years of being out of print.

March 17: the Board's Decision

On March 17, 2004 the CCL Board of Directors made its response to our negotiations and proposals. We received it on March 20, and I noted in my day book, "Received letter from [the CM] detailing Board position of no give and no compromise." Their position was that they were not bound by the written contract and that they could renege on the other agreements they had made with us. In the Random House *Compact Unabridged Dictionary* of 2,230 large pages, "renege" has two meanings. The first applies to card playing, and the second applies here: "to go back on one's word." That is precisely what the CCL Board was doing.

On Monday, March 22, we received an email from [the BM who visited us] in which he described the Board's position.

> This is a good Board. We have some immediate challenges, as you well know. These challenges need our full attention--

particularly with respect to securing CCL's financial picture, establishing quality control policies and procedures, and, in the end, making sure our teachers are teaching and teaching well.

The Board has a responsibility to make business decisions which protect the future of CCL. These business decisions are NOT being made in terms of being "pro-Kippley" or "anti-Kippley", but rather in terms of "what is best for CCL".

On a personal note, I firmly believe you have always had the best interests of CCL in mind when you directed the organization—and that you have made many personal sacrifices that put the organization ahead of your own interest. I don't for a minute doubt that. In fact, in my interactions with people, both within and outside CCL, I say precisely that. I have the utmost respect for both you and Sheila.

I replied on May 16th as follows:

While I appreciate your sentiments in the last paragraph, I have difficulties with the second paragraph above. I am not saying that I think that the Board is [trying] deliberately to hurt us, but I really have to question how you and the others conclude that what the Board has done is "best for CCL." In general, the [former CM] Board created conditions that made it impossible for us to work for CCL. It "constructively fired" us in November 2002. Then [the ED and CM] [disemployed] us in September 2003 for no cause other than [the CM's] personal desire to have no Board members working as employees. Then she wrote bylaws that weakened the control of the Board over teacher training and at the December Board meeting she created conditions that made it impossible for us to continue on the Board. Specifically:

As you know, the Board, through [CM's] letter of March 17, has refused to pay current royalties according to the contract and de facto has refused to make the most recent payment to us. As a lawyer, you certainly are aware that there is no better way to invite litigation than to unilaterally renounce a contract. How is it "best for CCL" to unilaterally decide not to pay its bills?

I had indicated that I would like CCL to return the publication rights to the Rosary booklet IF I could find another publisher. Instead, the Board unilaterally decided to cease publication and returned the publication rights, thus taking the publication out of print. Further, while having about 2,100 copies still in the warehouse, it took them out of its computerized inventory so that CCL cannot sell them. I went into the office prepared to pay for 20 copies and was told I could not BUY any because it was no longer on the inventory list. However, if I wanted to have all

2,100 copies, I could have them for FREE. I took 20 as a gift and told [the ED] to check with the Board before giving me the remainder. I didn't want to be accused of defrauding the organization. So who acted in CCL's best interests, the well-paid ED or me? I don't know who is running the show, but I suggest that whoever it is does not know how to run a small business. When publishing houses stop publishing a work, they normally do what they can to sell the remainder at a discount. Your staff was prepared either to trash or to give to one person an inventory with a face value of about $8,295. Since then I have had requests for multiple copies from two people. One from Hawaii had been told by the staff that they could not sell her the 30 she wanted to buy to distribute on a Mediterranean cruise and was told to call me in case I might have some extras. A call to [the ED] got that straightened out. Why is it "best for CCL" either to trash $8,295 of inventory or give it all to one person instead of trying to sell it? Why is it "best for CCL" to discontinue the publication of the Rosary booklet? It was not a moneymaker but it paid for itself. It was a good, low-cost premium, and some CCL people dearly love it. Why was it best for CCL to simply make it unavailable instead of giving me adequate time to look for another publisher?

On December 8, 2003, [the vice-Chairman] said that the Board regarded us as assets, wanted to treat us with respect, and wanted to settle our differences out of court. Aside from your visit on January 10-11 and your letter of March 22, we have seen nothing to indicate any of these. I will not comment further on the letter of March 17 or the [CCL attorney's] letter of May 6, 2004, a letter approved, I am sure, by someone on the Board. I would only ask what in those letters represents regarding us as assets, treating us with respect, or making any real effort to settle our differences out of court. If it was to be in CCL's best interests to treat us as [the vice-CM] had said, why is it best for CCL to act in the contrary way that we have experienced?

I'm not ready to accuse anyone of deliberate ill will, but I think the Board members need to re-evaluate what is best for CCL. Perhaps they would do better to ask, "Is this proposed action fair?" Or "Is this action something that we could point to with pride in a fund appeal letter?" In the Annual Report, is the ED prepared to explain paying $200 to $500 per hour for its three lawyers to lead the effort to renege on a good faith, valid publishing contract?

In your letter above, you mentioned "securing CCL's financial picture." Before you came on the Board, I had volunteered to balance the books on my back. That is, I had volunteered to work as the full-time ED for fiscal 2004 for the $1.00 a year or whatever minimum is required to be an employee. [The new ED] had initially sought volunteer work. He could have been hired as my assistant with right of succession for $30,000 per year to supplement his military retirement, and he would have had a full year of excellent training in all of CCL's operations including teacher training and the work of the regional field representatives. But [the CM] insisted on getting rid of the Kippleys and hiring [the new ED] at full-time, full salary. If the response to the last fund appeal was disappointing, it should not be a surprise. [The ED's] appeal letter was well intentioned but, in my opinion, quite inadequate. If there had been a commitment on the part of the Board to work out the publication and royalties matters through negotiation, both CCL and ourselves would have better bank accounts, but the Chairman has led the way on the path of confrontation. What has been "best for CCL" in all of this? If the Board is really interested in doing what is best for CCL, it will remove [the CM] and select someone who is committed to the principles enunciated by [the vice-Chairman] the morning of December 8th.

When the Board was being criticized for firing [the former ED], a prevailing theme was that because CCL is a spiritually based organization it has to be more than just legal—it has to be fair and just. Those statements resonated with Sheila and myself because we thought and continue to think that we were the ones who were being dealt with unfairly and unjustly. I think we treated [the ED] justly. He was given specifics and ample opportunity to change. On the other hand, I don't think the treatment we have received since September 3 has been fair, just, prudent, or even legal.

That's all for now. I know you wrote me in good faith. I hope that you will be able to bring about the realization among the majority of the Board members that it is best for CCL to fulfill its contractual obligations and to abandon the path of confrontation.

Sincerely,

John F. Kippley

To the best of my knowledge, the only good that letter did was to relieve a bit of the pressure Sheila and I were feeling at the time.

Larry and Isabelle Kane arrived early in the afternoon of March 25, and their visit was a welcome respite from the growing conflict. Larry had headed the Human Life Foundation established by the U.S. bishops right after *Humanae Vitae,* and now he was involved with archiving NFP materials. Kane's work is more fully described in Chapter 9. At 7:00 Mass the next morning, I introduced them to a CCL staffer, and the Kanes left about nine that morning for their home in Virginia.

By this time, our first attorney had put us in touch with a copyright attorney, and by this time he had drafted a "demand" letter which we reviewed. It certainly looked convincing to us the morning of March 26th, but with hindsight it might have been better if he had met CCL's attorney or attorneys for lunch and just asked them informally, "What are you guys trying to do? What do you really want?" That's what our litigation attorney did some five years later, and that approach had some success. But in March 2004 perhaps both parties were too convinced of their own case to negotiate.

Sheila and I took a three week vacation starting Tuesday, April 20th and returning Monday May 10th. On the way to the Outer Banks we toured the Biltmore Estate near Ashville, SC. We found it disappointing after all the hype. The area around Kitty Hawk was windy, of course. That's what drew the Wright brothers here to test their first airplane. We found the wet sand to be too difficult for bike riding even with our fat tires, but we enjoyed watching adults learn to fly with hang gliders. On the 25th we arrived at our daughter's home in the greater New York City area and spent the next couple days there, helping with the flower planting on Tuesday, April 27th, our 41st anniversary. We continued up the coast and on Thursday we biked around Block Island for our best biking of the trip. Got to Cape Cod the next day where we did some more biking over several days. On Tuesday we took a bus tour of Martha's Vineyard which we found disappointing. We really weren't interested in learning what big-name star lived here or there. On Wednesday we arrived at Mary's in the greater Boston area. We got a call from our copyright attorney who told us that he had received a total denial of the facts he had cited in his demand letter.

On May 11 we read the May 6th 14-page document from CCL's copyright attorneys. We thought that page 13 maybe illustrated half an olive branch. Our attorney responded on June 3 and cited a court case against their withholding the royalties due on current sales. On June 11, I appealed to [a BM], citing our past financial help to CCL and appealing for justice including the payment of the royalties that were legally due us. On the 17th [the BM] replied that the Board was not trying to hurt us. That was comforting. I wonder what more they would have done if they were actually trying to do so. By mid-June our attorney received another reply from CCL's copyright attorney, and our attorney thought it was infuriating. On the 24th he wrote their attorney asking for action regarding things in the letters of May 6th and June 3rd.

The expensive back and forth between the attorneys continued during the summer with sometimes lengthy intervals between responses. In mid-July I talked with CCL's vice-Chairman but found nothing to encourage us. On

July 30, their lawyer offered a settlement that included a non-compete clause that was absolutely unacceptable.

On August 4th, our attorney filed our copyright claims, and on the 6th of August I made what I thought was a generous counter-offer to the Board of Directors. They had made it clear that their holding the copyright to the Fourth Edition was non-negotiable. We had made it clear that our freedom to speak and write was non-negotiable. So in this letter we offered to concede regarding the Fourth Edition. We made a big concession on some money issues. But we reaffirmed that our freedom was non-negotiable. I also told them that our attorney had told us that he did not believe further efforts for a settlement are likely to be productive, but he did not object to our making one last effort to communicate directly with the Board. The CCL folks didn't like dealing with me directly, so our lawyer told them to regard it as coming from him.

On August 25th I reminded the Chairman that she had previously told me to tell her to resign if I thought she wasn't doing a good job, and so I complied with her request. On August 27th we sent a letter to a number of our CCL contacts and friends explaining what had been happening between the new management and ourselves. This was in response to what [the CM] had said at the 2004 CCL Convention. There, in her talk, she spoke thusly about us:

> John and Sheila Kippley have fully retired from CCL and the CCL Board of Directors on December 9, 2003. John and Sheila have decided that this time is best for them. I miss them but it was time for them to go. I didn't push them out. I want you to know that. They did leave on their own. They decided it was their time.

On September 7th, I wrote Bishop Victor Galeone, the Episcopal Moderator for Natural Family Planning on the USCCB Pro-Life Activities Committee—that is, the U.S. Bishops' man for NFP. I asked him to intervene to try to persuade CCL to enter a formal and binding conciliation process. On September 16th he wrote to the CCL Chairman and encouraged both sides to consider "reconciliation through an independent, mutually agreed upon arbitration process." He told me later that on November 20th he still had not received a reply. What he finally received, he told us, was just a reiteration of the CCL position.

On September 9th, one of the CCL copyright attorneys replied to my proposal of August 6th with a 13-point counterproposal that wanted us to surrender our rights to the first three editions of *The Art of Natural Family Planning*, and it also included a non-compete clause and a level of confidentiality that we considered a gag rule. The CCL attorney also made it clear that CCL did not appreciate our "missive" of August 27th informing other members of the CCL community about the recent events.

On October 1, I wrote the Board a letter and explained why we could not accept their 13-point proposal, and I repeated that while we had conceded on their non-negotiable, they were ignoring ours. I told them we regarded the endless back-and-forth as non-productive and expensive. I also told them that in the light of spiritual considerations we were not planning to start legal proceedings at this time. We called for negotiation within the parameters of both of our non-negotiables or for some sort of conciliation process. [The CCL attorney] replied to that on October 21st, asking for some clarifications, and I answered her on the 29th.

Now I need to interrupt this fascinating historical record with something having nothing to do with our disputes with CCL concerning publications and finances. It would be a dispute of a different nature.

New Directions

At the CCL Convention in June 2004, it appeared that CCL was moving away from the directions we had set. There was talk about change, and soon some of the changes were put in place. By late summer the Board announced that it would no longer support its teachers who taught in languages other than English and Spanish. Under our leadership, CCL had provided financial, technical, and moral support for teachers in the Czech Republic and Slovakia, and we had also provided non-financial support for teachers in Belgium and Poland. All of that was now being dropped by CCL's new management. They were also cutting the job of the Regional Field Representative (RFD) working in Louisiana, the only RFD not working in Cincinnati.

On October 17, we wrote the CCL Board about the history of CCL, its international outreach, and its RFDs. We couldn't save the job of the RFD, but we helped to persuade the CCL Board to continue its financial support to the two full-time CCL representatives in the Czech Republic and Slovakia through June 2005, at which time the gentleman in the Czech Republic would start receiving European social security income. The Slovakian gentleman and his wife were much younger and still had five children to raise and support.

We detected hints from the 2004 convention that CCL might be making changes that were contrary to the classic content of the Triple Strand approach we had brought to the founding of the League, and these changes would be made clear at the CCL convention in 2006. Dialogue with CCL was getting nowhere, so we decided that the only way we could ensure that the classic content was maintained would be to start another organization.

Natural Family Planning International, Inc.

We filed articles of incorporation for NFP International in November, 2004 as a way to keep alive the teaching that had been so successful since 1971 and also as a way to raise funds to maintain the CCL operation in Slovakia.

Thanks to the new CCL management, Sheila and I now had more than enough work to keep us busy full time, but a combination of the CCL conflict, the need for other activities to keep our minds off the conflict, and age-related reduced energy limited our useful hours to 20 to 30 hours of volunteer work per week for the most part.

The founding of NFP International was not done out of spite. When we resigned temporarily in November 2002, we kept working for CCL as volunteer Board members. When we resigned from the Board in December 2003, we had absolutely no intention of founding another organization. Even after the Board decision on March 17, 2004 to violate the written contract on *The Art of Natural Family Planning* and to renege on their agreements on the other publications, we did not plan to start another organization. It was only after CCL started to proclaim the age of change and then stopped its support of the two European programs that we decided that we had to start a new organization to maintain the traditional program. The internet now made it possible to communicate around the world without any paid staff.

Continued Conflict

I replied on October 29th to the letter of October 21st from CCL's copyright counsel. In her previous letter of September 9th, [a CCL attorney] had written that our "missive" to members of the CCL community was an attempt to "malign" the work of the new CCL management. Since I thought that was inappropriate terminology, I replied that we had simply described what had happened and that Board must be proud of what it has done since there had not been the slightest hint of apology or regret. So how could we "malign" by describing what the Board is proud of? Since [the CCL attorney] wanted clarification about where we stood on CCL's 13 points, I told her we fully agreed with only two of them. I also questioned whether she was authorized to do anything substantive or merely to keep us going around in expensive circles.

On November 12th and 13th, we finished and sent an email message to a wider group that included CCL Teachers and Promoters as well as our own special contacts. In a message on November 19th to Bishop Galeone, I wrote as follows about the response to it:

> Many found it shocking. Some now regard us agents of the devil; others seemed to think we were saints; others saw CCL as God's organization and beyond criticism. Etc. The enjoyable part of the week was simply hearing from people and being able to respond to their questions. We have been in isolation for almost a year, so the communication was satisfying.

The CCL staff responded on November 17th by sending to their Teachers and Promoters a brief letter of support for the Board. On that same day the

Board revised its decision regarding the Czech Republic and Slovakia. It would make a grant of $6,000 each to the bishops of the Czech Republic and Slovakia, saying they could use it to support the work of the CCL representatives if they wished. Fortunately, they did.

We were starting to hear reports that we had started a lawsuit, so on November 23, 2004 I wrote CCL's Executive Director:

> That is simply false. To consider litigation is far from starting it. We did not even seriously consider litigation until we received [the Chairman's] letter of March 17, 2004 that effectively repudiated the negotiations that had started in January 2004. We have never filed a lawsuit against CCL. We wrote as follows to the Board in my letter dated October 1, 2004, almost eight weeks ago.

I then quoted from the liturgical readings for Tuesday, September 7, and continued to quote from my letter to the Board:

> In the light of the above instruction [from liturgical readings on September 7th and others] Sheila and I have decided not to pursue litigation at this time. If we won [in a Federal Court copyright case], it would be almost as bad as if we lost. It would be a Pyrrhic victory because the cost to CCL would be disastrous, and it is certainly not our intention to harm this organized effort to promote marital chastity through the vehicle of NFP instruction. We have attempted to negotiate one-to-one, to no avail. We have communicated to just a few handfuls of others, and we know that some have written you, so far to no avail. We think that telling the church means telling anyone who is interested. We have thus far definitely limited our efforts to 'tell the Church,' but we are beginning to wonder if the Board as a whole wants us to expand our efforts in the public forum.

I also reminded the ED that as of November 20th Bishop Galeone had not received a reply to his letter of September 16th:

> I suspect that most bishops are not accustomed to waiting for more than two months for a substantive reply or even for an acknowledgement, but then, most bishops are not accustomed to dealing with the current CCL hierarchy.

On November 23rd, CCL's attorneys hand-delivered to our attorney a six-page letter from the Chairman responding to my letter of October 29th. It did not advance the resolution of the issues. On November 24th CCL's litigation attorney notified our attorney that CCL would send our resignation letters to inquirers. Those, of course, would be the short and conciliatory ones of

December 9th, not those of the end of December that told the reasons for our resignations from the Board.

On December 3rd I replied to the Chairman's letter of November 23 with a short one-pager. I told her that under the present circumstances it wouldn't be appropriate to respond point by point, but that we simply could not sign a settlement that would silence us. "Since we cannot sign such an agreement, negotiations that do not address this key issue except to say 'silence' are simply a costly exercise in letter writing."

That same day I replied to the ED and the staff regarding the ED's email of November 23rd that this whole situation is a distraction for the staff. I reminded them that one of the first management actions the ED took was to disemploy us shortly after he started his job in September the year before. I reminded the staffers of their own involvement.

> When [the current CM] first became chairman, she started to hear from you. She told us that she was getting unspecified negativity towards Sheila and me. Apparently she took your negativity very seriously. Further, you have actively involved yourselves in the current dispute by writing a letter to the Teachers and Promoters. I cannot understand why the CCL titular leadership wants the dispute increasingly aired in public, but it is to that public dispute that you have made your own contribution so you need to be informed.

I proceeded to let them know about a number of things that I suspect were only known to a very few, including what happened at the meeting on Pearl Harbor Day 2003 and our response. I noted that [the CM] was now accusing us of "going public," apparently forgetting that we were simply responding to her public statements that Sheila and I had retired and that she didn't push us out—her message at the CCL Convention that summer. As I reviewed it for this writing, I must say it was a pretty good review of the conflict in a brief three-and-a-half-page letter. It was certainly not sympathetic to their November 17 complaints that "the on-going tensions with John and Sheila have at times been very detrimental to our work environment."

The year closed with a letter from CCL's litigation attorney accusing us of libel. It was a great example of stating as facts what are not facts and thus inviting further response from the accused.

Despite all of this, the year 2004 had a number of highlights. We had enjoyed good health. We had formed a new NFP organization, and at the end of the year we were applying for non-profit status. We had experienced a pleasant three-week vacation in the spring that included visits with two of our daughters and their families. So there were lots of good things to compensate for the pain of our dealings with CCL.

17. Books, Health and Litigation

April 2005 opened with the news that the condition of Pope John Paul II was terminal, and on April 2nd he went to his eternal reward at 9:37 p.m. Rome time. Pope Benedict XVI was elected on Tuesday, April 19th.

Pope John Paul II was elected to the papacy on October 16, 1978, and he was formally installed on October 22, ten years and almost three months after the promulgation of *Humanae Vitae*. While Pope Paul VI, the author of *Humanae Vitae,* had apparently been so shocked by the rebellion against its teaching that he said little or nothing about it for the next ten years, Pope John Paul II made its reaffirmation the prime focus of his papacy for the next ten years. For a somewhat complete documentation of his tireless advocacy of marital chastity, see my book, *Sex and the Marriage Covenant,* described later in this chapter. He came to the United States on October 1, 1979, visiting Boston, Chicago, Des Moines, the District of Columbia, New York, and Philadelphia. I might have tried to attend his Des Moines farm-field celebration of Mass, but Sheila was due to deliver very soon. As it happened, our fifth child was born on October 12—Columbus Day and five days after the Pope had celebrated Mass on the Washington Mall. (It was our first home birth, a most gratifying experience for Sheila and me.) I wonder how many other Catholic boys born that day were named Christopher John Paul.

I was privileged to meet Pope John Paul II on two different occasions, both in the Vatican. The first time was in November, 1981, six months after he had been shot and just a few days before the publication of *Familiaris Consortio.* I had gone to Rome, as other NFP leaders had done, to let the Curia know about our organization and work in NFP. I also distributed copies of *Birth Control and the Marriage Covenant* around the Vatican. I gave one to Msgr. Carlo Caffara, President of the Institute for Studies of Marriage and the Family of the Pontifical Lateran University, and enjoyed a good conversation with him. He seemed receptive to the concept that the marriage act ought to be a renewal of the marriage covenant. I was granted a front row seat at the Pope's Wednesday audience in the Paul VI auditorium. After the formal part of the talk and ceremonies, the Pope personally greeted each of the first-row attendees, so that gave me an opportunity to hand him a copy of *Birth Control and the Marriage Covenant.*

My second handshake meeting with the Pope occurred in October 1986, and this time the audience was in front of St. Peter's Basilica. I was returning from a visit to England, Ireland, Belgium, the Netherlands, and a pro-life conference in Poland, and I recall that it was almost winter-like in Poland but the sun was very hot in Rome. As I looked closely at a photo of this meeting, it's a bit embarrassing as it appears I was giving the Pope a mini-lecture. In my hands to give to the Pope were *Birth Control and Christian Discipleship* which was a booklet for Protestants and Catholics who think like Protestants, a reprint of "A Covenant Theology of Sex" which was an article I had written for *Homiletic and Pastoral Review* in 1983, the latest edition of *The Art of Natural Family Planning*, and some other materials I can't identify some 24 years later. On top of all that was a yellow pad with my notes. Well, at least I was a believer with the Pope, and that wasn't the case with all the front-row attendees. While waiting for the ceremonies to start, I chatted with a Latin American dignitary who informed me that his wife was in charge of birth control in their country, but it was not a form of natural family planning. I was happy to exchange business cards but was hardly surprised never to hear from her.

Breastfeeding and Catholic Motherhood

As indicated previously, Sheila and I had written two books in the late Sixties that were the basis for our founding the Couple to Couple League. Whatever we may have thought about the completeness of those books when they were first published, continuing experience led us to write more in the same two areas. Sheila wanted to go beyond health and baby spacing, and I wanted to address additional issues in my book on sexual morality. These efforts were not made easier by our relationship with the League.

Sheila had given talks on breastfeeding at retreats and religious conferences in the past and wanted to write a book on the spiritual aspects of breastfeeding to give support to Catholic mothers. After the separation from CCL she had more time and was ready to write. Since she was still hurting from CCL's actions, however, and because she was hoping for a publisher with a wider distribution network, she asked Sophia Institute Press if they would be interested in such a book. Soon the book was in the making through Sophia.

In promoting the book, the Sophia editor wanted to associate her with the Couple to Couple League, but Sheila asked that CCL not be mentioned in the short biography. Her editor insisted that CCL was part of Sheila's history and wanted to include this organization, so Sheila sent some public information to her editor concerning the conflict with CCL so that the editor would appreciate where she was coming from. Duly informed, the editor agreed with Sheila's request. *Breastfeeding and Catholic Motherhood* was published in March of 2005. As of this writing, CCL has never promoted or sold it.

As indicated later in this chapter, in November 2005 we felt obliged to sue CCL for breach of contract because it was no longer paying us the contractual royalties on the 4th edition of *The Art of Natural Family Planning*. About two months later, February 2006, CCL countersued saying in one part of their lawsuit that *Breastfeeding and Catholic Motherhood* was "substantially similar to the edition of the breastfeeding book," referring to *Breastfeeding and Natural Child Spacing*, authored by Sheila since 1969. It was originally self-published, followed by a Harper & Row hardcover edition, then a Viking-Penguin paperback edition, and was later published by CCL. The lawsuits were, of course, public knowledge.

Sheila had checked with our copyright attorney in writing *Breastfeeding and Catholic Motherhood* and forwarded his counsel to Sophia. She did this to avoid any legal action from CCL, but obviously her efforts did not work. Sheila often referred to *Breastfeeding and Natural Child Spacing* in the Sophia book to increase, not decrease, the sales of her other book published by CCL. The only similarity in *Breastfeeding and Catholic Motherhood* was the use of the Seven Standards in one chapter because she had to show that God made women in such a way that frequent breastfeeding spaces babies. Those Seven Standards can be used by anyone and had been used by us since the 1970s. Like the Lactational Amenorrhea Method, the Seven Standards provide a method anyone can use or teach.

The Sophia book was a completely different book and in no way competed with Sheila's CCL-published book, *Breastfeeding and Natural Child Spacing*. The founder of the Catholic Nursing Mothers League, who is also a lawyer, was ready to come to Cincinnati to testify to the difference between the two books if we needed her. As she wrote:

> I am extremely surprised to hear that *Breastfeeding and Catholic Motherhood* is involved in CCL's countersuit. It is a substantially different book from *Breastfeeding and Natural Child Spacing*. BF&NCS is still offered by La Leche League, a non-sectarian organization, and is on its approved list because of its essentially secular approach. LLL would likely not carry—and might not even approve—*BF&CM* because it is specifically sectarian. It is addressed to CATHOLIC mothers. This really sounds like a legal strategy of "throw everything in including the kitchen sink" (email, February 10, 2006).

A well-known CCL author wrote a beautiful review of *Breastfeeding and Catholic Motherhood*, but the CCL Board of Directors voted not to promote the book in any way and would not accept the review for CCL's bi-monthly magazine, *Family Foundations* (email September 21, 2005). I am convinced that many CCL members would have benefited from reading Sheila's Catholic book.

Sex and the Marriage Covenant: A Basis for Morality

The first edition of this book was titled *Covenant, Christ and Contraception*. Published by Alba House in the spring of 1970, it was the book partially responsible for the start of CCL along with Sheila's book, *Breastfeeding and Natural Child Spacing*. In 1976, the Liturgical Press reprinted it with the title of my choice, *Birth Control and the Marriage Covenant*. In 1991 the Couple to Couple League published an expanded edition with a new title, *Sex and the Marriage Covenant: A Basis for Morality*. In the late 1990s, I prepared a slightly revised edition, but some of the staff members objected to the section on marital rape, thus leading to an extended out-of-print status. This was the book whose copyright had always been registered in my name but which CCL transferred to itself without my knowledge. When I learned of this at a Board meeting in mid-2003, I was so upset that I thought it prudent to leave the room for a bit. One employee who was involved with the copyright transfer of *Sex and the Marriage* Covenant to CCL later apologized, telling me he felt he had betrayed me. He was correct, but it was more than just saying something snide behind my back. The "transfer" of the copyright from the author—me—to the publisher—CCL—completely without my permission constituted the theft of the copyright, something so clearly unlawful that I still wonder why they did it. Certainly they had to realize that when I found out they would either have to reverse their action or find themselves in court. But that was management at the time. In addition, [the ED] contacted the Archdiocese of Cincinnati and had the Imprimatur lifted from the book.

Without going into the details, I eventually regained my copyright of the book and was allowed to seek another publisher. I also regained the *Imprimatur* for my book and was very pleased with the comments by the priest who did the ecclesiastical review. On February 5, 2005, Rev. Robert A. Stricker granted the *Nihil Obstat* (No Objections) to *Sex and the Marriage Covenant* saying:

> John F. Kippley in his manuscript "Sex and the Marriage Covenant" presents a very thorough theology of sexuality. Though he sometimes is at odds with the conclusion of certain reputable theologians, whose opinions have been accepted as valid probable opinions, I found nothing in this manuscript which contradicts the formal magisterial statements on sexual morality from the declarations by Popes Pius XI, Pius XII, Paul VI, John XXIII, and John Paul II, nor in documents issued by the United States Conference of Bishops, nor in the allocutions of Pope John Paul II. All of the author's conclusions flow logically from the above mentioned statements. So until such a time that Rome should render a negative opinion concerning any of the conclusions in "Sex and the Marriage Covenant," I believe they

express a probable theological opinion, if not a probabilior opinion. [Probabilior means "more probable. jfk]

This is the book, as *Birth Control and the Marriage Covenant,* that helped Kimberly and Scott Hahn to accept Catholic teaching against birth control when they were still Protestants. Ignatius Press published the revised version in September 2005. We are forever grateful to Fr. Joseph Fessio, SJ, for his interest in this book that had been out of print for more than three years.

A Matter of the Heart

Starting in the summer of 1999, Sheila and I had decided to do some regular bicycle riding as our form of exercise as a couple. I couldn't keep up with her on the tennis court, and Sheila wanted no part of golf. I think she would do well at golf because she has natural athletic ability, but it holds no attraction for her. So we compromised on bicycle riding, joined the Cincinnati Cycle Club, and went on our first evening group-ride—the Thursday night Tomb ride, so named because it starts near the tomb of former President William Henry Harrison whose chief claim to fame is that he delivered the longest inaugural speech on record. Unfortunately, it was cold and rainy on that March 4, 1841, and he caught a cold that eventually caused his death a month later.

The Tomb ride offered three options at the time. One route is essentially level since it follows the Ohio River west and then turns north along the Great Miami for a total of about ten miles to a resting area and then retraces itself to the starting point. The second route is three miles shorter and returns from the resting point via Dugan's Gap and Cliff Road. The Gap is a granny-gear (at least for us) uphill grind to Cliff Road which is a most enjoyable roller coaster in which your downhill momentum carries you well up the next hill. We opted for the level route, and at our return we were shocked to find that ours was the only car in the parking area. We were so far behind the others that Sandy, the group leader, had already left in his car to search for us.

Our surprise stemmed from the fact that we had already done a few longer daytime rides where lots of bikers with variable starting times and ride lengths resulted in a full parking lot for hours. So even though we were slow, we completed the short version of some rides long before many others who did much longer routes. To see an empty parking lot was a "what's happening?" event.

On the next ride, Sandy suggested I ride his lightweight bike to feel the difference—and it was considerable. So we bought some used lighter weight bikes that were still heavy compared to those of our fellow riders but a lot lighter than our mountain bikes.

In 2005 I hoped to do a better job of keeping up with the regulars in the slow group on the Tuesday night and Saturday morning rides. So on March 29th I bought a new and lighter bike, and that same evening I rode 18 miles with the slow group for a 13.7 average speed, good for me, and leaving me very tired. On the 31st I did a short training ride of nine miles on the Mount Airy park course. Then all sorts of things kept me off the bike until April 14th when I worked out for an hour on the bike. Next Tuesday, the 19th, the valve on my back tire broke as I was pumping up the tire, and for some reason that left me very depressed, but now I think it was providential. On Saturday, April 25, I entered a Senior Olympics race at Mount Airy. It was a cold day, and I was bundled up, but some of the other geezer jocks were shivering and raring to go in just their summer biking shirts. In the mile race, I came in third among the three in my 75-79 age group, proving that I was not in the shape they were. I didn't bother to stay for the 5K jaunt, but I might have if the weather was more congenial. On Thursday, May 5, we did the shortest version of the Tomb ride—leaving the car at the Cleves Drive-In and biking just a 12 mile level loop and then enjoying a good dinner.

On May 10th I didn't do the regular Tuesday night ride. In mid-afternoon Wednesday, Sheila and I started to walk to a nearby church for our quarterly blood donation, and about three or four houses down from ours, I experienced a feeling in my chest like I had never felt before. Not painful but stretching all across my chest and from the bottom of my sternum upwards. So we went home, got the car, and I waited while Sheila donated. I knew they wouldn't take my blood that day if I told them what happened, so I didn't even try. Back home I started to pull a few weeds around the patio, and I got the same feeling again. This time I figured I should have it checked so we went to the ER at the local Mercy Hospital less than a mile away.

They put me up for the night, and the next day I failed the treadmill stress test. I didn't want to push myself, and anyone who could see the monitor could tell there was something wrong. Where the spike should go up, mine was going down. The next day I was transported to Christ Hospital where Dr. Dean Keriakes, the most prominent angioplasty surgeon in Cincinnati, performed an angiogram and angioplasty, inserting five stents. Three arteries were partially blocked, one had two blockages, and one blockage was so long it took two stents. I was conscious during the procedure and could hear them talking. The day was Friday, May 13th, the anniversary of the first appearance of Our Lady at Fatima.

The worst part was immediately afterwards when I was required to lie motionless for an hour so that the groin incision would heal properly. Maybe the longest hour in my life. Staying at the hospital that night I needed pain medication and a sleeping pill, and the next day I went home just after lunch. I slept upstairs in my own bed but stayed downstairs all day Sunday. Monday everything was normal, and I started anti-cholesterol medications.

With hindsight, the events of the preceding six weeks were providential, including the date of procedure. When the tire valve broke on April 19th, that might have been a lifesaver because the halfway point on the Tuesday rides is generally the culmination of a gradual ascent that keeps me huffing and puffing, not a good place to have a heart attack. The race day's cold weather that helped me to go home early might have been another lifesaver. The docs made it clear that I didn't have a heart attack, but Dr. Jason Smith told me I flunked the stress test as badly as anyone he had seen. The bottom line, so to speak, was that this experience gave me a little more confidence that God still had some work for me to do. It's nice to feel useful.

Deal Breakers

Since 2004 had closed with a letter from CCL's litigation attorney stating that Sheila and I were libeling the CCL Board of Directors and the Executive Director, the first order of business in 2005 was to set the record straight. With the help of our attorney, we responded to each of his allegations. To describe truthfully what has happened is not libel. There were other allegations that stemmed from apparent misunderstanding of the facts, but the only interesting allegation was his assertion that we might be in violation of our obligations to CCL by forming a new and competitive organization. There was, of course, no such obligation.

In the middle of January we had an exchange of emails with the Board member who had formerly been the negotiator with us. That led to my drafting a point-by-point reply to the CCL attorney's proposal of September 9, 2004. Our attorney worked this over and made a formal reply to their attorney on February 23rd, and on April 13 a CCL attorney replied. In a nutshell, CCL continued to insist on levels of non-competition and of silence that were unacceptable to us. I replied with a three-page letter that I emailed on April 21st, giving reasons why we found their stipulations unacceptable. True, there was a non-compete clause in the contract for *The Art of Natural Family Planning,* but since CCL had unilaterally repudiated that contract, it seemed rather strange for them to think that we should abide by it. As for organizational non-competition, we had never agreed to not establish a competing organization. Further, we wrote, "until you abandoned the missionary work of the League in Eastern Europe last fall, it never entered our thoughts to do so." We also wrote:

> We would like very much to be able to respond to any inquiries about our relationship with CCL with words of peace and reconciliation, something along the lines suggested by [your attorney] on page 3 of her letter. We agree, however, with the basic theme of the encyclical *Populorum Progression* by Pope Paul VI, "If you want peace, do justice." Our conclusion to three and one-half years of conflict is a repetition of that same theme.

"If you want peace, do justice." Treat us with fairness and respect.

I indicated our willingness to remain at the negotiating table, and that same day I told our attorney we wanted him to register the copyright of our new online NFP book. Sheila also wrote a two-page letter. In it she referred to their lawyer's statement, "We are unlikely to get CCL and the Kippleys to ever agree to any single characterization of what happened regarding their decision to part ways with CCL." Sheila retorted:

> The facts speak for themselves. We have spoken only the truth. The CCL Board members should be happy about spreading the truth, especially if they are proud of their behavior toward the founders.

That exchange more or less ended the dialogue that started in January of 2004. After the word got around about my May 13 angioplasty, the ED sent me a sympathy note on May 19th.

On August 9th, Sheila wrote the ED on a different issue as follows:

> People are surprised that we are not on the fund appeal, CCL email and In House mailings. As founders and #1 Teaching Couple, we would like to keep up-to-date with the activities of CCL. Would you kindly place us on the above lists?

He sent the request to the Chairman who replied on September 12th:

> Although we continue to respect you as the League's founders, you have repeatedly publicly exposed your legal and business disputes with the League through mass emails and other means. CCL believes this unnecessarily raised tension and created confusion among some of our members and harm to the organization.
>
> Therefore you will continue to receive the *Family Foundations* magazine as permanent members of CCL, but we cannot grant your request to receive other communiqués.

We saw in that an implication that we had somehow taken the initiative in airing the dispute, so on October 25th I replied with a five-pager. I reminded the Chairman that after she and the ED had disemployed us in September 2003, "we did not raise any fuss whatsoever." With regard to publicizing our differences, I wrote:

> You broke things wide open with your talk at the CCL Convention in June 2004. It was bad enough that both you and [the ED] had written in *Family Foundations* that we had "retired" when you knew that was definitely not the case. But at the

convention you repeated that error. Further you said that we had decided that it was time for us to go. To cap it off, you said that you wanted your audience to know that you didn't push us. You and [the ED] disemployed us; then you gave your anti-Kippley talk at the Board meeting, and yet you could tell people that you didn't push us out! Absolutely amazing.

We thought it was time to set the record straight, and we did so.

I continued for another couple pages and concluded:

We would appreciate knowing by November 20 if you would like to enter arbitration or a negotiated agreement. If you believe that any fact is materially misrepresented in the letter, please let us know by email within 24 hours after you receive this.

Since this was the last substantive correspondence before we entered formal litigation, its entire contents is an appendix to this chapter.

The Chairman replied on October 28th that they would be happy to reopen negotiations and asked me to confirm that we are willing to pick up the settlement negotiations where we had left off. I replied on November 10th that their attorney had said that our refusal to go along with their desires for both a non-compete agreement and a broad confidentiality agreement would be a deal-breaker. I noted that a settlement agreement on the publishing contract should not be held hostage to agreement on these non-related issues. I recalled our previous willingness to accept a settlement of approximately two-thirds of the deferred royalties and that we had spent basically two years trying to avoid litigation.

But enough is enough. [The vice-Chairman] said on December 8, 2003 that the Board wanted to settle our differences out of court. I hope that the Board will revive that desire. Therefore by November 18th, please send us either the wording on an agreement that we could reasonably sign on those two unrelated matters, or let us know that you are dropping those issues, or that you want to enter arbitration. If CCL fails to respond adequately by Friday, November 18th, our attorney will file suit the week of Monday, November 21.

There was no reply, and we filed suit for Breach of Contract on November 22, 2005. That ended the year as far as CCL was concerned, but there was still one more important life event.

Glaucoma Surgery

If glaucoma runs in your family, you might learn a lesson from this. I knew it ran in my family. My maternal grandfather went totally blind, probably by the time he was 70, maybe suffering greatly reduced vision for a number of years before that. My mother had it, but not her identical twin sister. Mom caught hers early, took drops, and never complained about any loss of vision. I had my eyes examined about age 40 and there was no sign of it yet. I breathed a sigh of relief, and I didn't have my eyes checked for another 15 years. Even then it was just a routine eye exam. I simply figured it was maybe about time to have a new prescription.

At age 55, the glaucoma was well advanced in my right eye and evident in my left. That started years of efforts to keep the pressure low. The drops worked well in my left eye, but my ophthalmologist was concerned about the long-term prognosis for the right—the pressure wasn't staying low enough. That led to a laser surgery that makes little holes to let the excess aqueous fluid out of the eyeball, and that worked fine for a while until the holes clogged or sealed themselves. So we did a second one, and that eventually failed too. The only option to keep the pressure low enough so that further damage could most likely be curtailed or at least slowed significantly was trabucolectomy, generally referred to as a "trab" for obvious reasons.

This is surgery in a way that laser surgery isn't. It involves a knife. The doctor makes a very small incision, then cuts a small hole in the eyeball, and lastly sews a flap of eyeball tissue over the hole. The sutures are tied individually so he can take out as many as he needs to adjust the pressure. It also involves a number of checkups in the following days and weeks.

The day the doctor was available for the surgery could not have been better: December 13, the feast of Saint Lucy, patron saint of those with diseases of the eye. Absolutely providential. The surgery was highly successful, and my right eye pressure has remained low without using any drops for five years as I write this in December of 2010. My eye doctor told me that the trab would cause a cataract to form and that I most likely would need cataract surgery within two years. Well, yes, a cataract is forming, but very slowly. I can still read 12-point type on the computer screen at about 18 inches, but it's not good enough for duck or pheasant hunting, which I haven't done in years anyway. Thank you, Lord, for healing. Thank you, St. Lucy, for your prayers.

The lesson to be learned is this. If glaucoma runs in your family, get your eyes checked early and regularly. Even if it doesn't show up for years, don't assume that it has skipped you. If it doesn't run in your family, still get your eyes checked occasionally, say at least every five years once you are 25.

Dodging another Bullet: Prostate Cancer

While on matters of health, I might as well mention my experience with prostate cancer even though it didn't happen until late in 2006. Like many men my age, I had been having an annual physical including a check on my PSA—a blood test that can reflect prostate cancer. My PSA level had risen a year or two earlier, and my primary care physician had sent me to a urologist who told me that my elevated level was not out-of-line for my age. In 2006 it jumped up, and he did a biopsy that revealed cancer in my prostate gland. He wanted Sheila at the consultation, and when he told us the news, my immediate reaction was that it was no big deal since it was not at all uncommon among men in my age group. Sheila told our children, and one of them asked if she could share the info with her husband. Sure. Within about an hour I received a phone call from a man in her extended family who told me of his experience and strongly recommended the proton-beam treatment in Loma Linda, California. It turned out to be a most welcome call.

Mid-October 2006 found me ready to leave for nine weeks of this specialized radiation treatment affectionately called the "radiation vacation" by those who receive it. I rented a small apartment about a ten-minute walk from the clinic, and the actual treatment time took about an hour per day counting walking and waiting time. Actual daily radiation time was in terms of seconds. Basically, the proton-beam can be focused very closely on a small organ such as the prostate, and it can be controlled to go only so far and no farther. Thus it does less collateral damage than other forms of treatment. As it turned out, my Loma Linda doctor had reasons to think my cancer had spread beyond the prostate, so 25 of my 44 treatments were a broader form of radiation, but I still suffered no adverse effects of which I am aware.

There were well over a hundred men taking the treatment at the same time, and their age range was surprising. One gentleman was almost 90, but the surprising thing was the number of younger men, some in their forties and fifties. Prostate cancer has long been associated with aging, but it is also associated with prior vasectomy. Two studies in the December 1993 issue of *JAMA,* the Journal of the American Medical Association, reported that men who had a vasectomy had an 89% increased risk of prostate cancer 20 years later. So it's no surprise that men who have a vasectomy at age 30 or so are having prostate cancer in their fifties.

Sheila came out for three weeks in the middle of the treatment, so we did a bit of sightseeing. We also played tennis, and that was the occasion of my only real discomfort. I was running back for a deep one, hit it backwards over my head, and then did a quick stop and sharp turn to avoid running into the fence. That maneuver pulled a groin muscle that reduced my formerly brisk walking to a shuffle.

As I write this, it has been four years since the treatment, and the combination of a very low PSA level and the annual physical exam indicate that the cancer has been routed. Since that time I have been contacted by a couple of much younger men with the same condition. For various reasons they could not take the proton treatment, and the sufferings they endured during their difficult recoveries made me all the more grateful for the treatment that I experienced.

Other Milestones

Within a couple weeks after the May 2005 angioplasty I was biking again, and on Sunday June 12, Christopher and I did the River Rendezvous Ride. It starts across the Ohio River in Ludlow, then goes up the hill to the airport, gives you a few miles of only mildly rolling hills and even some flatness. At the second rest stop we asked a few questions about the route to Rabbit Hash, a quaint little village that once elected a dog as its "mayor," and I think we misunderstood what we were told about the hills. On the steepest hill, I granny-geared down to three miles per hour before walking the rest of the way. On the way back, without any pumping I was quickly enjoying the breeze at 42 miles per hour. We made a big mistake by not going a bit out of our way to stock up on liquids and calories at the snack stop for this part of the ride, and by the time we got to the last leg along the river, I was so dry and weak that I was walking up just little rollers. When I noticed that a gentleman mowing his lawn had an old pickup in his driveway, I offered him five dollars to take me the mile and a half to our starting point. Chris declined the ride, wanting to be able to say he made the 55 miles on his own. I was too tired to care.

The lesson: when doing that sort of biking, make sure you stock up on your fluids and calories at every chance.

- In mid-June 2005 we traveled to Pittsburgh for Sheila to compete in Senior Olympics tennis. On Tuesday, the 14th, she won her first two singles matches, but on Wednesday she lost her third match, and we headed home.
- The next Monday we traveled to Niagara Falls to meet with David and Mishka Prentis who head up the NFP program we helped them to start in the Czech Republic.
- In the first three weeks of July, Chris and I put on new decking after Chris removed the old material.
- On September 11, Sheila and I biked the Horizontal Hundred in Findlay. The name denotes that the only elevations in the ride are highway overpasses. Sheila did 64 miles and I did 75 to celebrate my approaching 75th birthday.
- Sheila and I attended the Fellowship of Catholic Scholars conference in Charlotte, NC.
- A routine age-related colonoscopy showed no problems. I was told to have it repeated in three years.

All in all, the year 2005 had many blessings for Sheila and me.

Appendix

The following letter to the Chairman of the CCL Board constitutes a summary or review of events, most of which are already recorded in this and previous chapters. Thus there is some direct repetition.

October 25, 2005

Chairman, Board of Directors

Dear [Chairman]:

On this past August 9th, Sheila wrote [the ED] a short email message that read as follows:

> Dear [ED],
> People are surprised that we are not on the fund appeal, CCL email and In House mailings. As founders and #1 Teaching Couple, we would like to keep up-to-date with the activities of CCL. Would you kindly place us on the above lists?
> Thanks, Sheila"

He responded: "I will forward your request to the Board. Respectfully, [ED]"

Sheila's email was prompted by a discussion with an active Teacher who found it quite strange, almost unbelievable, that we are not on those lists. That teacher thought that if one of us asked in a non-threatening way, the request would be granted.

On September 12, you replied in the negative. You wrote:
> Although we continue to respect you as the League's founders, you have repeatedly publicly exposed your legal and business disputes with the League through mass emails and other means. CCL believes this unnecessarily raised tension and created confusion among some of our members, and harm to the organization.

It appears to me that you have forgotten some important details that lead Sheila and me to a different conclusion.

After you and [the ED] disemployed us in September, 2003, we did not raise any fuss whatsoever. The Board was honoring the publishing agreement on *The Art of Natural Family Planning*, and it was also honoring its decision to grant royalties on *Marriage Is for Keeps*. I continued to help you with the bylaws. We had founded an organization, guided it through what may have been the worst 30 years of the Church vis-à-vis promoting and teaching chastity, worked faithfully and hard, and you and [the ED] terminated our employment by the simple expedient of giving us no work to do. Other CCL employees have been permitted to work well into their 70s and to choose the time of their own retirement, but you made an exception of us. Yet we made no outcry.

At the Board meeting on December 7, 2003, you engaged in an attack upon our characters, painting us as rip-off artists. I responded and demonstrated that we have been one of the chief donors to CCL. However, apparently you succeeded in significantly damaging our reputations with the Board, for there has never been the slightest hint of an apology for that assault. The value of the deferred contractual royalties on *The Art of Natural Family Planning was* slightly over $145,000. In addition, I had reduced my salary by about two-thirds beginning in January, 1966 (from $44,000 to approximately $15,000) and the savings to CCL from that voluntary action on my part amounted to approximately $100,000 up through June 30, 1999, assuming a regular COL increase. (I understand the actual savings may be somewhat less because there was not a COL increase each year.) I also put myself on part-time when [a former staffer] was made ED in April 1999, thus creating additional savings for CCL. The CCL records also show that we had made direct cash gifts of $38,015 to CCL over the years. Because CCL was fulfilling its contractual obligations on the royalties, I donated my time (full time at the office) from May to September, 2003, thus saving CCL another $16,500. From the information available to me at present, it appears to me that Sheila and I have donated approximately $150,000 to CCL in addition to helping CCL with its cash flow problems by deferring the royalties mentioned above. Regardless of the precise amounts, I suggest that we are among the top donors to CCL. All this information was available to you from CCL records (that's where I got most of it) before you chose to portray us as you did.

You have argued that the royalties should be reduced because of a decision of the Board in late 1991 that the royalties on the proposed Fourth Edition of *The Art of Natural Family Planning* should not exceed "the average of the amount received in the last 5 years." I admitted to the Board that I completely forgot about that five years later when it would have gone into effect. Nobody else on the Board remembered it either, nor did [the] business manager. I also assured you that if I had remembered it in 1996, I would have either persuaded the Board to reverse itself, or I would not have reduced my salary by $30,000 per year. That is the sort of thing that can be negotiated or brought to fair and impartial arbitration.

You also conveyed your impression that we had created special and favorable deals on the royalties. In point of fact, Sheila's contract with Harper and Row stipulated a 15% royalty. Her contract with Sophia Institute for her new book carries a royalty of 12%. Ignatius Press offered a 10% rate on *Sex and the Marriage Covenant*. Thus the CCL royalty rate of 10% on all its books is quite standard. It is "special" for *Breastfeeding and Natural Child Spacing* only in the sense that it is lower than the standard rate offered by others for the same book or type of book, and it is identical to the standard rate offered by Ignatius.

Your performance and the lack of any apology by the Board or the few staff persons in attendance contributed greatly to our decision to resign from the Board. After all, how could we function in a situation of such suspicion? Still, we remained silent. When we later asked one of the attendees why he didn't say anything about your presentation about us, he replied that he knew it wasn't true.

Hoping for a negotiated agreement on several issues, we met with [a Board member] in January, 2004. It was an entirely amicable meeting. I told [this BM] how much I enjoyed speaking at the seminars and would like to continue doing this. Several days later, both Sheila and I were taken off the speakers list at the CCL website. [The BM] asked about *The Art of NFP*, and I offered to do both an abbreviated version and a fifth edition.

You replied on March 17, 2004 on behalf of the Board, and unfortunately you repudiated everything we had discussed in the negotiations. Further, although CCL had been paying royalties on *The Art of Natural Family Planning* during 2003, you repudiated the publishing agreement. You also repudiated the previous Board decision to grant us royalties on both editions of *Marriage Is for Keeps*. You left nothing on the table except the assurance that even though the Board believed it was not under a legal obligation to do so, the royalty "payments will continue to be paid by CCLI using this same formula (applied during 2003) as long as the Fourth Edition of *The Art of Natural Family Planning* remains in print." CCLI has never made any such payments.

Regardless of copyright ownership, the publishing agreement was and still is a valid contract. There is nothing in law or precedent that prevents an organization from entering into a publishing contract with an employee, even if the work is registered as a work for hire. The case your attorneys are fond of citing, *CCNV vs. Reid*, specifically noted that the "work-for-hire" criteria do not apply if there is a written contract. If you doubt this, I challenge the Board to come with me to Court for a simple declaratory judgment on that fact. If the judge agrees with me, CCL agrees to fulfill the terms of the contract. If the judge agrees with you, then I will withdraw my claim that you have acted unjustly toward us regarding the publishing agreement.

If your counsel has advised you that [CCL] can repudiate the contract, I believe you have been poorly served. Professor Gerard Bradley, a legal scholar at the University of Notre Dame Law School, researched *CCNV vs. Reid* on our behalf as a disinterested party. He recently wrote me: "You ask whether CCNV prohibits a corporation from having a publishing agreement with an employee. Answer: definitely not." I also asked him if CCL has <u>any</u> basis in law to repudiate the publishing agreement. He replied: "No they cannot simply (i.e., unilaterally) repudiate the contract. Basically, no one can do that without incurring liability for damages."

Still, we did not make an outcry in the spring of 2004. Instead, we wasted thousands of dollars in legal fees and basically a whole year in negotiations made fruitless by CCL's insistence that we accept a gag rule. We had made it clear in 2002 and repeatedly during 2004 that we would not accept a gag rule, but you kept dragging things on, refusing to talk with us except through lawyers. In these negotiations, you offered us an amount that would have been acceptable as payment for back royalties up through 2002. Unfortunately, you made it dependent upon a gag rule, thus making it appear to be hush money and thus unacceptable. We are quite willing to sign a standard confidentiality agreement about the details regarding an agreement, but we cannot sign a total gag rule.

You broke things wide open with your talk at the CCL Convention in June, 2004. It was bad enough that both you and [the ED] had written in *Family Foundations* that we had "retired" when you knew that was definitely not the case. But at the convention you repeated that error. Further you said that <u>we</u> had decided that it was time for us to go. To cap it off, you said that you wanted your audience to know that you didn't push us. You and [the ED] disemployed us; then you gave your anti-Kippley talk at the Board meeting, and yet you could tell people that you didn't push us out! Absolutely amazing.

We thought it was time to set the record straight, and we did so.

You may be correct in stating that our response to your allegations raised some tension and created some confusion among some CCL members, but you must take full responsibility for that. You are not God. Your word does not create the facts. If you choose to say things about us that don't square with reality, you are inviting a response. We had tried to keep things within the immediate family, so to speak. We had asked [the editor of the CCL magazine] not to publish responses to your invitation. She agreed, but the "Thank you" responses were published anyway.

While we have exposed the truth about our disemployment, we have not widely exposed the truth about our legal dispute regarding *The Art of Natural Family Planning*, contrary to what you implied in your recent letter. The truth of the matter is that we have a valid publishing agreement with CCL for that publication. Nor have we widely exposed the reality about the deferred royalties. The truth is that when CCL was having cash flow problems about the time the Fourth Edition was published, we deferred the royalties in order to help CCL, and there may have been other times when we either deferred the royalties or outright gifted them back to CCL; I presume that [the business manager] has such records. The deferral of royalties was done in good faith with the anticipation that we would receive those royalties when we had a greatly reduced cash flow in our Social Security years. ***What you have done is to break a good faith agreement and thus deprive us of a significant part of our income in our Social Security years.*** This is a gross injustice.

The Gospel for the first Sunday of September was and is pertinent to our dispute. We believe that in the words of the gospel, our brother has sinned against us. We attempted negotiation, and [the BM] brought a draft to the Board. Instead of agreeing or coming back with something a little bit different, you repudiated it completely. If your brother doesn't listen, "take one or two others along with you so that every fact may be established on the testimony of two or three witnesses. If he refuses to listen to them, tell the church." In September 2004, we appealed to Bishop Victor Galeone, the USCCB bishop for NFP. He in turn asked you to submit the disputes to binding arbitration. After seven weeks in which you did not even acknowledge receipt of his letter, you and the Board refused his reasonable request. Thus, we have tried the gospel approach, and the current CCL management repudiates it. Any further telling of this unhappy story is simply an extension of telling it to the church. It's not that we enjoy telling the story. People have a very difficult time understanding why or how an organization can simply dismiss its founders unless those founders had done something really bad. They also find it quite difficult to fathom why an organization that likes to be thought of as Christian would repudiate the effort by a Catholic bishop to achieve justice and peace, maybe even some form of reconciliation. If you would like us to refrain from telling this story, simply remove the cause—CCL's injustice toward us—and we will have nothing to talk about.

You accuse us of having done some unspecified harm to the organization. On the contrary, it seems to us that we care more about CCL than you or anyone else. For four years Sheila brought quality assurance problems to management, and she got a thorough-going whistle-blower treatment. With her efforts repudiated by current management, three out of four consecutive issues of *Family Foundations* contained mistakes in the CyCLe column (November-December 2004 through May-June 2005). To add insult to injury, one of the mistakes was plagiarized from an article I had written more than four years previously, but the plagiarists failed to copy the chart correctly and therefore published an erroneous interpretation, and they have refused to apologize for the plagiarism. It seems to me that poor quality will do more harm to CCL than anything we could ever say or do. You will remember that poor quality assurance was the Number One reason Sheila and I gave for our resignations from the Board. As I told you in my letter of resignation, I did not want to be part of a lawsuit legitimately filed against CCL for clearly mistaken teaching.

If CCL has been harmed, it is you and the rest of the Board who have harmed CCLI by burdening it with the spiritual deadweight of gross injustice. As the *New Oxford Review* stated in two recent issues (June and October, 2005) an organization that is founded on injustice and deception is not worthy of support.

You have further harmed CCLI by abandoning Headquarters' support of the non-English, non-Spanish branches of CCLI. You have given up those parts of the world to others. On the contrary, we are doing what we can to support CCLI in Slovakia and elsewhere. The operations that we support are still called CCL of Slovakia.

The refusal of the Board of Directors to publish Marilyn Shannon's beautiful review of Sheila's new book, *Breastfeeding and Catholic Motherhood*, does additional harm to CCL. First, your refusal portrays the Board unfavorably. "Petty" and "incredibly small" are the reactions we hear. Second, it deprives many CCL members of the best opportunity they have of discovering this book that would encourage them or affirm their decision to breastfeed and/or enable them to encourage others to do so. Third, CCL could probably sell at least a thousand copies a year in the next few years, thus earning gross profits of about $4,400 per year. CCL could most likely ring up sales of at least 300 copies per year of *Sex and the Marriage Covenant* just released by Ignatius. The combination would probably exceed the $6,000 net income you reported for fiscal 2005. This would be a risk-free investment, but you have chosen to refuse this opportunity. [CCL presently sells *Sex and the Marriage Covenant*.]

A friend who believes that CCL has been specially blessed by God over the years once told [the ED] vis-à-vis your treatment of us that CCL is making it hard for God to continue that special blessing. Do you really think that your continued injustice toward us is pleasing to God? We believe that this gross injustice is a millstone that will continue to harm CCL. Since we would like to see CCL help the Church meet the challenge of marital chastity today and in the future, we pray regularly for CCL.

I believe that a just solution to the current situation will be mutually beneficial. If you think that your actions are already fair, I challenge you to submit them to a fair and impartial arbitration board. I can think of only three reasons not to do so—1) you and the Board know in your hearts that the current situation is unjust and therefore fear an impartial review; 2) you really want to litigate the contract issue, using donors' funds quite unnecessarily for legal fees; or 3) you want to avoid arbitration and litigation by working out a just and mutually beneficial agreement on the publishing contract. We stand ready to work with you on the latter.

We would appreciate knowing by November 20 if you would like to enter arbitration or a negotiated agreement. If you believe that any fact is materially misrepresented in this letter, please let us know by email within 24 hours after you receive this.

Sincerely,
John F. Kippley

18. Two Settlements

Once our attorney formally filed suit for breach of contract in late 2005, the matter proceeded according to established legal procedures. The CCL attorneys replied with a countersuit against us and specifically against Sheila for the publication of her book, *Breastfeeding and Catholic Motherhood* published by Sophia Press in 2005, alleging it was a violation of the non-compete clause of their publishing contract for *Breastfeeding and Natural Child Spacing*. Sheila had discussed this with our attorney who saw no competition and assured her that CCL would not contest it if they were reasonable. But it provided them with titular grounds for a countersuit.

In 2006, after the initial exchanges, our attorney suggested a combination of arbitration and mediation, and they accepted. Our meeting on May 31, 2006 lasted for more than 12 hours. What was actually agreed upon is a matter of confidentiality, but we can certainly report our reactions. Both Sheila and I were adversely affected by sadness. I was upset for at least a week and Sheila for another week.

While the mediation-arbitration concept is good, the execution can be very painful. We were left completely by ourselves for long periods of time while our attorneys conferred with theirs, and we did not appreciate this at all. Second, when the day stretched into the night hours, we felt greatly disadvantaged. We are not night people. We were very fatigued, and we should simply have said, "See you tomorrow." As a result, when the pressure was put on us by the arbitrator-mediator, we made concessions that we seriously regretted the next day. The best thing that could be said from our perspective is that it brought an end to the long settlement process that started after the Board meeting in November 2002. We would not recommend the mediation-arbitration process as we experienced it unless all parties are meeting in the same room with only brief breaks for each side to confer among themselves.

Continued Conflict

What was supposed to be the end of the process didn't turn out that way.

A CCL staffer made me the butt of his humor at the CCL convention in June 2006, just weeks after the settlement.

At the same conference, CCL Board member Father Richard Hogan criticized my covenant theology of sexuality as "deductive, objective and principled" and then dismissed it as not being relevant today because people are more in tune with being inductive, subjective, and so on. In addition, he indicated that one had to be a Scripture scholar to learn the covenant theology.

The EWTN Flap

On Wednesday, September 13, 2006, three CCL representatives—the Board chairman, the ED, and Board member Fr. Richard Hogan—were interviewed by Father Mitch Pacwa, S.J., on his prime-time EWTN program (8:00 p.m. Eastern time). During the program Father Hogan argued that in standard NFP instruction there is no need to teach about the need to have a sufficiently serious reason to use NFP. Specifically, Fr. Hogan said he was "on a campaign" to delete mention of grave or serious reason from regular NFP instruction.

Further publicity was given to the views of Father Hogan in an interview in the November 22 issue of the *National Catholic Register*. Then things got interesting for a while.

December 4. Pam Pilch, founder of the Catholic Nursing Mothers League, blogged on the *NC Register* interview at the "Heart, Mind and Strength" weblog. Fr. Hogan had told a little story that used the example of a couple having four children in five years, and Ms. Pilch used this to launch her advocacy of ecological breastfeeding and its customary natural spacing of babies. Sheila got notice of this blog almost immediately, and I replied the same day.

First I noted that in his story Father Hogan displayed little appreciation of the difficulties involved with very close birth intervals, and I related a true-life story that illustrated one of those difficulties. I also opined, "Every priest should understand ecological breastfeeding and recommend it at every opportunity. They need to appreciate God's own plan for spacing babies. Priests should become well informed before putting themselves out as experts on natural family planning." Then I continued:

> In his September 13 EWTN interview, Fr. Hogan announced that he is on a campaign to delete from regular NFP instruction any mention of the need to have a serious reason to use systematic NFP. That is, he is on a campaign to censor sections 10 and 16 of *Humanae Vitae*. True to form, he said nothing about ecological breastfeeding, the only kind of NFP for which you do not need a serious reason to use it. In fact, given all the information now available about the benefits of breastfeeding, a couple need a very good reason not to breastfeed.
>
> In my opinion, any priest who publicly campaigns to censor an important part of *Humanae Vitae* disqualifies himself from

participating in any leadership position in the Church and the NFP movement until such time as he publicly changes his position.

Then Ms. Pilch chimed in again and quoted a paragraph from Father Hogan in which he was responding to the question, "Why is the Couple to Couple League changing its curriculum?" In his interview in the *National Catholic Register,* Fr. Hogan was quoted this way:

> It has been 30 years since it was first done by John Kippley in 1971. The old curriculum was based on covenant theology, which was very prevalent at the time. Covenant theology isn't wrong. But arguably, it is less easily understood than the theology of the body.

Blogger Pam Pilch explained her problem with that as follows:

> As a non-theologian, I don't exactly understand this point. I came to CCL in 1996 and I thought that John's covenant theology made a lot of sense. The upshot of it in my mind was that the marriage act is a renewal of a couple's wedding vows—that it expresses with our bodies the truth that in marriage we take each other fully and unconditionally and give fully, holding nothing back.
>
> I thought it was easy to understand. The Theology of the Body, on the other hand, with words like "nuptial meaning" does kind of confuse me, at least if I had to give a definition of it on my own. I guess when I started reading about it (some years into my familiarity with NFP) I thought it pretty much meant the same thing as the covenant theology. (In fact the first time I heard a summary of the TOB I thought to myself—Hey I wonder if the Pope got that from John Kippley?) Only the idea of sex being a bodily renewal of our wedding vows was a sort of quick and easy way of understanding it.

That was the gist of her eight-paragraph response, and at this point Dr. Gregory Popcak, moderator of the blogsite, added his two-cents worth (his terminology) with an intervention about what he calls "Integral Procreation," the Theology of the Body, and the findings of neuroscience about the good effects of attachment parenting, and he concluded.

> Taken together, integral procreation and the TOB present a strong argument for Ecological Breastfeeding, Attachment Parenting and the willingness to submit to at least the natural child spacing that results from these methods.

December 5. Dr. Popcak added this comment.

I will just say that, on second read, I'm not sure I understand how Fr. Hogan could be saying, on the one hand, that we should have children one on top of the other while saying that we should eliminate the need for serious reasons to use NFP on the other. Perhaps, barring clarification, it would be best that we assume that there is some misunderstanding here and be as charitable as possible in our reading of the work of the two men [Fr. Hogan and Kippley] who are laboring faithfully in the vineyard.

December 7. Pam Pilch, Sheila, and readers wrote more than three pages of blogs dealing with ecological breastfeeding and what CCL would be doing on the subject in the future.

December 10. Sheila contributed a short blog on the difference between Ecological Breastfeeding and the Lactational Amenorrhea Method.

December 12. Greg Popcak introduced the replies of CCL's Executive Director and Father Hogan. The ED wrote the following twofold accusation:

In at least one of the [recent] postings [on this weblog], "Father Richard Hogan was disparaged" and "his words were taken out of context."

Father Hogan then provided a six-point response to the criticisms of his EWTN comments on September 13. In the sixth point he wrote:

Sixth, when I said on the EWTN program that I had a campaign against the language of serious or grave reasons I meant two things. First, I do not think the translation is as accurate as it should be. I do prefer "just causes" for the Latin "justae causae." Second, grave or serious reasons for having recourse to the infertile times should not be imposed as a prerequisite on couples beginning their lives together. Rather those very virtuous reasons are the result of NFP.

December 13. Theologian Kevin Miller responded to Father Hogan's comments. He cleared up the translation issue. Yes, "just causes" is the proper translation of "justae causae," but that isn't the issue. Dr. Miller also used "serious reason" as the translation of "seriis causis." He also addressed Fr. Hogan's unusual interpretation of *Humanae Vitae*. After stating that we cannot ignore the language of "serious," he added,

Nor do I see anything in the text that suggests that Paul VI isn't talking about couples at the beginning of their married life, as well as those who've been married for some time.

Moderator Greg Popcak then closed the discussion. "As far as this blog is concerned, we're done with this topic." I didn't appreciate being accused of disparagement and taking Fr. Hogan's words out of context and then being denied an opportunity to respond, so I wrote the moderator to that effect but to no avail.

The *New Oxford Review* Flap

On November 14, 2006 the USCCB issued a small booklet on natural family planning titled *Married Love and the Gift of Life*. I thought that *Married Love* could have been better and wrote a commentary that was published in the March 2007 issue of the *New Oxford Review* (NOR). In it I criticized Father Hogan for his comments in the EWTN program of September 13, 2006. I thought it was universally understood among people who appear on public television that public statements are open to public comment including criticism.

In a CCL-related chat room, a CCL Promoter drew attention to my NOR article, and the CCL ED immediately replied, "In Kippley's article, Fr. Hogan's words have been taken out of context and incorrect conclusions and innuendos have been made." In one sentence, the ED accused me of three offenses—taking Fr. Hogan's words out of context, drawing incorrect conclusions, and making innuendoes. I wrote a reply and asked the Promoter to post it to the chat room. She apparently tried, but it was not published. Instead the chat-room moderator wrote me that it was "most uncharitable" for someone to let me know that the Promoter had called attention to the article and that the ED had responded.

So I wrote another short letter about the chat room practice in which CCL management can criticize a person who says or writes something the management doesn't like but the person thus criticized cannot make a reply in the chat room. Needless to say, that was never published either.

Fortunately, it was just at this time that our website developer suggested that we start to blog. We took his suggestion and posted our first blog on April 23, 2007. If we had started the blog just two months earlier, there might have been some interesting dialogue. As it was, we had no means by which to reply to the three accusations made by CCL's executive director.

The Blogs

In our blogs we felt free to express our disappointment with the direction of the new CCL management. It was apparent that CCL was dropping its former promotion and teaching of ecological breastfeeding, so on May 27, 2007 Sheila offered her comments and published many and stronger comments by others. On June 27, I offered my opinion that CCL was ethically and professionally obliged to tell couples about Rule K, the temperature-based rule that sometimes yields the start of Phase 3 a day earlier than any of the other Sympto-Thermal rules. On November 18, 2007, Sheila noted that the new CCL manual contained, in two different areas, a seriously incomplete and therefore possibly misleading statement about exclusive breastfeeding and infertility. She also drew attention to the fact that people had told her that they received no reply from their letters of complaint to CCL, and she drew attention to her role as the whistleblower during her last years of CCL employment. On December 2nd, 9th, 16th, and 30th she blogged again on the breastfeeding issue, but most of the blogs consisted of readers' comments.

Our blog of January 6, 2008 had more readers' comments, not all of them critical. Three blogs in January and February showcased CCL's "Extreme Makeover" of December 12, 2007 which was negative about its former program and then CCL's subsequent comments on January 9 that acknowledged that the "old program served us well." Yes it had, and we continue to believe that there are no good reasons to drop the classic content of the Triple Strand we had brought to the founding of the League in 1971.

We also noted CCL's financial strength reported as of June 30, 2007 and that shortly thereafter it had disemployed one part-time and two full-time staffers. In mid-February 2008, we used the word "disemployed" to refer to the termination of our employment by CCL in September 2003. An article in the January 6, 2008 issue of the *National Catholic Register* also quoted us as using that term to describe the termination.

The folks at CCL apparently did not appreciate our comments, and thus on February 22, 2008 the legal process started again. It went back and forth periodically until we finally ended up in a second mediation meeting on November 11, 2008. Perhaps it was fitting that it occurred on Armistice Day. In this meeting, there was no arbitrator, although that was the fallback position in the event our mutual mediation meeting failed. Also in this meeting, all the parties were in the same room for all the discussion except for a few breaks when the respective parties went to separate rooms. In the end, we had another settlement agreement that we signed on December 18.

19. The Extreme Makeover

Starting in 2004, the CCL management talked about the changes it would make in its teaching program. Finally, on December 12, 2007 the changes were announced as the EXTREME MAKEOVER with a widely distributed promotional kit and press release whose first sentence stated that it was an answer to the problem of "stale materials and a skeptical audience." (The all-capitals usage comes from CCL's promotion materials.)

In a supplemental sheet, its description of our founding of the League in 1971 was correct as far as it went, but it omitted three important purposes that had shaped the CCL instructional program since the beginning.
  1. To promote and teach ecological breastfeeding as a form of natural family planning.
  2. To use the covenant theology of sexuality to explain and support the teaching of *Humanae Vitae*.
  3. To teach a freedom-of-choice version of the Sympto-Thermal Method of systematic natural family planning.
  Those were the characteristics that for 36 years had distinguished the Couple to Couple League from other NFP organizations.

Unfortunately, all three of these distinguishing characteristics were deleted in the EXTREME MAKEOVER. We agree with the long–time CCL member who told us that it appears that "CCL was getting rid of anything related to the Kippleys." Of course we can't state that with any factual certainty, but we can say that the changes certainly have that appearance.

Deletion of Ecological Breastfeeding
The biggest surprise was the deletion of ecological breastfeeding as a form of NFP. In its Capital Campaign literature of 2006, CCL promised that the new course would continue to provide "Promotion of ecological breastfeeding." The chairman had also stated that ecological breastfeeding was a very important part of the CCL program. Now it was gone.
  To be sure, CCL continues to say nice things about breastfeeding including some reference to delayed fertility, but that simply makes it resemble all the other NFP programs. Everyone today says nice things about

breastfeeding. Sheila heard nice things about breastfeeding when she went to her first childbirth education course in 1964. Those comments led her to La Leche League where she also learned about the baby-spacing effects of breastfeeding. So she breastfed our first baby with some anticipation of delayed fertility, but her first period occurred at three months postpartum even though she was nursing frequently, day and night. Why? With our second child, Sheila had better advice from another doctor, and her first period occurred at 12 months.

What caused the difference between these two experiences? Sheila wanted to know, so she did both forms of scientific research. First, she reviewed all the then-published English-language research dealing with breastfeeding and the return of fertility. Second, she developed a survey and included this in her then self-published book, *Breastfeeding and Natural Child Spacing*. From these surveys it was clear that the frequency of nursing was the key element in the delay of fertility. From conversations with many moms, she had learned about the various styles of breastfeeding and about many of the breastfeeding and mothering substitutes. So she developed a set of "guidelines" to steer mothers away from devices and practices that reduced the amount and the frequency of suckling. As Sheila gained more experience with mothers who dropped one or another of the guidelines and then complained about an early return of fertility, she realized that the term "guidelines" could be interpreted very loosely and needed to be strengthened, so she changed the word to "Standards."

It was so clear that the effects of frequent breastfeeding were different from the effects of cultural nursing that she gave it a name—"ecological breastfeeding"—to distinguish it. By the time Harper and Row published the hardcover edition of her book in 1974, she had developed a subtitle so it read, *Breastfeeding and Natural Child Spacing: The Ecology of Natural Mothering.*

This was unique. The scientific literature has reported on the frequent nursing patterns of mothers in primitive cultures and developing countries, but no one had tried to translate that information into standard maternal behaviors that could be followed by mothers in the United States and other developed countries. No one had ever before developed a program—simply a short list of do's and don'ts—that combined scientific research and a mother's common sense to achieve something close to the normal infertility built into breastfeeding by the Creator. I write "something close" very deliberately. Our research that was published in 1972 and 1986 demonstrated that American mothers doing ecological breastfeeding experienced an average of 14.5 months of breastfeeding amenorrhea with a range from 1 to 30 months. However, in primitive cultures with patterns of more frequent suckling, the duration of breastfeeding infertility is even longer, and that is probably closer to what our early ancestors experienced. (In our published research we did not include three surveys that reported 41,

41, and 42 months of amenorrhea because we feared they might skew the statistics and become a distraction from the overall findings.)

All of this was done before our first NFP course in the fall of 1971. That meant that Sheila brought to the founding of the League something unique, something that had never been done before. This part of the NFP program we developed served mothers well for 36 years and continues to do so through NFP International. I have read in the business literature that successful businesses emphasize what is unique about their product or service. But CCL chose to repudiate this part of its history and to become just another NFP program that says nice things about breastfeeding but fails to promote the Seven Standards of Ecological Breastfeeding as a true form of natural family planning, a beautiful form of child care and a natural baby spacer.

Deletion of the Covenant Theology of Sexuality

The deletion of the covenant theology of sexuality was not surprising to anyone who thinks CCL was making changes to delete the Kippleys' imprint, but it was surprising in another way. In orthodox Catholic circles, it is common to talk about the Theology of the Body (TOB) developed by Pope John Paul II. This is a series of 129 lectures delivered in his Wednesday addresses between 1979 and 1984. They are a first-rate intellectual effort to show that the teaching of *Humanae Vitae* flows from our very nature as man and woman created in the image and likeness of God. The lectures are not, however, easy to read, and it is not easy to see how they all fit together. I confess that I read them as they were published but did not truly comprehend the grand design. I would frequently read a sentence, agree that I had read something good, but found that I could not remember what I had read. The writing style of John Paul II with sentences that can go on forever does not lend itself to easy comprehension.

Several books explain the papal Theology of the Body, and some speakers make it sound as if it will bring great numbers of Catholics to accept *Humanae Vitae* if only they are given an opportunity to hear it. I hope they are right. What I know, however, is that when the Pope was trying to reach the more ordinary laity in 1994, ten years after the completion of his TOB lectures, he did not urge them to read his lectures or books about them. Instead, he incorporated the basic statement of the covenant theology.

> In the conjugal act, husband and wife are called to confirm *the mutual gift* of self which they have made to each other in the marriage covenant. The logic of the *total gift of self to the other* involves a potential openness to procreation: in this way the marriage is called to even greater fulfillment as a family. Certainly the mutual gift of husband and wife does not have the begetting of children as its only end, but is in itself a mutual

communion of love and of life (*Letter to Families,* n. 12, February 2, 1994, italics in original).

As noted several times previously, the covenant theology of sexuality can be stated in 17 words: "Sexual intercourse is intended by God to be at least implicitly a renewal of the marriage covenant." Such a statement is open to considerable explanation, but that's it in a nutshell. In my opinion, the Pope has incorporated the same thought into his own writing above.

The Couple to Couple League could have called attention to this identity, showing that it had been teaching a simple-to-understand "theology of the body" since its beginning, but it chose instead to drop it entirely. In its place, they have tried to incorporate the papal TOB into their materials, and they have a priest trying to explain and apply his interpretation of it in their instructional audio-visual program.

Given all the talk about the papal TOB, it was not surprising that CCL wanted to become like everyone else. However, what is surprising is that an overall theme of the EXTREME MAKEOVER is the claim to simplicity. The switch from the covenant theology to their interpretation of the papal TOB is just the opposite. It is a switch from the simple and easy-to-grasp to the complex and difficult-to-comprehend.

More Abstinence

The third major change announced in the EXTREME MAKEOVER was an alleged simplicity in its version of systematic NFP. With the help of Dr. Konald A. Prem, we had developed four sympto-thermal rules and one temperature-only rule for determining the start of postovulation infertility. The reason for having four STM rules was to have one very conservative rule and three that would provide the earliest start of Phase 3 consistent with the charted evidence. In some situations, the mucus sign seems to provide the earliest start, and in other situations, the temperature seems to do so. In all the sympto-thermal rules, the signs have to cross-check each other.

That *looks* or *sounds* complicated the first time you see or hear it, but we had successfully taught these distinctions for more than 30 years. In an NFP course, each rule takes about five or ten minutes to explain and then apply to a chart. The whole purpose of having more than one rule is to allow couples to select the earliest possible start of Phase 3 consistent with the charted evidence.

The new management of CCL decided it would prefer to teach only one Phase 3 rule. Certainly that sounds simpler and easier to teach, but the reality is that the one rule becomes three rules when applied to different situations. One significant difference between the old and the new is that the new system has dropped the rule that was based on a very strong temperature pattern with a minimum of two days of cross-checking from the mucus sign. In some cases, this rule (Rule K) indicates the start of Phase 3 a day earlier than the other STM rules. The CCL position is that couples can always wait another day.

Well, yes and no. In many cases, yes. But what about the spouse who won't be around the next day because of necessary travel? That could entail not just another day but another week or even months in the case of military deployments. The approach we took in the old CCL (and that we take now in the current NFP International) was to let the couples make those decisions by themselves. We provide them with the information, and they can decide in the given situation whether to wait another day or to celebrate their marriage with the marriage act that evening.

Three things had made CCL unique in the NFP movement—ecological breastfeeding as a form of natural family planning, the covenant theology of sexuality, and a version of systematic NFP that sought to minimize abstinence by identifying the earliest possible start of Phase 3. All three unique characteristics were dropped in the December 2007 changes. We agree only with their terminology about the changes: they are extreme.

An Injustice?

Injustice involves the violation of a right. Is this applicable to the extreme changes made by CCL? Is this applicable to the NFP movement as a whole? The reader will have to be the judge.

God made woman in such a way that the frequent suckling of her baby normally postpones the return of fertility for more than a year. This is simply God's plan for spacing babies. Do women have a right to know this information? That's a key question. We believe that every woman has a human right to know this part of God's plan for love and life. Furthermore, research has shown that only the frequent suckling pattern outlined in the Seven Standards of Ecological Breastfeeding provides, on average, more than a year of breastfeeding amenorrhea. In a culture with various patterns of baby care and nursing, women have a right to know what sort of breastfeeding actually will provide extended natural infertility and what kinds won't. This is why we are convinced that every woman has a God-given right to learn about the seven standards of ecological breastfeeding.

If this is a God-given right, then don't those who provide and teach natural family planning have a corresponding God-given obligation to teach this information? And doesn't that mean that dioceses should require the NFP programs offering services in their jurisdiction to teach the seven standards of ecological breastfeeding? And doesn't that mean that individual programs should be doing so even without diocesan instructions?

And what about teaching all the signs of fertility? God made woman in such a way that her cervix secretes mucus during her fertile time. This is common knowledge, and we are pleased to join with almost everyone else in the NFP movement in teaching this information.

God made woman in such a way that her cervix undergoes certain physical changes during the fertile time, changes that can be discerned and evaluated by ordinary women once they have been properly instructed. We find it regrettable that most of the NFP movement still does not share this common knowledge with those they teach.

God also made woman in such a way that after ovulation her waking temperature rises sufficiently to enable the couple to discern the start of post-ovulation infertility. We find it regrettable that much of the NFP movement fails to teach this important information to the couples they teach.

Lastly, what is done in the various NFP programs to place the physiological information in the context of Christian discipleship and the call to generosity in having children? I am convinced that couples have a right to know what the Catholic Church teaches on these issues, and I think they also have a right to know an easily understood explanation such as the covenant theology that Pope John Paul II incorporated into his own teaching. It's unfortunate that CCL has stopped using the simple renewal-of-the-marriage-covenant concept the Pope himself used when he was reaching out to the ordinary laity.

20. NFP International

Sheila and I founded Natural Family Planning International in 2004 to carry on the work we had started in 1971 with the Couple to Couple League. When things went badly for us in 2002, we had no intention of founding a new organization, and we were happy to keep working with the people at CCL in 2003. After the meeting on Pearl Harbor Day in 2003 and our resignations from the Board on December 9th, we still had no thought of founding a new organization. My thinking was that I didn't like what was happening to us but that at least the organization would be keeping alive the core concepts we had brought to the founding of the League in 1971. That proved to be wishful thinking.

Why NFP International?

We had structured CCL as a missionary organization. Over the years we had tried to employ regional field representatives (RFD) to work in areas away from Cincinnati, but without much success. The most successful effort was in Louisiana, and in 2004 the new management shut it down. They offered the RFD a position in Cincinnati, but family considerations made that all but impossible. The new management also decided to discontinue its support of the CCL program in areas where the language of instruction was not English or Spanish. This affected CCL's missionary efforts in the Czech Republic and Slovakia. I mentioned this in a previous chapter and bring it up now only to illustrate why we formed NFP International. This will not be the only repetition as I explain our new organization that continues the work of the CCL that we had founded.

We filed for incorporation of NFPI as a not-for-profit organization in the State of Ohio in November 2004, and in early 2005 we filed for federal recognition as a 501 (c) 3 organization, which was granted. We hoped that this would enable us to raise funds to support the NFP mission in Europe.

We had founded the Couple to Couple League on three basic concepts that we have previously described as the Triple Strand approach to NFP. That approach had served extremely well during our 32 years with the League (fall 1971 through the end of 2003) and continued to serve well through 2007. It was unique in the NFP movement, so it distinguished CCL from the other NFP providers. Thus, the primary reason for the existence of

NFPI is to promote and teach the classic content of the Triple Strand approach to natural family planning.

Natural Family Planning: The Complete Approach

Our first big task was to write a new manual for users and teachers alike. The result was an entirely new manual with a question-answer format that makes the information more readable than previously. We titled our first version of this manual *Natural Family Planning: The Question-Answer Book*. Its cover was simply the words in green ink on white paper, and it contained only 100 pages. By late 2005 it was posted on the NFPI website and was available as a free download, chapter by chapter, thus making NFP instruction more accessible than ever before.

In the summer of 2005 we learned about print-on-demand (POD) publishers, and that was a great discovery for authors with a book to publish but no money for inventory. POD publishers use a computer-driven printer that requires little or no setup and can print one book at a time.

On January 9, 2008 at the invitation of our pastor, we began an NFP course in which we taught directly from the new manual without any slides or PowerPoint. We liked teaching this way, and our attendees preferred it, saying it was more personal. They can also follow the text, observe sample charts, do the practice work in the manual, and with a detailed index they know exactly where to find things for review.

During 2008 we made further revisions, worked with a POD publisher, and published it in early 2009 with the title, *Natural Family Planning: The Complete Approach*. This version of 156 pages has full-color front and back covers, and it's available in both a perfect-bound edition and a coil-bound edition. We prefer the latter for teaching because it lies flat. Finding room for improvement, we published a slightly updated edition in February 2010.

On March 26, 2010 we made it downloadable as one PDF file from the NFPI website, and we also started to require a limited registration before downloading. On May 13, South Dakota filled out the roster of all 50 states, and on December 12 and 13, registrations from Saudi Arabia, Belize and the Isle of Man brought the international total to 71 countries. Registrations in February, 2011 from Bolivia, Oman, and Hungary raised that total to 80.

The NFPI Website, www.NFPandmore.org

As indicated by the above figures, the internet has been of immense help for sharing faith, information, and insights with people throughout the world. In addition to registrations for the online manual, this website has been accessed by people in over 100 countries. We have tried to make our website the "go-to" site for information about natural family planning information and related issues. We intend to publish as much original research as we can so the website will be of increasing value to students and other researchers. For example, on March 15, 2010 we posted the temperature-only NFP study by Dr. G. K. Doering that was first published in a German medical journal in 1967. We think this is the first time this study was made available in English. In October 2010 we posted Dr. Edward F. Keefe's 1977 article on the cervix changes, "Cephalad Shift of the Cervix Uteri."

The "and more" part of the website title is significant. The NFPI website offers not only NFP instruction, but it also offers NFP research and articles, related Church teaching, and spiritual support by way of the Seven Day Bible Rosary and a prayer book. The "And More" sidebar offers support for Protestants ("Not Just for Catholics") and links to some of the on-site articles such as "Understanding *Humanae Vitae*" and the "Sexual Revolution."

We started work on the website in the spring of 2005 and had its first version online by the fall. You can read into those generalities that you need to record significant milestones right when they happen. Details you think you will never forget do manage to get lost in the shuffle after a few years.

Blogs. Our webmaster suggested that we blog to bring more traffic to the site, so we reluctantly started blogging on April 23, 2007. Readership was very limited at first but gradually grew so that in the four months of July through November 2010 we averaged over 21,000 visits per month. Our policy has been to publish only one blog per week except for daily blogs two weeks per year—NFP Awareness Week starting around July 25 and National Breastfeeding Week in August.

Instruction. In contrast to some NFP websites, the NFPI site offers actual instruction. Readers can download the entire manual for self-study, and the requested donation for this ranges from free (to the poor) to almost free ($10.00) for everyone else. Free NFP charts can also be downloaded from the website. Interested parties can take a guided home-study course that includes testing on the basics and the interpretation of charts. A certificate of competence is awarded upon successful completion of these exercises.

The Right Kind of Instruction

The reason for this effort is to provide the right kind of instruction in natural family planning, something that is much more than "Catholic birth control." The right kind of instruction in NFP has to address the whole person. Within the Catholic Church, the entire body of Catholic teaching on love, marriage and sexuality needs to be presented in the context of Christian discipleship. The NFP course and the rest of the marriage preparation need to present Jesus as the reason for all teaching about love. He is love incarnate, so it is a great omission to try to teach about love and marriage, including sexual love, without letting Jesus show us the way.

The right kind of instruction is both negative and positive, and everyone has a human right to learn both. There are serious problems with unnatural forms of birth control, and they need to be addressed. Hormonal birth control (the Pill, injections, implants, and coated intrauterine devices) can have long-term harmful effects. Everyone should learn that every form of hormonal birth control has the potential to cause an early abortion. Every couple deserves to know that the Pill increases the risk of breast cancer. They should also know that vasectomy is associated with an increased risk of prostate cancer. Lastly, they should realize that the traditional barrier methods of birth control are by no means 100% effective. If this information does not help a couple to eschew all unnatural forms of birth control when they start their marriage, at least it may help them to discontinue these unhealthy and immoral practices in the future.

The positive aspects of natural family planning are beautiful in themselves and even more attractive in comparison with the unnatural forms of birth control. What follows in the next section has been said before, but I wanted to repeat it here for completeness about the NFPI program.

The Positive Aspects

God made woman. God Himself made woman in such a way that the frequent suckling of her baby at her breasts postpones the return of fertility. Scientific research has demonstrated that frequency of suckling is the key to the normal postponement of fertility. Mothers who practice ecological breastfeeding according to the Seven Standards will experience, on average, 14 to 15 months before their first postpartum menstruation. These mothers will also provide the best nutrition for their babies and gain significant health benefits for themselves; and they will save well over a thousand dollars with each baby—funds not spent on formula and baby foods. Every engaged and married woman deserves to know this part of God's creation.

God Himself made woman in such a way that pre-ovulation estrogen causes a healthy discharge of mucus from the cervix. God Himself made woman in such a way that pre-ovulation estrogen also causes several physical changes in the cervix. Both the mucus changes and the cervix changes can be detected and evaluated by informed women. Every engaged and married woman deserves to know these aspects of God's creation.

God Himself made woman in such a way that post-ovulation progesterone causes her basal (i.e., resting) temperature to rise enough that the upward shift can be readily noticed with accurate temperature taking and recording. A sufficiently elevated temperature pattern of at least three days provides a positive assurance that she is past ovulation. The NFP husband can become involved in the process of fertility awareness through the simple act of giving the thermometer to his wife in the morning, taking it back after a minute or so, and recording the temperature on their chart. Every engaged and married couple deserves to know this aspect of God's creation.

One sign or cross-checking signs? It is sometimes said that a one-sign approach is easier to use than cross-checking signs. That can be said about any of the signs, and I know couples who have used a one-sign approach with each of the signs—cervix, mucus, and temperature. That, of course, is their choice, but it's a choice they can make best only after they have learned all the signs and how they can work together. It also needs to be recognized that in comparative studies the cross-checking systems have yielded higher pregnancy-avoiding effectiveness rates than mucus-only systems.

Renewal of the marriage covenant. God Himself created the marriage relationship and ordered sexuality exclusively toward marriage. The Bible and sacred Tradition make it clear that God intends sexual intercourse to be, at least implicitly, a renewal of the marriage covenant. That is, in God's plan, sexual union is exclusively a marriage act that reflects and renews, at least minimally, the faith and committed love of the marriage covenant and is not deliberately closed to the transmission of life. As mentioned in the previous chapter, Pope John Paul II incorporated this basic understanding of the marriage act into his *Letter to Families* ten years after he completed the lectures that make up his *Theology of the Body*. "In the conjugal act, husband and wife are called to confirm in a responsible way *the mutual gift* of self which they have made to each other in the marriage covenant" (n.12.12, his italics). In practice, these concepts are easily expanded to explain more fully the marriage covenant. Every engaged and married deserve to learn this basic understanding of their marriage covenant and how it applies to love and sexuality.

God made marriage for family. The right kind of NFP course will help couples understand that marriage is for family and that they are called to be generous in having children. NFP is not "Catholic birth control." Specifically, the NFP course should transmit standard Catholic teaching that couples need a sufficiently serious reason to postpone or avoid pregnancy in order to use systematic NFP. Some NFP promoters want to avoid the term "serious reason" (HV 10 and 16) and substitute "just cause" (HV 16). While both terms are used in *Humanae Vitae,* I think that "just cause" is psychologically inadequate if used separately instead of as a supplement to "serious reason" in the present circumstances. "Just cause" terminology carries the risk of sounding like "just 'cuz" as in "just 'cuz we don't want the inconvenience of kids or more kids."

Aside from wanting to do what's best for the child, "serious reasons" are not needed to use ecological breastfeeding with the hopes of a year or more of natural infertility. In fact, considering all the benefits of EBF to both mother and baby, couples should have a truly good reason not to breastfeed.

Walking with Jesus. While it is true that systematic natural family planning can stand on its own merits as a method of birth control, it is also true that periodic abstinence can test our resolve and offer us real temptations to engage in immoral sexual activities during the fertile time. Through faith we know that the narrow way of Jesus is the only way to true happiness, and we know that He calls us to take up our cross daily and to follow him. We know that Jesus came to save us and to teach us how to love. Even so, we are weak and we can feel like St. Paul who wrote about his weaknesses. We need the help of the Lord to overcome these temptations, and we need to remember that He revealed to St. Paul that He provides the grace necessary to overcome temptations (see 2 Cor 12:9). It is unwise to think we are not going to be tempted, and it is stupid not to pray to the Lord for the graces we need to overcome them.

Obedience. That brings us to the last point that needs to be included in a complete course on natural family planning: obedience to the Lord who continues to teach in and through his Church. Sometimes we can be tempted to think that because we understand and teach the reasons for Catholic teaching against contraception, or because we now have the Theology of the Body and the covenant insight, we no longer need to teach obedience. In an anti-authoritarian age, we might feel uncomfortable talking about the teaching authority of the Church.

On the contrary, however, it is helpful to remember that, although Jesus possessed all the virtues, the only virtue of the Lord Jesus specifically mentioned in the New Testament is obedience. Further, how can any of us dare to teach that it is seriously immoral to engage in contraceptive behaviors without relying upon the Magisterium of the Church founded by Christ and guided by the Holy Spirit through the centuries? How can we expect couples to believe that contraceptive behaviors are the grave matter of mortal sin if all we present is a theological statement? What sort of force does mere argument have today? Obedience is the fruit of a heart that is open to the Lord Jesus who is the reason for being a Catholic and for following his teachings in and through his Church. All of our theologizing exists to support the biblical-Catholic authoritative teaching, but our theology does not stand by itself. To omit reference to the Magisterium is to short-change those we seek to teach.

Results. I think that with this sort of course and reinforcement from the pastor and the rest of the marriage preparation program about 25% of couples will start their marriages with marital chastity. Further, the seeds that have been planted will continue to grow, and many of the contraceptors will experience for themselves the wasteland of secular sexuality, so I expect a gradual increase in the numbers of couples who repent and accept full Catholic teaching on love, marriage and sexuality. With help from the pulpit and an overall parish environment that promotes authentic Catholic spirituality and sexuality, I think that by their tenth anniversaries at least two-thirds of couples who experienced the right kind of marriage preparation and NFP course will be fully practicing Catholics.

What is difficult for me to comprehend is that in December 2010 only six dioceses are making any kind of NFP course a required part of preparation for marriage. Why does any priest or any bishop NOT want Catholic engaged and married couples to know everything I have described as the content of the right kind of NFP course? It's all basic and easy to understand, and it can be taught modestly, even in mixed classes. I would like to think that even those who think of themselves as "liberal" or "pro-choice" on birth control would want their people to know all of the above.

After all, how can people make an informed choice without this information? To paraphrase Romans 10 again, how can people act rightly unless they believe? And how can they believe unless they are taught? And how can they believe and act rightly unless they have the right kind of instruction? And in today's context, how will they experience such instruction without being required to do so?

Summary

I have described seven subjects that need to be taught in an adequate NFP course.
1. Ecological breastfeeding as a form of NFP
2. Changes in cervical mucus and in the cervix
3. Temperature changes
4. The marriage act as a renewal of the marriage covenant
5. Generosity in having children
6. Walking with Jesus
7. Obedience to Christ speaking through his Church

All of this information can and should be taught very economically. I cannot find any good reason why any informed bishop or priest or family life director would not want engaged and married couples to know all of these seven positive dimensions of chaste natural family planning.

What Is Unique about NFP International?

We believe that NFP International offers the most complete approach to natural family planning.
- It teaches all the common signs of fertility, the seven standards of ecological breastfeeding, the need for sufficiently serious reason, and relevant Catholic morality. Its instruction addresses the whole person, not just symptoms of fertility, and places the "methods" explicitly in the context of Christian discipleship.

- Most persons of average intelligence can learn both systematic natural family planning and ecological breastfeeding by reading the NFPI manual.

- Its low cost makes it universally available. That is, its question-answer form of instruction can be taught directly from the NFPI manual without slides or PowerPoint, and thus it can be taught in poor conditions where electricity is not always available.

- In the United States, for our classroom course we request a donation of less than two days minimum wages, and that includes a printed version of the NFPI manual plus a thermometer, charts, and instruction that lasts a lifetime.

- The NFPI manual, *Natural Family Planning: The Complete Approach,* can be downloaded for free for the poor.

- Free charts are available at the home page of www.nfpandmore.org.

- NFPI provides a very reasonably priced home study course for learners and engaged persons preparing for marriage.

- NFPI provides free teacher training for those who are convinced about the NFPI Triple Strand and want to teach from the NFPI manual.

Natural Family Planning: The Complete Approach

- This is the only American NFP text that teaches ecological breastfeeding as a form of natural baby spacing. NFPI instruction does not force anyone to breastfeed for any specific duration, but it does empower a couple to make a well informed choice.

- It is the only American NFP text that uses the simple-to-grasp covenant statement of sexuality to explain and support the teaching of *Humanae Vitae.*

- It is the only American NFP text that teaches the cross-checking signs in such a way that couples can determine the earliest start of post-ovulation infertility consistent with all the evidence. Thus the start of Phase 3 may be recognized one or two days earlier than with other rules.

This manual also teaches
- All the fertility signs and their rules
- Generosity in having children
- The need to have a sufficiently serious reason to use systematic NFP to avoid or postpone pregnancy

- Catholic teaching about the meaning of human sexuality
- Fertile-time chastity when avoiding pregnancy
- How to determine pregnancy and accurately estimate the due date.

The Importance of Teaching Chastity

The price of teaching chastity is very small. The cost of not teaching chastity is extremely high.

Priestly unchastity has scandalized millions, provided a lavish source for criticism of the Church, and bankrupted several dioceses.

Marital unchastity has undermined countless marriages, and it has played a major part in the decline of vocations to the priesthood. It has led to a Catholic birth rate just at or below replacement level, setting the stage for our descendants to be living in a country dominated by Muslims whose parents and grandparents didn't stop at two children.

When you read this, I hope you can say that at least the preparation for marriage in the Catholic Church in the United States has improved remarkably. That's the required preparation for the remedy of the other sexually related ills that afflict the Church and the entire culture in the West today.

The history of the NFP movement has clearly demonstrated that no organization can do much by itself and that most diocesan NFP programs leave much to be desired. It is clear that the effort to bring about a rebirth of chastity and a culture of life within the Church and the culture requires the cooperation between the hierarchy and lay organizations envisioned by the Fathers of Vatican Council II. The NFP International organization is such a lay apostolate and can be an effective vehicle for building a culture of life when it is properly utilized by dioceses and parishes.

The International Character of NFP International

The first day of November 2010 brought an email message from France that illustrates the international character of NFP International. The process actually started in April when the writer registered to download *Natural Family Planning: The Complete Approach,* and I sent him a registration survey. When he returned the survey in November, he wrote:

> Thank you for your excellent books *Breastfeeding and Natural Child Spacing* and *The Seven Standards of Ecological Breastfeeding*. I translated "the Seven Standards summary" for my wife and for the nun teaching NFP in the hospital where our children were born. What we found in your books, we found nowhere else!

He also summarized his wife's breastfeeding experiences. With her first two babies she did not do EBF and experienced six and 9.5 months of amenorrhea respectively. With her third baby, she did ecological breastfeeding for 15 months and weaned for one month, and she experienced 15.5 months of amenorrhea.

I asked him if they would like to start the French version of NFP International, but he replied that he did not have the time for that sort of task. He added,

> I think that EBF teaching should be the priority in France. Indeed, French Catholic couples who know Catholic teaching and the Billings method totally ignore EBF.

After two more paragraphs describing some unfortunate aspects of the breastfeeding situation in France he added:

> To conclude, there is a big need for the teaching of ecological breastfeeding in France. I am sorry because I have no time to translate (except for the little PDF I sent you). [A listing of the Seven Standards in French is available at the NFPI website.]

Our hope is that in a few years that situation is radically changed for the better. We are grateful that people in over 80 countries have made good use of services at the NFPI website.

21. Matters of Justice

Justice matters. Justice matters for the culture and society. Justice matters for individuals. The entire body of Catholic teaching about justice is ultimately focused on the dignity of the individual person and the effort to achieve and to protect the rights of individual persons.

It is commonly believed and taught by Christians that when an individual has suffered an injustice, the victim is called by God to forgive those who have done wrong to him or her. That is true, but it is not the whole story. Forgiveness does not preclude the effort to achieve justice, whether for a third party or for oneself. Pope Benedict XVI was very specific on this point as he addressed the issue of sexual abuse. On May 11, 2010, in a plane en route to Portugal, he stated very clearly:

> This too is something that we have always known, but today we are seeing it in a really terrifying way: that the greatest persecution of the Church comes not from her enemies without, but arises from sin within the Church, and that the Church thus has a deep need to relearn penance, to accept purification, to learn forgiveness on the one hand, but also the need for justice. Forgiveness does not replace justice.

Accountability

Within the Catholic Church, there are several levels of authority and responsibility. The Popes exercise their teaching and governing responsibilities and rights with several different kinds of documents that have different levels of authority such as encyclicals, exhortations, and personal directives called *motu proprio* (by his personal initiative, literally, "by his own motion"). Bishops exercise their teaching and governing responsibilities and rights through Church-wide Councils, national councils, and as the chief shepherds in their own dioceses. Pastors exercise similar responsibilities and rights within their own parishes. That much is quite clear.

It also seems quite clear that the diocesan bishops are responsible for implementing the teachings of the Popes, Church-wide Councils, and their own decrees. That's how the teaching of the Church is to be brought to bear on world, national, and local cultures, at least within the Church.

But who is responsible for blowing the whistle when local pastors and bishops fail to apply the teachings of the Church within their own areas of responsibility? Who will hold them accountable? Who is responsible for trying to bring the teachings of the Church to bear on situations not subject to the control of the bishops? Is no one accountable? Is everyone equally accountable? Do some laity and priests with special competencies have more responsibilities than others?

Perhaps I have not been reading the right things or attending the right lectures, but I haven't seen or heard much about accountability. It seems to me that injustice will thrive unless bishops and priests teach regularly and also act when circumstances require it, but who will hold them accountable to do so, and how does one hold a bishop or priest accountable? If a priest refuses obedience to the liturgical norms and instead changes the words of the Mass, should he be held accountable? And how? If bishops publish a document on marriage in which they pledge to cooperate with every provider of NFP instruction, should they be held accountable and what would that mean? Injustice will also continue to thrive if the laity do not support, both emotionally and financially, the efforts of their fellow laity to remedy issues of injustice.

Rules of Engagement

The Great Scandal of 2002 was obviously caused primarily by priests who violated the moral teaching of the Church, but it was aggravated by both bishops and laity who were excessively reluctant to admit or expose the corruption of morality within the Church. As a result, the effort to avoid scandal led to an even greater scandal. Most of this reluctance is due to the great respect that almost all Catholics have for almost all priests. Some reticence is due to having unrealistic expectations of universal perfection and sanctity in priests. Some people become unduly scandalized when they learn of the serious sins of a priest. I have been told of people who held a particular priest in such high regard that when he failed, they lost their faith. I know of people who say they have lost faith in the Church because of the Great Scandal. Perhaps, but perhaps the Scandal offered them a convenient excuse to give into their own anti-religious sentiments imbibed from the culture.

So it seems to me that the first rule of engagement is that all parties need to recognize the Judas principle. One of the original Twelve Apostles was unfaithful. That's 8.33 percent of the first group of bishops. The percentage of priests who abused young children and adolescents was about 2.0 percent. I suppose that unhappy spirit of Judas will always infect a few of our bishops and priests, but we need to keep those failures in context. We need to realize that the Church is always in need of reform. When injustice rears its ugly head within the Church, we need to try to remedy it, and we also need to put such efforts explicitly in the context of the Judas principle.

The second rule of engagement is that the demands of justice within the Church need to be taught in Catholic seminaries and houses of formation, in diocesan continuing education for priests, and somehow the Pope needs to teach his fellow bishops. Laity who are active in apostolic efforts and dependent upon free publicity through the parish bulletin should not be discriminated against because, for example, they ask for the correction of liturgical abuses or other injustices.

The third rule of engagement concerns real efforts instead of gossip. Mere gossip can be a real scandal, and that's why efforts need to be made through the appropriate channels first. Unless the problem is already public, "going public" should occur only when such efforts have failed.

Simply put, the traditional phrase, "The Church is always in need of reform" doesn't refer to doctrine but to the individual members of the Church and their relationships with each other.

A Review of Issues in My Memoirs

The Regina experience. This was a breakdown of justice within the Church at all three levels—Archbishop, pastor, and some of my fellow laity. On the other hand, it was the witness of my fellow Catholics who were well educated in both Catholic social justice principles and in secular business justice who supported me and who led the public opposition to the parish-related injustices. It was obviously not a sexual abuse, and the incident clearly shows that not all abuses within the Church are sexual in nature.

On the downside, I heard rumors that one person was so scandalized upon learning of these injustices that he or she left the Church, and I still regret that happening, if it is true, and I have prayed many times for that person's return to the fullness of the Faith. We tried to put the case into perspective, but we waited too long. We should have started our public efforts with a statement of the Judas principle. On the upside, several years later a priest told me that my actions had improved things in Regina, whatever that meant.

The firefighter experience. The bothersome thing about this incident is that no one else stepped forward. There were thousands of homeowners and business owners whose lives and property are dependent to some degree upon the proper performance of their local firefighters. There were educated Catholic laity and priests, people who knew Catholic social teaching and who could name the great social encyclicals that affirm the right of workers to organize and to be treated decently. Of course, I don't know what behind-the-scenes efforts they were making. Maybe some had already tried talking with the city safety director, but I never heard about any such efforts before or after my visit to City Hall.

On the upside, the firefighters were encouraged that someone who taught theology at a Catholic college would support them. The apparent downside was that my efforts probably cost me my teaching job, but with the benefit of hindsight that was beneficial because it led to our move to the Twin Cities where we were able to work with Dr. Konald Prem and begin our ministry of teaching natural family planning.

The dormitory debate. Objections from students were understandable. Some possibly did regard their rooms as "living rooms" where only innocent conversation would occur. Others possibly wanted to fornicate in their bedrooms behind locked doors. But the chaplain should have known better than to use the pulpit to accuse me of not understanding what was going on. Again, this was at a time of significant theological confusion among priests and seminarians, some of whom believed the anti-Catholic-morality teachings in the books they read and the lectures they heard. It was the same theological environment that gave rise to the Great Scandal.

On the downside, it was disappointing that my department chairman did not publicly support me. He knew the overall situation at the college, and his own reaction was to switch from the theology department to the music department. On the upside, it probably helped me to realize sooner rather than later that I would never be granted tenure no matter how many books or other publications were on my record, no matter what my value might be as a witness to Catholic teaching. That realization, in turn, helped with the decision to work full-time in the natural family planning movement.

The dismissed teacher. This experience illustrated corruption within the Church at several levels. It started with a religious sister and her principal teaching false sexual doctrine in the classroom. It was greatly aggravated by the Archbishop's unwillingness to back up his own decision that the principal couldn't fire the innocent teacher for seeking to correct the situation. The corruption became precedent setting when the due-process board ruled that although the principal had, in violation of the Archbishop's order, fired the innocent teacher, she had a right to discriminate so she would feel comfortable with her staff. The fact that no one else protested this injustice illustrated an unhappy combination of ignorance of the demands of justice, indifference to the fate of a Catholic teacher simply doing his job, or cowardice masquerading as prudence.

The downside was the collective actions of the sister-teacher, the principal, the disciplinary failure of the Archbishop, and the decision of the due process board. All of these illustrated the corruption dealing with sexual morality in the Archdiocese of Cincinnati in the Seventies. The upside was threefold: the sister and her principal left the school, I joined the ranks of those who had little confidence in Archbishop Bernardin, and the innocent teacher became a lawyer who later successfully blew the whistle on theological corruption at the archdiocesan seminary.

The dispute with CCL. We had a valid signed publishing agreement that stipulated royalties on *The Art of Natural Family Planning.* At official meetings, the Board of Directors had also voted to provide royalties on two of my other publications. I believe it was an injustice to violate the publishing agreement and to renege on their Board agreements. I believe that the lengthy and expensive legal costs constituted another form of injustice against us and probably against donors who did not contribute funds for such litigation.

The biggest injustice, in my opinion, has been the "Extreme Makeover" which retained the "Triple Strand" label but radically changed its contents. In the Extreme Makeover, CCL dropped both the terminology and the concept of ecological breastfeeding as a form of natural family planning. Every adult has a right to know this aspect of God's creation.

I think that couples have a right to know the rules that will provide the least amount of abstinence, but in the Extreme Makeover, CCL dropped a temperature-based rule (we call it Rule K) that sometimes provides a start to Phase 3 one day earlier than the other STM rules as well as two days earlier than mucus-only rules.

When it comes to explaining the teaching of *Humanae Vitae*, the Church has a right to expect that NFP programs will convey its teaching on the need for serious reason to use systematic NFP for pregnancy avoidance. If there are both simple and difficult ways to explain the teaching of *Humanae Vitae*, couples have a right to hear the easy-to-grasp explanation. Ten years after he finished his *Theology of the Body*, Pope John Paul II used the idea that the marriage act should be a renewal of the marriage covenant in his *Letter to Families.* He did not tell couples to read and study his 129 lectures, valuable as they are. I think that justice and common sense require us to use the simple "renewal of the marriage covenant" concept in the very limited time available in any NFP course.

Management positions. CCL produced two manuals that contained errors that could lead to unintended pregnancies. In the case of its new user's manual titled *The Art of Natural Family Planning: Student Edition,* we pointed out the mistake and even offered to write a corrective text, but the management refused to insert an error sheet even though that's a common publishing industry practice.

Some mistakes are inevitable, but I believe that the whistleblower treatment given to Sheila and the Board's failure to correct this situation was an injustice to her and potentially to the candidate teachers and those whom they would instruct.

Transferring my copyright on *Sex and the Marriage Covenant* to the Couple to Couple League without my authorization was clearly an injustice.

Sometimes the line between simply lousy management and injustice becomes blurred. Examples of these include the refusal to address the issue of bullying behavior in the office, the complete lack of any consequences for calumny, and the complete lack of any apology for the treatment Sheila and I received at the Board meeting on Pearl Harbor Day 2003.

The Greatest Injustice

The greatest injustice in the world today is the killing of unborn children. It is massive and has been with us so long that too many of us regard it as an unchangeable evil unless the Lord Himself intervenes in some catastrophic and prophetic way.

Closely related to abortion is the injustice of contraception. It is related to abortion in three ways. First, all of the hormonal forms of birth control have the potential to cause an early abortion by thinning the endometrium so that implantation of the newly conceived baby does not occur. Second, the social and legal acceptance of abortion started with the social and legal acceptance of contraception. Third, the social and legal rejection of abortion is probably dependent upon the social and legal rejection of contraception. Many are working hard to stop abortion completely or reduce its frequency while saying or doing nothing to oppose contraception. In one sense, I hope they are successful and I wish them well. In another sense, I think that efforts to stop abortion through legal processes will succeed only through a rebirth of chastity, and that will involve the rejection of marital contraception and the acceptance of natural family planning when needed.

Whatever the relationship between the acceptance of natural family planning and the social and legal rejection of abortion, two things ought to be clear. First, couples who practice ecological breastfeeding and systematic NFP are pro-life and will vote pro-life when properly educated. Dioceses and parishes need to do everything in their power to educate all those whom they can reach. Second, the failure of Catholics to accept Catholic teaching on love, marriage and sexuality not only endangers their own salvation and harms the Church as a social and spiritual body, but it also has the ballot-box effect of helping to promote the culture of death.

Therefore, education in marital chastity, eco-breastfeeding, and systematic NFP is not just "nice." It is so necessary for the good of the couples, babies, the Church, and society that it is an injustice not to insist on such education as part of preparation for marriage.

Other injustices. We have learned personally of other situations that involve the loss of apostolates by their founders. I will address some of these indirectly in the next chapter.

22. Learning from Mistakes

In the previous chapters I have more than once revealed my mistakes and those of others, and some of them are repeated in this chapter. This book has been written largely in the hopes that at least a few people can benefit from these mistakes. As George Santayana has noted, "Those who do not remember the past are condemned to repeat it." I am sure that you will make your own mistakes, whoever you are, but perhaps the mistakes related in this book can help you avoid some of mine and those of a few others.

Injustices to individuals and to groups are an unhappy fact of life, a testimony to the enduring effects of Original Sin. Prior to the Second Coming of the Lord Jesus, they will not be completely eliminated. That leads to two possibilities.

1. You may be offered the opportunity to help others when you witness an injustice. The great temptation is to do nothing. In some cases, it may be prudent to limit your response to prayer. In other cases, it may be Christian prudence to pray and also to engage in some sort of action. Not all action will influence the result, but some forms of action will at least provide moral support for those whose rights are being denied.

2. If you recognize the widespread effects of Original Sin, you have the opportunity to protect yourself and your endeavors as well as you can. In other words, it is imprudent to assume that everything will go as it should. Considering the human condition, it is a matter of Christian prudence to imagine a worst-case scenario and then plan accordingly. Here a word of caution is necessary. No matter how well you arrange matters to protect yourself and your endeavors, there can be no guarantee that someone will not try to deny you justice. The point is, however, that if you arrange things prudently, efforts by others to deny you justice are less likely to succeed and your efforts to defend your rights and those of others may be less costly.

Setting Up Your Organization

Let's assume you are Catholic and have an idea that you think will help the Church. Let's assume that you want to build an organization to carry that idea beyond your neighborhood parish and want to serve the Church universal. Let's also assume that your idea is fully orthodox, addresses a key area of concern where Catholic teaching is ignored or rejected, and is therefore controversial. You know ahead of time that widespread acceptance of your idea will not be immediate. You have a number of decisions to make.

For-profit or not-for-profit. There are advantages and disadvantages to each form of organization. Both forms of organization have to make a profit or they will go out of business, and every organization is truly a business. The difference between the two is not the need for profit or at least a breakeven, but what happens to those profits. In not-for-profits, the profits have to stay in the organization (or be given to other non-profits when it ceases to do business). On the other hand, if you have money you want to invest in the organization, the non-profit organization limits the percentage of the revenues you can donate. The federal government seeks to prevent the formation of non-profits as tax dodges for the wealthy.

Control. Do you want to be in control or do you want others to be in control? Don't be too quick to say that you want others to be in control because you think they will bring in the needed funds and support. That may be true in a localized community where name recognition is important, but it may not have any relevance for an organization that seeks to serve the Church universal. Further, the contributions by some Board members may be surprisingly small.

There are two ways in which you can retain control. The most obvious is to keep the Board of Directors very small. The late and great Father Paul Marx, OSB, wrote in his autobiography, *Faithful for Life*, these heartfelt sentences:

> The decisions and actions of the board convinced me, as nothing else could, of what I already knew, that good pro-life work does not get done by a large committee or board. I do not know of a single flourishing pro-life effort in the whole world that is conducted by a large administrative board (112).

He spoke favorably about a married couple who maintained control of their organization by keeping their Board size at three persons including themselves. Remember two important points: 1) The larger the Board, the more opportunities there are for politics and factions to develop. 2) You can always expand the Board, but reducing its size will be almost impossible if factions have developed.

The second way of maintaining control is to write the Code of Regulations in such a way that you and one or two other people, depending on the legal minimum, are the only members of the controlling Board of Trustees who then set up a Board of Directors. The Trustees can then dissolve the Board of Directors if it does things that the Trustees deem incompatible with the organization's mission. It is my understanding that this form of organization is quite common. In fact, when Sheila and I separated from the Couple to Couple League, some folks who were acquainted with the Trustee form of control were shocked that we had not set up our organization in that way.

The bottom line is that this is something you will want to discuss with competent legal counsel.

If you choose to keep the Board very small, you probably need to develop and then actually use an Advisory Board. You may be able to get on your Advisory Board certain people with great expertise who would never want to be on your Board of Directors simply because they don't have the time to attend Board meetings. Some advisors like to be used, and you need to keep them informed.

Your Business Is a Business

You might like to think of yourself and your volunteers and employees as just one big family, but the reality is that your organization is a business, and that's not a bad word. You need to keep certain records, and you need to follow applicable laws and regulations. You need to run your organization in a business-like manner. That and what follows may seem all too obvious to state, but we have seen examples that illustrate the extremely high cost of not doing things in a business-like manner.

I repeat here three huge mistakes I made by way of not being business-like, and they proved very costly to me and Sheila. We had a publishing agreement with CCL for *The Art of Natural Family Planning,* and two of the mistakes dealt with that publication. First, without realizing the importance of copyright ownership, I wrote "Copyright 1996 by the Couple to Couple League" in the Fourth Edition. The previous editions had been copyrighted in the names of John and Sheila Kippley. Second, about the time the royalties were due on the Fourth Edition, I became eligible for Social Security, and our financial situation seemed more flexible than CCL's, so I deferred some of the royalties. My big mistake was that I treated this informally as in "we're all family" with the business manager, and it did not get entered into the accounting system. I should have told him to enter it into the accounting system as "Deferred royalties." I also should have notified the Board what I was doing and gotten a Board action to approve this and to approve in advance that the royalties would be paid us upon our request.

My third big mistake was that when I started to get Social Security I reduced my salary from $44,000 down to the $15,000 allowed by the IRS. (In 1997, if you were receiving Social Security, were under 70, and were still earning income, you had to pay back to the IRS one dollar for every two dollars you earned over $15,000.) My mistake was that I was still in the "we're all family" mode and made no restrictions on this gift. I should have structured it as a loan callable upon my departure from full-time employment. The last two mistakes left CCL with a significant war chest to carry on our legal battles that began after they refused to pay the contractual royalties, both current and deferred.

Contracts. Written contracts are legal documents provided they meet the requirements which are frequently minimal. They record an agreement between you and another party at a certain date. They can be changed if both parties agree to the change. They are important both as simple reminders of what the parties agreed to at the time and as a vehicle for helping to prod each party to live up to their agreement. If things turn sour, they provide a third party such as an arbitrator or judge or jury a basis on which to form a judgment about the respective obligations of the parties.

It is not being legalistic or untrusting to have contracts. It is just a matter of common sense recognition that parties can forget the details. Good contracts can and should spell out how to handle differences of interpretation or what to do if things turn sour. In the event of the death or incapacitation of one of the parties, a contract is a great service to those who inherit the responsibilities and the rights dealt with in the document. I know of a situation in which a bishop was helping a small organization, and he helped even more by putting his intentions into contractual language so that continuity would be assured when the next bishop was assigned. On the other hand, I have seen situations where the lack of a contract such as a publishing agreement has caused pain that otherwise would have been completely avoided.

To repeat something my lawyer son-in-law told me, it is much less expensive to spend a few hundred dollars for competent legal counsel and a good contract when starting a legal relationship than to have to spend thousands of dollars in litigation later to fight for your rights after they have been violated or simply threatened because of a lack of written clarity and contracts.

If you sign a contract, be sure to read it first. Better yet, if the contract has to do with anything affecting the future of your organization, have a competent attorney read it and tell you what it means. If the contract is between you and another organization that is larger and better financed, be doubly sure that you have your attorney read it. The same holds true for contracts between you and other individuals, especially if they have much more money than you and can thus afford extended legal expenses if things turn sour. You can be reasonably assured that the other party's legal counsel either drafted or reviewed a proposed contract. If the other party puts pressure on you for a prompt signing, state very simply that it's your policy not to sign important documents without a review by your legal counsel. Hint: Write this into your bylaws. If it's in your by-laws, you can deflect any pressure by telling the other party truthfully that you need to follow your by-laws.

This may seem too obvious to write, and I wouldn't write it if we didn't know some folks who suffered significant losses because they caved into pressure to sign before a careful review. From their previous conversations with the other party, they thought the agreement was mutually advantageous, so they signed the agreement without reading it. They soon wished that they had sought legal counsel before signing. If they had been dealing with a completely secular organization, they might have been a bit skeptical, especially when confronted with time-related pressures to sign now instead of later. But they were dealing with their co-religionists.

Lastly, but certainly not the last word on this subject, periodically review your organization's contracts and your policy handbook. This is especially important if there is a major change within your organization or some key employees move from one location to another.

Publications. Most organizations produce publications ranging from brochures to books. Who owns them? If they produce revenues, who gets the revenues or how are they to be shared? If the author leaves the organization, can he take his works with him to be published by a new publisher?

As an author, be aware of and be wary of the work-for-hire legal doctrine. That doctrine can be applied by your employer to mean that anything you write on company time belongs exclusively and totally to the employer even if you have a unique talent and even if the document in question could not be written by anyone else. Some employers might even stretch it to mean that anything you write while you are their employee is their intellectual property, even if you write it on your own time. When I wrote that last sentence, I thought I was really imagining things, but within a month I learned of a case where that was exactly the employer's claim. The work-for-hire doctrine means that your employer can deny you any royalties for such work unless you have a written contract. As an employee, you may not have much leverage, but you might do well to contract with copyright counsel to represent you to work out a publication agreement that is fair to both parties. One way of handling significant publications is to have the value of the employee's writing time deducted from the royalties earned before he starts to receive actual payment. Something similar might be said also about patents, but I will stick to writing.

As an employer, use the work-for-hire doctrine fairly. Develop a written policy on publications so that everybody knows the ground rules, and have it signed as a contractual agreement, but beware. If you make your policy too stringent in favor of the employer, your best writers may decide to do their best work at home in the evenings and weekends and find another publisher. Don't kill the goose that lays the golden eggs.

On the other hand, every author, either published or still hopeful, knows that the value of his or her time is only one of the costs of publication. That's why publishers pay royalties of only 10 or 15 percent on trade books and sometimes lower on high volume textbooks or other books that require an extraordinary amount of work by others. Copyright counsel is more expensive than basic legal counsel, but expertise at the beginning can be helpful to all parties in the long run. Good counsel can also help both parties to understand common practices in the field and to do what is right and not just legal.

Another reason for publishing contracts is that they establish who owns what. We know of an organization that published a book written by a non-employee without any sort of contractual agreement. Then an employee left the organization and took the book to another organization. I can't guess the legality of that, but it seems to me that the first organization paid a high price for being too much in the "we're all family" mode.

Charity. If your organization is a recognized not-for-profit organization, your own contributions are tax-deductible, but they are limited. For a publicly-supported 501(c) 3 organization, the founders can donate only two-thirds of the organization's annual revenues. That is, at least one-third of the revenues have to come from the public. These things can change, and this is not legal advice, so check these things with competent legal counsel.

You may also plan to leave a substantial portion of your estate to your organization if it outlives you, but you also need to be aware that the organization that you founded may be changed profoundly after you leave the helm, and that might be years before you die. It may change so much that you would not want to fund it.

We made a mistake in this area. At the first Board meeting after a new executive director had been installed, we became very wary of some new directions that we could not support. We were under a duress of time because we were leaving on a plane trip very shortly. Since planes go down occasionally, we promptly changed our Will to exclude our own organization. So far, okay. Then I made the mistake of telling the Board we had done so. My wishful thinking was that the Board might take another look at the way it was going. The reality was that informing them did no good and may have deepened the growing alienation.

Commonsense Ways to Stay on the Same Page

The person with sufficient business experience will find what follows to be so elementary that it's not worth reading, but many of us have not had such experience. So here are a few items that will seem very obvious once you read them.

Mission statement. Be sure you have a basic mission statement. Keep it short enough that almost anyone can memorize it. If you can't write it by hand on a standard business card, it's probably too long. You can always explain its ramifications in subsidiary sentences.

Then make sure that every employee and Board member knows it and accepts it wholeheartedly. Make it part of the employee application and job description.

Use it as your guide whenever you are considering new projects. Keep asking, "Does this advance our mission?"

Background checks. Do a background check on every candidate who seems to have the basic abilities and requirements for the job and whom you consider a serious contender. If you are not experienced in these matters, you might do well to contract with a specialist. Former employers may be quite reluctant to say anything truly damaging but truthful about their former employee, but an experienced person should know the right questions to ask and how to follow up on any comment that is less than a full endorsement.

Job descriptions. Have job descriptions that are sufficiently realistic so that both the candidate and the manager will have the same basic understandings of what is needed and expected. If the job requires travel, make sure that's in the description with a realistic estimate of time away from home. Review the job description with the candidate and consider having the candidate sign and date his or her acceptance of the description.

Religious discrimination. If agreement on articles of faith is important to the organization, specify this in the handbook and the job descriptions. It is my understanding that every religious organization can discriminate on the basis of religion, but check that with competent legal counsel. How can an organization seeking to promote the full Catholic way of life hire a contracepting Catholic or non-Catholic?

Employee handbook. You will need an employee handbook to codify your organizational policies and practices. This can and should include the sorts of things carried regularly in the business pages of newspapers. Dress code. Personal use of phones, email, internet, cell phones, texting. Work at home. Business hours. Expected hours for non-hourly employees. Lunch hours. Flex-time or fixed hours. Ownership of whatever is sent via company equipment such as emails. Copyright and royalty policies.

Work ethic, full-time or part-time. In light of your company policies about business hours and possible overtime, discuss the candidate's work ethic. Review your own expectations. Is it reasonable to expect overtime except in very unusual situations? Make clear whether the job is a full-time breadwinner position or for part-time supplemental income.

In-house or outsourcing. If possible, determine very early in the game what services you need to keep in-house and what you can outsource. What is best for your mission and the people you want to serve?

Consultants. Consult a handbook on standard business practices, and after you have done your best to cover the basics of employment policies and practices, don't be afraid to consult a management advisor or legal counsel.

Management. Lastly, it may help to keep in mind that management is primarily about helping others to do their jobs well and better. Expect people to make some mistakes, and help them to learn from them. On the other hand, if an employee either cannot or will not do what needs to be done, be prepared to administer discipline, even termination, in a way that is fair to all parties. Termination is sort of an industrial capital punishment, so be sure that it is the discipline of the last resort.

As the boss, you need to be a leader, and you will have an easier job if you try to remain positive and look for ways to help those who need help. Have an open-door policy, and be willing to talk with those who want to talk.

Bosses don't need to be bossy to manage well. Leaders who attempt to pull their subordinates along with them will generally be more effective than bosses who try to push—lay a string on a table and try to push it. .

Conflict and Phasing Out

One area for which you need to develop a worst-case plan is serious conflict with your own Board of Directors or with key employees who have the ear of the Board members. This may seem unimaginable, and that's why you have to imagine it. You may think that because you are the founder or a long-time leader there will be such a residue of gratitude that your ouster is unthinkable. Think again. While the Board may be reluctant to oust you in a public manner, it can make life so difficult for you in the working environment of the office that you will feel you cannot continue. You may even fear for your own bodily safety, as I did. So you may figure the only thing to do is to resign. That was one of my mistakes. Of course, if you have properly structured the organization, you can disband the Board and appoint others or simply reduce its size to the legal minimum.

Resignation. The time will come when you will want to resign if for no other reason than you are getting older, have less energy, and want to spend more time with your family. If your reason for wanting to retire is simply a matter of less energy, be sure you get a thorough health checkup. We know a gentleman who had developed a worthwhile apostolate but felt he should resign for reasons of health. After he resigned his job as Executive Director, he suffered a medical incident that he survived very well. After entering a rehabilitation program, within a few months he was feeling better and more energetic than he had in the previous five years. His reason for resignation vanished and he wanted to return to his job as the ED, but it was too late.

Under ideal conditions, you will hire your own replacement. I had wanted to do that, but the budget was insufficient for two salaries. I would have been better off, once I had reached the Social Security age, to diminish my own salary to a low level, even to that of a dollar-a-year, in order to bring in someone whom I could train and trust. As it happened, I reduced my salary to $15,000 and deferred our royalties, but I failed to use those savings to hire the right person. At a time of crisis in 2003, I offered to work for a dollar-a-year, but by that time the new chairman would not agree to that even for one year.

Conditions vary so widely that no one can tell you what to do ahead of time, but my experience leads me to suggest a couple of things not to do.

1. Don't resign abruptly. That may be just exactly what certain parties want, but it may not be in the best interests of yourself or your family or the organization you founded. It may be helpful to seek counsel of some professionals who can help you negotiate the terms of your resignation.

2. Don't put your job on the line. That makes it too easy for your opposition. We made that mistake, and the Board only had to refuse our demand to demote the ED whom we were convinced was not up to the demands of the job. So they did nothing, and we followed through with our threat and resigned, and it was most certainly not a negotiated resignation. (When the ED was let go about five months later, we came back as employees, but that did not last very long and we were permanently disemployed about four months later.)

3. Don't place too much trust in any one person who is in a position to help you or hurt you. From my conversations with a particular Board member, I was sure of that person's support at the November 2002 Board meeting, but at the crucial time that support evaporated.

4. Don't accept a gag rule. Transparency is important. This is not to say that all the dirty laundry needs to be cleaned in public, but if what is happening in your organization is truly unfortunate, sometimes the only leverage you have for constructive change is the threat that you will let interested parties know about the problems and their causes. While you are still an employee, you may have certain legal rights to use the organization's email system that you will not have as an ex-employee. Check it out. If you cannot communicate within your organization, you may find that certain newspapers or bloggers might be interested.

This is why you need to negotiate the terms of your resignation as an employee, as distinct from resignation from the Board of Directors, while you have a constructive relationship with the Board. In our case, we should have had a written agreement that our deferred royalties would be paid to us upon our retirement. As mentioned previously, we should have structured my salary reduction as a loan payable upon our resignation as employees. Faced with that sort of financial liability, the Board might have acted differently.

5. Be truthful. We read the following item on Friday, November 22, 2002 shortly after a Board meeting that left us unemployed and very unhappy. It resonated so much that we clipped and filed it, and we recently rediscovered it.

> When tempted to obfuscate or answer obscurely—that means tell a lie—better think again, Ray Capp says in *When You Mean Business About Yourself: Achieving Personal Success through Lessons from the World's Best Corporations*. "Honesty is the smartest option," he says. "Being honest is the most efficient way to operate. The truth requires the least energy to explain and maintain. It allows people to choose to interact with you time and time again."
>
> —John Eckberg, "Today's Career Talk," *The Cincinnati Enquirer*

When All Is Said and Done…

We live in a fallen world burdened with the effects of Original Sin which G.K. Chesterton wonderfully described as the mystery which explains the mystery of the human condition. In this concluding chapter I have emphasized things that you can do to help protect yourself in various ways. This should not be interpreted as meaning that you can't trust anyone. You simply can't have a decent life without trusting lots of people almost all the time.

We are all called to trust that God will sustain us and take care of us, but that doesn't mean we are called to abandon prudence. For example, it would be highly imprudent not to seek an education that will enable you to serve others including your family or future family. We are called to believe and to trust that God does bring good out of evil, but that doesn't mean that we are not called to do what we can to prevent evil and to seek justice in the face of injustice.

God has taken good care of Sheila and me and our family. Our two years in Regina gave Sheila the opportunity to start the first chapter of La Leche League in the Province of Saskatchewan, and it gave her very easy access to a health sciences library where she did so much of the research that culminated in her book, *Breastfeeding and Natural Child Spacing*. The unemployment injustices we suffered in Regina gave me the time to write my book first published as *Covenant, Christ and Contraception* and later revised and expanded to its current 2005 edition published by Ignatius Press as *Sex and the Marriage Covenant: A Basis for Morality*.

As the first draft of *Battle-Scarred* was concluded, it was just over seven years since our complete separation from the Couple to Couple League. We have been very unhappy with the changes that its new management has made since the separation. It is not easy to see the core principles on which we founded the League flushed down the drain. Those principles or charisms served well for 32 years, and we have yet to see any validating reason for dismissing them. We have not yet clearly seen what good God is bringing or plans to bring out of that. Perhaps it is the work we are currently doing in NFP International. Perhaps those core principles will be adopted by more NFP organizations now that they are no longer associated exclusively with one large program. We don't know.

However, we have had some great satisfactions in our life with NFPI. From letters we have received, we know that our work is still helping people in very significant ways. For example, in mid-November, 2010 Sheila received this email note from a blogger. I inserted the [just] in line 4.

> Continue your good work and don't grow weary. Our prayers are coming your way. Please don't ever forget what good scientific information you have given to the masses. The "work" that you and your husband have given people is not [just] a helpful aid to fertility monitoring, but instead, it is a way of living, a way of embracing marriage selflessly, a way of nurturing our children, and a way of growing a family in the love of Christ. As I breastfeed my fourth child, I thank you for helping me to be the mother I am proud to be. I will never regret mothering using ecological breastfeeding. It is so funny to even give "it" (ecological breastfeeding) a name because it just seems so natural to do—like I was always meant to mother this way.
>
> Praise be to the Kippleys for using the talents God has given them to nourish the Body of Christ.
>
> Many blessings to you in the upcoming Advent season.

Admittedly, the second-to-last sentence is a bit heavy, but all the writer is saying is that the Lord gave us some gifts and that we having been sharing them with others. And why not? The breastfeeding insight, the covenant insight, and the commonsense recognition of the value of crosschecking signs—all of these were not the results of great study and research but simply gifts to be shared with others. We are grateful to all of those couples and individuals who have helped us to share these gifts over the past 40 years, and we invite all those who share our convictions to help us share these gifts ever more widely and for many years to come.

One last paragraph

I wrote this paragraph in October 2010 just two days after the televised announcement of the use of a person's own stem cells to heal his or her damaged eyes. One of the researchers said on camera that all the work that went into this advance would be worth it if only one person regained his or her eyesight. The same sort of thing can be said about our work. If we help only one couple to abandon the sinful practices of contraceptive behaviors, our work has been worthwhile, and we hope to enjoy that couple's friendship in heaven. That, after all, is one of the great purposes of life.

* * *

Author contact source: www.battle-scarred.info